The Gift of Creation

The Gift of Creation

Theological Reflections on Ecology, Metaphysics, and Politics

EDITED BY
Mátyás Szalay

☙PICKWICK *Publications* • Eugene, Oregon

THE GIFT OF CREATION
Theological Reflections on Ecology, Metaphysics, and Politics

Copyright © 2024 Wipf and Stock Publishers. All rights reserved. Except for brief quotations in critical publications or reviews, no part of this book may be reproduced in any manner without prior written permission from the publisher. Write: Permissions, Wipf and Stock Publishers, 199 W. 8th Ave., Suite 3, Eugene, OR 97401.

Pickwick Publications
An Imprint of Wipf and Stock Publishers
199 W. 8th Ave., Suite 3
Eugene, OR 97401

www.wipfandstock.com

PAPERBACK ISBN: 978-1-6667-3708-0
HARDCOVER ISBN: 978-1-6667-9618-6
EBOOK ISBN: 978-1-6667-9619-3

Cataloguing-in-Publication data:

Names: Szalay, Mátyás, editor.

Title: The gift of creation : theological reflections on ecology, metaphysics, and politics / edited by Mátyás Szalay.

Description: Eugene, OR : Pickwick Publications, 2024 | Includes bibliographical references.

Identifiers: ISBN 978-1-6667-3708-0 (paperback) | ISBN 978-1-6667-9618-6 (hardcover) | ISBN 978-1-6667-9619-3 (ebook)

Subjects: LCSH: Creation.

Classification: BT695 .G48 2024 (paperback) | BT695 .G48 (ebook)

VERSION NUMBER 11/04/24

Scripture quotations are from The Catholic Edition of the Revised Standard Version of the Bible, copyright © 1965, 1966 National Council of the Churches of Christ in the United States of America. Used by permission. All rights reserved worldwide.

To Mons. Francisco Javier Martínez Fernández
Archbishop Emeritus of Granada, Spain

For from the greatness and beauty of created things
comes a corresponding perception of their Creator.
—WIS 13:5

Contents

Contributors | ix

Introduction | xi
—Mátyás Szalay | xi

1. "Faith Is Obvious": The Apologetics of Creation | 1
   —Mary Taylor

2. Rhetorical Style as Real Substance: Interpreting the Work of Creation and the Novels of David Adams Richards | 31
   —Norm Klassen

3. Re-Homing the Human: Reflections Arising from *Laudato Si': On Care for Our Common Home* | 45
   —Jeffrey Dirk Wilson

4. "*Nulla mortalia efflavi*": The Living Universe of Hildegard of Bingen | 68
   —Miguel Escobar Torres

5. *Ordinatissima Pulchritudo Huius Mundi*: St. Augustine's Image of Creation | 91
   —Salvador Antuñano Alea

6. Creation and the Gift-Task of the Human Person in the Thought of Ferdinand Ulrich | 110
   —Michael Dominic Taylor

7. The Return of the Angels: The Ecological Turn as a Conversion to the Theology of Creation and to Natural Law | 130
—Rocco Buttiglione

8. Differences and Similarities in the Initiatives of the Catholic Church and the European Union to Protect Our Common Home | 142
—Lóránd Ujházi

9. Being, Creation, and Education: The Gift of Distinguishing What Is Real from What Is Not | 159
—Alejandro Serani Merlo

10. A Field Hospital for Catholic Bioethics: The Conciliar Methodology of *Laudato Si'* and *Fratelli Tutti* | 170
—M. Therese Lysaught

11. The Opposite of Anthropocentrism: Commodity Fetishism, Ecological Crisis, and a Sacramental View of the World | 198
—William Cavanaugh

Contributors

(by surname)

Salvador Antuñano Alea (PhD, University of Barcelona; PhD, Pontifical Athenaeum Regina Apostolorum)
Chair of Ancient and Medieval Philosophy, Francisco de Vitoria University, Madrid, Spain

Rocco Buttiglione (PhD, Sapienza University of Rome)
Member, Pontifical Academy of Social Sciences, Rome, Italy

William Cavanaugh (PhD, Duke University)
Professor, DePaul University, Illinois, USA
Director, Center for World Catholicism and Intercultural Theology

Miguel Escobar Torres (PhD, University of Seville)
Professor, Rey Juan Carlos University, Madrid, Spain

Norm Klassen (DPhil, University of Oxford)
Professor, St. Jerome's University, Ontario, Canada

M. Therese Lysaught (PhD, Duke University)
Professor, Loyola University Chicago, Illinois, USA

Alejandro Serani Merlo (PhD, University of Toulouse-Le Mirail)
Professor, San Sebastian University, Santiago, Chile

Mátyás Szalay (PhD, International Academy of Philosophy)
Research Professor, Pázmány Péter Catholic University, Budapest, Hungary
Head of the Department of Philosophy of Religion, Episcopal Theological College, Pécs, Hungary

Mary Taylor (PhD, Rey Juan Carlos University)
Consulting Editor, *Communio: International Catholic Review*
Vice-Director, Pax in Terra, Connecticut, USA

Michael Dominic Taylor (PhD, Rey Juan Carlos University)
Teaching Fellow and Dean of Students, Thomas More College of Liberal Arts, New Hampshire, USA

Lóránd Ujházi (PhD, Pontifical University of the Holy Cross; PhD, National University of Public Service)
Professor, Pázmány Péter Catholic University, Budapest, Hungary
Professor, Ludovika University of Public Service, Budapest, Hungary

Jeffrey Dirk Wilson (PhD, The Catholic University of America; PhL, The Catholic University of America)
Research Associate Professor, The Catholic University of America, Washington, DC, USA

Introduction

Mátyás Szalay

What does it mean to consider creation as a divine gift? Distinguished scholars coming from different countries, with diverse intellectual backgrounds and working in varying academic disciplines, have produced this collection of essays that address this important and timely question. Whenever our intellectual endeavor is serious enough—an effort not directed toward resolving problems or attending complex issues, but that rather dwells in the mystery of being as it presents itself to us—we are engaged in something more than making sense of reality *individually*. We do what Edgar Morin called "rethink thinking,"[1] reconsidering our tradition in light of an encounter with a novelty that presents itself as an appeal: we are called to work in a living community of thought-exchange, a *Denkgemeinschaft*. The face of the earth renewed through Christ cries out for a new intellectual approach, here represented by a community that feels grateful and thus responsible for our common home.

Over the years, the authors contributing to this volume became involved in the intellectual and pastoral initiatives of Mons. Francisco Javier Martínez Fernández, former archbishop of Granada, Spain, and an institution that he founded, the Edith Stein Institute of Philosophy (Instituto de Filosofía "Edith Stein," or IFES). Thanks to Don Javier's efforts to inspire a wide-reaching intellectual movement toward renewing Christian culture, in 2021 IFES organized the Eighth International Symposium "Beyond Secular Faith," entitled "The Gift of Creation." This book is a continuation of the polyphonic dialogue began at the symposium, which laid the foundation for a systematic and profound re-examining

---

1. Morin, *Tête Bien Faite*.

of the Christian doctrine on the gift character of being and creation. The volume's wide scope is due to the fact that the gift character of being invites us to recover and deepen our study of the unity of the sciences, philosophy, arts, and politics within the fundamental dimension of the human person as created for the gift (to be received and given).

Just as Mary Taylor reminds us, the gift character becomes visible for those with a renewed vision. In her quest for a Christian apologetics of creation, the way to reach the point at which faith becomes obvious leads necessarily through the imagination of the child, who can receive the gift with joy. "What is needed for a return to the joy of childhood, though in a new and more profound register, is a re-engagement with the whole of life—how we live, all of what we are as persons in community, our imagination, a full and embodied catholic reason in harmony with faith."[2] Ferdinand Ulrich, one of the most vibrant voices of the contemporary critical revision of Thomism, rightly characterizes modernity as a tragically failed attempt to leave this childhood behind; we seek to become independent of the father's gift, incapable of gratitude toward the auto-revelation of the divine self.[3] Recovering the child's imaginative capacity, capable of wonder beyond certain modern perspectives, requires the introduction of new, more poetical terms; these must capture the dramatic encounter with love, which is both personal and universal, eternal and temporal, gratuitous and yet necessary. Gratitude is a response to this complex experience. When fully realized—as ontological gratitude for the whole given as a divine gift—it marks a specific style of thinking as well as expression.

Norm Klassen challenges us to think about ecology in rhetorical or even poetic terms while thoughtfully analyzing the novels of David Adams Richards. Through calling the reader's attention to the "slightly off" syntax,[4] which reveals the drama of human encounters with nature as well as with challenging cultural and social inequalities, Klassen masterfully shows the theological complexity of our ecological concerns. Appraising the large scope—so uniquely characteristic of *Laudato Si'*—that connects the dots between human trafficking and global warming, Klassen argues that "'care for our common home' is susceptible to bureaucratization. It may seem obvious that ecology means concern with life itself,

---

2. Mary Taylor, "'Faith Is Obvious,'" 3.
3. Ulrich, "Gott ist Unser Vater."
4. Klassen, "Rhetorical Style," 39.

but untethered from a view of the real suffused with the presence of God, it represents a simulacrum."[5]

Jeffrey Dirk Wilson's essay on "Re-Homing the Human" sheds a certain light on this unsettling simulacrum when he critiques Heidegger's idea of *Dasein* as the "uncanniest . . . —the most not-at-home—thing in the world,"[6] whose homecoming and self-determination in reality is only possible through violence toward nature. Wilson, being a farmer himself, knows exactly how dramatic and complex it is today to "care for our common home"[7] not just theoretically but practically. He carefully interprets scripture passages on creation, from man being placed in the garden, to his expulsion therefrom, to Jesus being mistaken for the gardener in John 20. His reflection on the complex relationship between man and garden results in his claiming: "The human is doubly co-creator with God. God made the world as a garden, but he charged the human to go on creating a garden out of the world."[8] Wilson argues with Wendell Berry that man is a creature that, just like Odysseus, must overcome estrangement with nature—even his own nature—in order to find the way home. "Re-homing the human" means resuming the responsibility to be a good gardener, which also includes restoring marriage and the political community.

Miguel Escobar Torres calls our attention to one of the best gardeners of all time, a sainted woman from the Middle Ages whose tremendous knowledge of nature, as well as music and paintings based on mystical experiences, helps us to understand the cosmic stewardship man is called to assume. He details how insightfully St. Hildegard of Bingen critiqued the *magistri* (the medieval theological masters), claiming that only a trinitarian vision that contemplates through the *viventis oculi* can capture the complex interconnectedness of all things, leading to a cosmic liturgical understanding of creation. Differentiating the parts—moments of joy, vulnerability, and hospitality—of the divine-human drama is certainly a distinct intellectual operation from isolating them. Separation never adds up to wisdom (*sapientia*), but rather divides the Creator from creation and man from nature—in short, what Escobar Torres calls "an obsolete modern paradigm."[9] Hildegard may indeed help us to transfigure our view of a world "permeated with *viriditas* and full of God," but also

5. Klassen, "Rhetorical Style," 43.
6. Wilson, "Re-Homing the Human," 50.
7. Francis, *Laudato Si'*.
8. Wilson, "Re-Homing the Human," 55.
9. Escobar Torres, "*Nulla mortalia efflavi*," 73.

and consequently not to consider man as an isolated subject looking at the world from the outside.[10] Rather, he should be seen as the subject who is called to be "the guarantor of cosmic order and beauty in a humanized ecosystem, in which he reigns *with* the other creatures."[11]

In a similar vein, although this time through the lens of St. Augustine, Salvador Antuñano Alea invites us to rediscover the theological implications of the *imago mundi* as a cosmic order. It is still exemplary and informative for our contemporary understanding of the cosmos how Augustine was eager to avoid three main dangers: Manicheanism, Pelagianism, and Donatism. Antuñano Alea offers a masterful systematic interpretation of Augustine's trinitarian vision of creation and elaborates on the implications of *creatio ex nihilo*. The world as *vestigium* is an expression to be perceived and understood by man. The Christian vision (*videre*) of creation that has measure, number, and weight gives rise to a metaphysical account of "*contextio creaturarum*," according to which each creature has its own place in a perfect network of mutual relations. The order and unity of all creatures is an *ordo amoris*, for it is given through and in Christ and is accessible therefore through the logic of *caritas*. What ignites desire and triggers love is the expression of beauty found in all things created, a beauty that reflects the original divine goodness and glory ("*ordinatissima pulchritudo*"[12]). Encountering the beauty in all species is a dramatic experience for Augustine as well; he distinguishes two basic attitudes toward created things: *uti* and *frui*. According to Antuñano Alea, Augustine invites us thereby to "treat things according to the truth they express, in consonance with the original divine intention by which they were created—without divinizing them, without enslaving ourselves to them, and acknowledging all the ontological depth and meaning they have."[13]

The ontological meaning of creatures can by further elaborated by bringing Ulrich back into the conversation. Michael Dominic Taylor rightfully stresses that the mysterious nature of creation is not only a theological truth, but that it is also an important starting point for any true metaphysical account. It is to be acknowledged that all created beings are "complete and simple, yet non-subsistent." In this presentation of the thought of Thomas Aquinas and Ulrich, we learn that man has

10. Escobar Torres, "*Nulla mortalia efflavi*."
11. Escobar Torres, "*Nulla mortalia efflavi*," 89.
12. Antuñano Alea, "*Ordinatissima Pulchritudo Huius Mundi*," quoting Augustine.
13. Antuñano Alea, "*Ordinatissima Pulchritudo Huius Mundi*," 104.

an exclusive position in nature because he alone can return to his full essence through his word—by naming all things—whereas all other creatures can only share in the human person's subsistence. Man is capable of acknowledging the radical contingency of all beings and thus of understanding the unique data of being: while *esse* is the ultimate condition of being in order to subsist, it must give itself away as a true gift. Taylor draws a powerful conclusion from this metaphysical insight: "This is the fundamental pattern of the cosmos. It can be seen, analogically, in the interrelatedness of organisms in the trophic webs describing ecosystems, in the bonds that unite a family, and it is ultimately a reflection of the Holy Trinity itself."[14] Along the lines of Ulrich's reflections, Taylor wonderfully delineates the paradox of the *Esse Subsistens*—being poor and wealthy at the same time—which is at the very heart of understanding the self-emptying mystery of love. Given that the intellect, being both passive and active, simultaneously possesses a similar wealth and poverty, it is this very paradox that analogically helps us to properly understand man's vocation to love. In contrast to modern and postmodern dualistic interpretations, it is an act of the integral person whose intellect and will are in harmony. Taylor ends his meditation on metaphysics and ecology with a *plaidoyer* for a kind of thinking that is essentially thanking: a praiseful "yes" that is able to name things properly.

Rocco Buttiglione's take on *Laudato Si'* begins by appreciating Pope Francis's response to the mounting anxiety regarding the state of the environment: a deep reflection on creation, which is gratuitously given by God and is renewed by Christ. Pope Francis, like his predecessors, intends to establish a new synthesis between theology and scientific thinking. Any real synthesis—if it is more than just a pious idea—is also an invitation to personal conversion. The pope, however, encourages us not only to convert to God but also to convert to nature; Buttiglione interprets such conversion in terms of a rediscovery of the natural law, which reinforces the fact that we live in the world of God. The rediscovery of nature as being permeated with the divine presence requires a transformation of our attitude regarding it. From a rather utilitarian, active technical approach toward nature, we shift to an esthetic vision that is more receptive to the form and inherent *logos* of things and their deep religious symbolism. While the sciences study nature in a compartmentalized manner, thus reducing the original richness of meaning encountered, metaphysics and

14. Michael Dominic Taylor, "Creation and the Gift-Task of the Human Person," 115.

theology are called to consider nature's transcendent reference to the divine and thereby grasp "the whole in the fragment."[15] That does not necessarily lead to hypostatizing the meaning of natural entities, i.e., divinizing natural phenomena and thereby rejecting the monotheistic vision; rather, it invites us to resist the disenchanting of the world. The recovered human gaze toward nature, which captures the natural forms and lawful functions in the creature's divine origin, is characterized by Buttiglione as "the return of the angels."[16] He concludes that such a refined, ecologically responsible vision of nature bears striking similarities with Aquinas's concept of the natural law: there are immanent laws of nature that guide the proper behavior of all species, especially humans. Disregarding these laws damages the ecosystem and threatens the disappearance of species. Since both nature and mankind were created through the same *Logos*, the immanent law that governs nature is the same that regulates human relations. Accordingly, when faced with demanding societal issues, man is responsible for offering intelligent answers and taking reasonable actions while also respecting the laws of both social structures and the ecosystem. The dramatic question we face concerning the natural and social contexts is the same: complementing nature or destroying it. Rediscovering the natural law in this new sense, however, does not mean that we are taking a step backward; instead, it presents a new challenge to integrate the rich Latin-American religious culture that Pope Francis has placed at the forefront of Western theological thought. Buttiglione highlights some of the important metaphysical implications of Latin American popular religiosity concerning its complex idea of man's interdependence with nature, which is guided by higher powers. While insisting on monotheism, the recognition of some of these cultural insights may be helpful for illuminating man's responsibility of stewardship toward nature.

Loránd Ujházi envisions the cultural and social task of Catholic theology similarly to Buttiglione, inasmuch as the Catholic Church must not be afraid of the new challenges put forward by the ecological movement. As the Hungarian priest points out, there may even be a fruitful dialogue and action plan that the Catholic Church can collaborate on with European lawmakers and administrators. Ujházi describes in detail how the Second Vatican Council marked a more positive attitude toward international organizations, and how Pope Francis, faced with an

---

15. Balthasar, *Das Ganze im Fragment*.
16. Buttiglione, "The Return of the Angels."

environmental crisis, urged us to develop a public policy system based on common values and theoretical orientation. (A prerequisite for joining forces with policymakers concerning the environment would be a careful delineation of the differences and similarities of the two agendas.) With regards to such a collaboration, Ujházi is keen on presenting the continuity between Pope St. John Paul II, Pope Benedict XVI, and Pope Francis. The current pontiff's innovation—among other things—is due to the transdisciplinary method introduced in *Veritatis Gaudium* that is also present in *Laudato Si'*.[17] He regards as Pope Francis's main merit "that he has raised to a high level of communication the idea that the only solution is to change our lifestyle."[18] This was important for his predecessors as well, but while "they linked the protection of creation to individual areas of Catholic social teaching . . . [t]he encyclical *Laudato Si'* does the opposite: its starting point is the created world, to which other societal challenges are connected."[19] In order to protect our common home, it is not enough to improve an individual person's moral behavior; systemic injustices need to be addressed and the misuse of wealth ended, which again implies changing the current logic of economics. The insufficiency and inefficacy of the EU's green policy reveals the core issue, so difficult to admit both politically and personally: we must all live a more modest and less consumption-oriented life. By assuming this certain poverty, we would become more receptive to higher gifts and the plenitude of reality.

But can man even distinguish between what is real and what is not? Alejandro Serani Merlo calls our attention to this special quality of being human. In contrast to all other creatures, human beings do not only live in reality, but they also "apprehend[] 'reality as reality,'"[20] i.e., only human intelligence is capable of consciously and freely appreciating creation as a gift. By engaging classic authors on the differences between human and animal nature, such as Jakob von Uexküll, Ivan Pavlov, and B. F. Skinner, Serani Merlo comprehensively differentiates between human and animal intelligence. Contrary to modernist reductions of human perception, the Chilean doctor and philosopher insists on commonsense realism by arguing that human intelligence captures more than just properties: it comprehends the things in themselves. He offers an analysis of Piaget's account of children's cognitive processes and thus of contemporary

17. Ujházi, "Differences and Similarities," 149.
18. Ujházi, "Differences and Similarities," 152.
19. Ujházi, "Differences and Similarities," 153.
20. Serani Merlo, "Being, Creation, and Education," 159, citing Zubiri.

constructivist theories. In opposition to what he calls a sin against intelligence, Serani Merlo posits that the main acquisition of early childhood is the awakening of intelligence and that proper human education must support the child's realism, encouraging it to flourish. This is certainly a hard task that takes time and effort, but it culminates in the child's grateful recognition of the reality of goodness, being, truth, beauty, and unity. Distinguishing what is real from what is not concerning each of these transcendental domains is crucial to appreciating creation as gift. In order to strengthen this capacity, and thereby the recognition of the natural and supernatural gifts of creation, Serani Merlo proposes a radical revision of Western education.

In order to properly appreciate the gift of creation—besides rethinking the process of the acquisition of knowledge, and thus also of education—we must reconsider our basic concepts of the health sciences. M. Therese Lysaught focuses on recent developments in Catholic bioethics, offering—like Serani Merlo—a criticism of the modernist tendency to propose a glorified independence of the human self, the consequences of which are the separation of God and nature (natural and supernatural reality), the division of man and nature, the compartmentalization of the sciences, and even further, the fragmentation of the self. Lysaught, when interpreting the development of moral and social theology, promotes a rediscovery of the vital relationship between Catholic teaching on bioethics and social doctrine. She states, "In *Laudato Si'* and *Fratelli Tutti*, Pope Francis is calling us to a vibrant and powerful anthropology, grounded in a robustly theological vision of the Trinity, that is lived not as adherence to commandments, norms, and precepts, but as the constant embodiment of the divine character revealed in Christ via scripture, the Good Samaritan, and the *alter Christus*, St. Francis: openness, hospitality, joy, dialogue, vulnerability, love, care, and interconnectedness."[21]

In his essay on *Laudato Si'*, William Cavanaugh also insists—against the famous critique of anthropocentrism described as "the historical roots of our ecologic crisis"[22]—that the scripture-based Christian worldview is not anthropocentric but God-centered. A trinitarian understanding certainly does not separate or oppose man and nature to each other: instead of claiming that man is free to exploit nature, it promotes stewardship. Although Cavanaugh acknowledges certain merits of the critique of

---

21. Lysaught, "Field Hospital for Catholic Bioethics," 188.
22. White, "Historical Roots."

anthropocentrism, he points out several other, more significant factors underlying the present ecological crisis. He explains with Ivan Illich and Karl Marx how commodity fetishism—centering our lives around things rather than people—deforms all intersubjective relationships as well as our relation to nature. Cavanaugh further develops Marx's theory, taking into account recent economic developments (such as online shopping) as well as various studies depicting consumerism as a powerful new religion. But contrary to Marx, who offered a kind of solution that would entail more anthropocentrism, Cavanaugh is clear that Christianity advocates for a different answer: the healing of all relationships. Included here would be the restoration of our relationship with creation and material goods, which would only be possible by returning to God. The conversion from commodity fetishism as a semi-religious worldview to a theocentric vision of reality is a long journey of the longing heart's gaze, exhausted by the idol until it rests on the icon. Here, Cavanaugh brilliantly connects commodity fetishism with self-idolatry. He argues with Chryssavgis that "the twinned narcissisms of consumerism and the degradation of human labor stem from the loss of the human person's fundamental role as liturgical celebrant of the sacramental reality of the world."[23] Cavanaugh extends the working mechanism of the icon, described by Jean-Luc Marion, to all created beings. When we rediscover the iconic character of material things as well as our fellow creatures, we are resituated in a cosmos with a living divine center, around which the whole creation, with humans at the forefront, moves in a cosmic sacramental liturgy.

The different voices represented in this collection of essays unite to sing a humble hymn of gratitude for the gift of creation, and in praise to the creator God who became one of us: a creature to fully restore the gift of creation. We hope that the reader, with his or her particular community, culture, and concern over what is often referred to as the "environmental crisis," will raise their own voice and join us.

Bibliography

Aquinas, Thomas. *De Potentia Dei*. Translated by the English Dominican Fathers. Edited and revised by The Aquinas Institute. https://aquinas.cc/la/en/~QDePot.
Balthasar, Hans Urs von. *Das Ganze im Fragment: Aspekte der Geschichtstheologie*. Einsiedeln: Johannes-Verlag, 1990.

---

23. Cavanaugh, "Opposite of Anthropocentrism," 212, citing Chryssavgis.

Chryssavgis, John. *Creation as Sacrament: Reflections on Ecology and Spirituality.* London: T. & T. Clark, 2019.

Francis. *Laudato Si'.* Encyclical, May 24, 2015. https://www.vatican.va/content/francesco/en/encyclicals/documents/papa-francesco_20150524_enciclica-laudato-si.html.

Morin, Edgar. *La Tête Bien Faite: Repenser la Réforme, Réformer la Pensée.* Paris: Éditions du Seuil, 2014.

Ulrich, Ferdinand. "Gott ist Unser Vater." *Communio Internationale Katholische Zeitschrift* 4 (1975) 29–38.

White, Lynn. "The Historical Roots of Our Ecologic Crisis." *Science* 155.3767 (1967) 1203–7.

Zubiri, Xavier. *Inteligencia Sentiente.* Madrid: Alianza y Sociedad de Estudios y Publicaciones, 1980.

I

"Faith Is Obvious"

The Apologetics of Creation[1]

MARY TAYLOR

> I am so resplendent in my creation,
> In the sun and the moon and the stars
> In all of my creatures . . . .
> And especially in children . . .
> And the gaze of children is purer than the blue of the sky,
> than the milky sky, and than a star's rays in the peaceful night.[2]

Introduction

THE STARS PROCLAIM, "HERE we are!" and shine with gladness for God who made them.[3] The voice of day and night "goes out through all the earth," pouring forth knowledge.[4] Dante tells us, "The heavens call to you and circle about you, displaying to you their eternal splendors."[5] In the

---

1. A previous version of this chapter was originally published in *Communio*: Taylor, "'Faith Is Obvious.'"
2. Péguy, *Portal of the Mystery*, 3–4.
3. Bar 3:34.
4. Dan 3:59; Ps 19:1–4.
5. Dante, *Purgatorio*, 14.148–49 (153).

Psalms and in the Canticle of the book of Daniel chanted in Morning Prayer, the life of nature—sun and moon, birds and beasts, lightning and clouds, fire and frost, mountains and hills, the entire cosmic order—joins in the litany of praise and awe and surpassing splendor. We are surrounded by and immersed in a world of miracles and wonders, of breath-taking and breath-giving beauty, of "the river of thy delights."[6]

Any parent knows that young children express an enchanted joy and astonishment when they encounter something in nature they have never seen before—a translucent jellyfish, the shimmering iridescence of an insect's wing or a peacock's feather, a new-born lamb—even a slug! The philosophical rule that "being is only encountered in beings" is a child's quotidian, concrete experience, opening to infinite horizons of discovery; children are astonished at being itself, life itself, and not at conceptual abstractions. Nor do they feel themselves to be abstracted subjects confronting alien objects: to watch, for example, a child and a puppy playing together is to witness something real, true, beautiful, and good that seems to be mutually unfolding and enfolding. Children don't imagine themselves as "consciousnesses" constructing what they experience; they are receivers of gifts from an inexhaustible trove of treasures: a lobsterman pulls up his trap and a little boy waits with bated breath to see the surprises it contains. Little children live in the perpetual surprise of Christmas morning; their stance before reality is one of open receptivity and trust.

It is a truth known to the poetic and prosaic alike that after childhood things are quite different. One ages, one is busy about many concerns, one must put away childish things, and more than anything else, temptation and sin cloud the horizon. Joy, wonder, and astonishment in all their immediacy fade, and our deeply intimate relationship with everything around us breaks apart. This rupture from a reality that does not depend on us but is given to us from nature, not merely in the modern ecological sense but in the classical sense, as that which is given to each being at its birth (*natura*) and thus is only understood "in relationship to an end (*telos*) that was already in some way present in the original meaning of each being,"[7] manifests itself in separation and alienation from God, from the image and likeness of God written into our own being, from community with other persons, and from harmony with creation.

---

6. Ps 36:8.

7. Quesada, "Nature, Culture."

"Faith is obvious," writes Péguy. "Faith can walk on its own. To believe you just have to let yourself go, you just need to look around."[8] He echoes St. Paul: people are "without excuse," for "ever since the creation of the world his invisible nature, namely, his eternal power and deity, has been clearly perceived in the things that have been made."[9] Faith should be obvious: why does that not seem to always be the case, given the splendor of creation? Edith Stein—St. Teresa Benedicta of the Cross—says of the prophets that they hear God's voice in nature, but it is not the case that natural revelation is accessible only to these chosen people. "The whole point of their mission rather assumes that others, too, can find God along this path . . . . Their only task is to bring people who hear their words to the point where they learn to see through nature."[10] To "see through" is to see both the gift and the presence of the Giver in the gift. "Creation" has a double meaning, referring both to the continuous act of the Creator himself, and to the created order; these are clearly distinct, but just as clearly intrinsically related, and should be mutually illuminating.

This is the task of a true apologetics of creation: to bring us to the point where faith is obvious. Apologetics is more than simply responding to each thrust of rationalistic arguments, clarifying terms, or untangling some logical impasse or another; though those things might be necessary, if done in abstraction they are as effective as cutting off one of the Hydra's heads. Rather, apologetics should reveal Christianity as a new light in which *everything* is recast. What is needed for a return to the joy of childhood, though in a new and more profound register, is a re-engagement with the whole of life—how we live, all of what we are as persons in community, our imagination, a full and embodied catholic reason in harmony with faith. It is often said that apologetics involves not only argument but invitation, for outside of the practices of the community—the Eucharist, the prayers, the acts of charity—Christian rationality

---

8. Péguy, *Portal of the Mystery*, 9.

9. Rom 1:20.

10. Stein, *Knowledge and Faith*, 100. See also Balthasar: "Visible form not only 'points to an invisible, unfathomable mystery; form is the apparition of the mystery, and reveals it" (Balthasar, *Glory of the Lord*, 1:151). It is easy to see how without a deeper understanding of creation, without the analogical imagination, "seeing through nature" could appear dualistic. Environmental ethicist Eugene C. Hargrove says that "a Medieval Christian, when confronted with natural objects . . . automatically tried to find Christian religious significance in them by associating them with parables and key remarks in the Bible," whereas modern people, when shown a picture of a fish or a bird, "thought about real fish and birds" (Hargrove, *Foundations of Environmental Ethics*, 34).

is sterile. Sometimes the best conclusion to a syllogism is an action: "The *Logos*, the reason for hope," says Benedict XVI, "must become *apo-logía*; it must become a response."[11] We are to take our part in carrying out our role as "co-operator with God in the work of Creation."[12] To witness to the faith is not so much to proselytize as to draw people into participating in the life of Christ and his body, the church, and thence into a giving-out, into her mission of the reconciliation of ruptures:

> In intimate connection with Christ's mission, one can therefore sum up the church's mission, rich and complex as it is, as being her central task of reconciling people: with God, with themselves, with neighbor, with the whole of creation.[13]

One of the problems in turning attention to creation is that too many see it as only of secondary importance, as if, against everything Scripture and our own experience tell us, God's entire non-human creation were nothing more than an inert and disposable backdrop.[14] Heidegger speaks of the "forgetfulness of being" and Robert Spaemann of the "forgetfulness of persons"; "forgetfulness of creation" is the third sister, inextricably intertwined with the others. Benedict XVI says that "to omit the creation would be to misunderstand the very history of God with men, to diminish it, to lose sight of its true order of greatness."[15] The first article

---

11. Benedict XVI commenting on the First Letter of Peter: Benedict XVI, "Meeting with Representatives," para. 11.

12. John Paul II, *Centesimus Annus*, §37. And see Benedict XVI: "God himself is the Creator of the world, and creation is not yet finished. God works, *ergázetai*! Thus human work was now seen as a special form of human resemblance to God, as a way in which man can and may share in God's activity as creator of the world" (Benedict XVI, "Meeting with Representatives," para. 10).

13. John Paul II, *Reconciliatio et Paenitentia*, §8.

14. Frank Sheed says:

> It is no compliment to God's omnipotence to treat what He has made of nothing as if it were little better than nothing. It is no compliment to a poet to be always seeking him and resolutely refusing to read his poetry. God is communicating with us, telling us something, by way of his universe. There is something verging on the monstrous about knowing God and not being interested in the things He has made, the things in which His infinite power is energizing. The logical development of so strange an attitude would be to love God so exclusively that we could not love men—an exclusiveness which He has forbidden. (Sheed, *Theology and Sanity*, 366)

15. Benedict XVI, "Easter Vigil Homily." "Our profession of faith begins with the words: 'We believe in God, the Father Almighty, Creator of heaven and earth.' If we omit the beginning of the *Credo*, the whole history of salvation becomes too limited and too small" (Benedict XVI, "Easter Vigil Homily," para. 3).

of the *Credo* affirms our belief in God the Creator; understanding our origin incorrectly leads only to incorrect understanding of everything else. The first error is that if God is not a true creator *ex nihilo*, if his "being" is not analogous but identical to that of creatures, then he becomes nothing more than the most supreme being and another "mechanical" cause, himself bound by something that exceeds him. Next, secular arguments against creation dismiss a God they paint as a distant, monolithic entity, but never consider the God-with-us of the Incarnation, nor the relationality of the Trinity. If divinity and humanity meet in the person of Christ, then in that radiant Form all the various metaphysical fractures—between God and the world, time and eternity, history and ontology, soul and body, obedience and freedom—are healed, and the limits, imperfections, and finitude of humanity and of all created being are not tragedies but signs of goodness and grace. If in the Trinity there is both difference and unity within the very heart of the Godhead, then both the human longing for unity with creation and with others and the simultaneous recognition of our differences are reconciled.

Errors about God are followed by errors about creatures.[16] Within the technocratic mindset, not only the things of nature but persons as well become mechanisms,[17] while in ecological philosophies of identity, the boundaries between persons and created things dissolve, and both become nothing more than projections of "abstract interpretive schemata . . . upon the incessant play of phenomena."[18]

Additionally, errors about creation lead to divisions within the community of believers; the current and recent popes repeatedly remind us of the need for "human ecology" and the deep and intimate connection between integral human development (in terms of life, family, and culture) and the created order, yet many behave as if these were mutually exclusive.[19] They reduce creation to "the environment" and reach a détente with secular ecologists. As a result, we lose what is distinctively Catholic:

---

16. Conversely, "errors about creatures sometimes lead one astray from the truth of faith, so far as the errors are inconsistent with true knowledge of God" (Aquinas, *Summa Contra Gentiles*, bk. II, c. 3, 1 [32]).

17. See, for example, Heidegger, "Question concerning Technology."

18. Michael Zimmerman on Arne Naess: Zimmerman, *Contesting Earth's Future*, 124.

19. In speaking of human ecology, Benedict XVI says that "the book of nature is one and indivisible: it takes in not only the environment but also life, sexuality, marriage, the family, social relations: in a word, integral human development" (Benedict XVI, *Caritas in Veritate*, §51).

we may not see ourselves as thieves, extracting natural resources in a frenzy of Baconian power and utility, but we do not seem able to conceive of ourselves as anything more than good stewards of the earth—that is, hired managers, who, as everyone knows, care less for what they guard than do the owners. We lose the far deeper ontological relationality of *children* of our Father and thus *heirs* to his kingdom.[20] This means that a Catholic apologetics of creation must address not only unbelievers, but believers as well.

The fissure with reality experienced by the maturing individual person has been widening intellectually and culturally as well, first in a mechanistic-reductionist approach and then in various self-referential manifestations, eventually culminating in skepticism, relativism, and nihilism. After the turn to the subject, the Kantian turn, and the turn to language, the turn to the created order understood as "ecology" or "the environment"[21] appears to open a door to nature as a place of true contact with concrete reality in all its wondrous particularity. It is, as Benedict XVI says, "a cry for fresh air," though it "has not exactly flung open the windows."[22] In the next section, we will consider four different ecological philosophies. In all these cases, creation as "act" is denied, and though creation as "created order" appears to be affirmed, there is little consistency about which lives are worth protecting along with a chilling flirtation with the concept of "life unworthy of life." We lose persons in exchange for the environment—an unnecessary exchange if creation is seen in its totality: a whole that includes the realities of environment, persons, and wonder. The loss of the child is the most acute version of our loss of persons. Given that children have such an affinity for creation and

---

20. Rom 8:16–17. I would like to thank André Houssney for suggesting the comparison.

21. A series of "turns" progressively moved philosophy away from the realist metaphysics and participatory epistemology of the ancient and medieval world. Descartes turned to the subject, splitting it off from and opposing it to the object, as the primary focus of philosophy. Kant's "Copernican Turn" abandoned metaphysics (what he saw as the study of the unknowable thing-in-itself) for appearance and the structures of the mind. The early twentieth-century positivists thought that, though we cannot say anything about the way the world really is, at least we can say something about what we *say* there really is. The postmoderns discovered that language is a far more elusive and slippery thing than previously imagined. With each of these turns, there was a corresponding skepticism about the possibility of knowledge and truth. For some philosophers, the shift to ecological philosophy was hoped to provide a return to some of what had been lost, and an end to the slide into nihilism.

22. Benedict XVI, "Listening Heart," para. 8.

live in a dimension of original unity, it would seem that the child holds a key to any true communion with creation, yet

> Everywhere outside Christianity the child is automatically sacrificed.... The Child-Word in his quiet powerlessness can be so easily and by a thousand means rejected and got rid of, almost without believers noticing it (in the same way that human society is built on the tacit, thousandfold murder of the unborn, as if there were no need to waste words over that).[23]

We end up with a world in which "Thank You for Not Breeding" signs punctuate ecological events, and the proclamation on a California billboard ("What Have Future Generations Ever Done For Us?") replaces a welcoming, generative hope. Not only is the child, in all his wonderment and awe, the proper human response to creation, but how we as a culture treat the child is indicative of our stance toward creation as a whole. One could say that the child—both in his action, and his reception by the world—is the continual reminder and symbol that creation is a gift.

An apologetics of creation, like all apologetics, must begin and end with the Incarnation. All things are created through Christ, the *Logos*, whose "identity is inseparable from his being a child";[24] after the ecological theories, we turn to Edith Stein's incarnational "catholicity of reason," and in the last section we return to Christ, the quintessential child. Only in Christ is the mystery of man made clear, and "only the Christian view of the mystery of childhood can offer a counterweight today to the heedlessness of the belief in progress, whether it appears in anti-Christian, or neutral, or even Christian guise."[25]

Four Ecological Philosophies

Giving a specifically intellectual defense of the faith seems harder than ever. Christianity's opponents operate under assumptions that simultaneously refuse to acknowledge any alternative viewpoints and provide ultimately empty answers. On the other side, many Christians, deceived into thinking that everyone is working within the same conceptual framework, accept the stripped-down presuppositions of the technocratic definitions, ontology, and anthropology of their opponents, with

---

23. Balthasar, *Man in History*, 257, 251.
24. Balthasar, *Unless You Become*, 11.
25. Balthasar, *Man in History*, 257–58.

predictable results. Among the usual suspects: (a) granting to science the realm of efficient/material causes while claiming for religion the formal and final causes, thus mischaracterizing the complementary integration of causes; (b) maintaining that science deals with fact, reason, and logic, while faith concerns values and emotions, thus capitulating to an irrational fideism that denies that both science and faith apprehend being, reality, and truth, though they ask different questions; (c) suggesting that only a "God of the gaps" can explain irreducible complexities and discontinuities, or the immense probabilities that had to coincide for there to be life at all, thus reducing God to a hypothesis that would no longer be needed as soon as science came up with an explanation; (d) arguing for a "creationism" in which creation becomes another mechanism competing with evolution;[26] or (e) making a case for "Intelligent Design" theory: though nature does indeed appear to be the design of a luminous intelligence, a God who could be deduced from such a design would not be the God of faith, of children, of the saints.[27]

1. Attacking these five attempts is the stock-in-trade of the spate of "New Atheist" books. These books do not advance the discussion; their various ideas—that a purported "pure nature" or "pure science" can be neutral or free of metaphysics;[28] that creation is a mechanism; that "first" and "cause" mean only "temporally first" and "mechanically caused"; that the Genesis story is a form of primitive, bad science, rather than, for example and among other things, a grand polemic against determinism[29]—these have all been refuted with great care and profundity, and those refutations have never been answered.[30] The books clearly have ideological purposes, and are built on a reductive science, a strictly and brutally utilitarian ethics, a mechanistic ontology, and an anthropology destructive of human life, freedom, and dignity. A great deal is presumed,

---

26. In recent years, much apologetics concerning creation has focused on the evolution debate—a war of bumper stickers in the popular mind: the Christian fish, inscribed ICTHYOS, or the fish with legs, inscribed DARWIN.

27. See for example Edith Stein's discussion: Stein, *Finite and Eternal Being*, 109–10.

28. "Naturalism . . . is a metaphysical (which is to say 'extra-natural') conclusion regarding the whole of reality, which neither reason nor experience legitimately warrants. It cannot even define itself within the boundaries of its own terms, because the total sufficiency of 'natural' explanations is not an identifiable natural phenomenon but only an arbitrary judgment" (Hart, *Experience of God*, 17).

29. See, for example, Ratzinger, *"In the Beginning."*

30. Two suggestions for further reading: Hanby, *No God, No Science?*; and Cunningham, *Darwin's Pious Idea*.

including a biblical literalism that even the earliest church fathers would have rejected. The authors are intelligent people who are quite capable of understanding what theology actually teaches, yet, disingenuously, each "Christian" position they present is what one wag calls a "straw son," the descendent of a straw man: a position obscurely descended from one that was never held to begin with.

While one might be tempted to say with Dante that these writers have "lost the good of intellect"[31] and it would be best simply to "look, and pass";[32] their perspective, or something like it, has become the very fabric of the culture, and since apologetics is the evangelization of the culture, we desire dialogue that excludes no one, including "those who are hostile to the Church and persecute her in various ways."[33] Some New Atheists call themselves "Brights," but the light they imagine they emit is the harsh and artificial glare of a bare light bulb in a cold-war Eastern Bloc stairwell, claustrophobic, devoid of beauty, luminosity, and splendor. There is something inhuman about the "self-proclaimed exclusivity [of] the positivist reason which recognizes nothing beyond mere functionality."[34] Wonder is eclipsed and freedom shrivels; wonder, says D. C. Schindler, "can be held open only if questioning receives a positive answer that is, in itself, inexhaustible,"[35] yet there are so many questions one is not even permitted to articulate.[36] Nothing grows here; in fact the very notion of "life" disappears, as does nature itself. In the end, it is the world of Enoch Emery in Flannery O'Connor's *Wise Blood*. Enoch steals a shrunken, desiccated, mummified man—a substitute Holy Child, a new Jesus—from a park museum, no longer even understanding the inborn longing to worship that he retains in a materialistic world that

> resembles a concrete bunker with no windows, in which we ourselves provide lighting and atmospheric conditions, being no

---

31. Dante, *Inferno*, 3.18 (25).

32. Dante, *Inferno*, 3.51 (27).

33. John Paul II, *Fides et Ratio*, §104; referencing Paul VI, *Gaudium et Spes*, §92.

34. Benedict XVI, "Listening Heart." "The windows must be flung open again, we must see the wide world, the sky and the earth once more" (Benedict XVI, 'Listening Heart,' para. 7).

35. D. C. Schindler, *Catholicity of Reason*, 226.

36. A fellow student once said to Edith Stein, in reference to a professor who "reduced to silence by his superior dialectic and biting irony" anyone who disagreed with him (or sought to introduce an unapproved perspective): "There are things which one dares not even think during Hönigswald's seminar. Yet outside of class, I cannot ignore them" (Stein, *Life in a Jewish Family*, 186).

longer willing to obtain either from God's wide world. And yet we cannot hide from ourselves the fact that even in this artificial world, we are still covertly drawing upon God's raw materials, which we refashion into our own products.[37]

The Péguy poem with which we opened continues, "In order not to believe, you would have to do violence to yourself. Harden yourself. Run yourself backwards, turn yourself inside-out, thwart yourself."[38] The reference to Enoch's mummy as the materialist's Holy Child is not far from the mark. The deformed view of creation under a technocratic mentality opens the door to a heart-hardened hostility to children, who become products of their parents' arbitrary choices rather than the fruit of their love, or cancers on the earth and rivals to endangered species, or resources to be harvested for parts, or nothing more than carriers for "selfish genes," or violent interlopers, as in Judith Jarvis Thompson's well-known "violinist" analogy for abortion.[39] These evince an astonishingly mechanical and extrinsic notion of relationship that radically falsifies, in fact annihilates, the very meaning not only of "mother" and "child" but by extension our relationship with the natural entities of creation and with God. The culture that makes these arguments draws the hearer into the circle of loss, a loss of ontological goodness, beauty, and truth, where there is no vision of freedom as embodying the mutual good of persons, where even one's own child is seen as an oppressive and degrading burden, not a gift and blessing. Why would anyone want to live like this, in this inhuman understanding of, and rupture from, ourselves, the natural world, and each other?

2. Excessive regard for technical making empties the world of the wonder that comes so naturally to children, wonder at newness of being, "the same absolute wonder which is the basic attitude of philosophy."[40] Other ecological philosophies would like to recapture it. A second group, the various "sciences of complexity"[41] such as emergence theories, want

---

37. Benedict XVI, "Listening Heart," para. 7.

38. Péguy, *Portal of the Mystery*, 3–4.

39. Thompson, "Defense of Abortion." We are asked to imagine a woman who is kidnapped and then hooked up to a dying violinist against her will; if she unhooks herself, he will die. She is entitled to do so, she says; the analogy concedes the personhood of the unborn child but argues that one still is not morally bound to that child.

40. Balthasar, *Man in History*, 258.

41. Emergence theories reject reductive mechanistic accounts and say that the behavior of higher-order systems cannot be deduced by analysis of the elements that go into it. Similarly, for chaos theory, "the interaction of components on one scale can lead

to bring back a sense of enchantment, generated by the notion that the universe itself is responsible for the forms of nature that emerge within it.[42] The claim is that all forms are included, and that spiritual and moral attributes are natural forms. A representative example is that of the "emergence" of gratitude:

> Gratitude is the most important facet of the spiritual life, allowing us to acknowledge and express our awe and our reverence. A universe that "spawns because it is" generates our capacity to spawn because we are, inviting us to wrap our arms and minds and hearts around this astonishing whole to which we owe our lives and of which we are a part, and gasp our stammering gratitude.[43]

This sense of gratitude should not be disparaged, and surely its awakening is greatly preferable to the mechanistic indifference of the New Atheists. But what does it mean to direct our gratitude to the "astonishing whole" from which nothing escapes? Nothing transcends this whole, for even transcendence itself is captured and renamed "horizontal transcendence."[44] Within this flat horizon, one is left puzzled at what there

---

to complex global behavior on a larger scale that in general cannot be deduced from the knowledge of the individual components" (Crutchfield et al., "Chaos," 56). Obviously these theories do have great explanatory value in many contexts.

42. "The entities, precisely the sub-intellectual art works of . . . creative Nature, bear the mark of an unconditionally original imaginative power to which one must be blind if one—I do not say classifies their forms within the evolutionary process, but [rather] explains them entirely on the grounds of their position within this process. [Their beauty and perfection] presupposes . . . a superior and playful freedom beyond all the constraints of nature" (Balthasar, *Glory of the Lord*, 5:620–21).

43. Goodenough and Deacon, "Sacred Emergence of Nature," 868. Stein and the *Catechism of the Catholic Church* remind us that Augustine said, "Si enim comprehendis, non est Deus" (If you comprehend it, it is not God) (Augustine, "*Sermo* 117," §5 [663]).

44. "Transcendence is commonly used to denote a discontinuity, as in the 'top-down' agency of transcendent deity. But transcendence also aptly describes the phenomenon of emergence, where discontinuities ('something elses') arise from, while remaining tethered to, their antecedents ('nothing buts'). This mode of understanding transcendence [is called] . . . 'horizontal transcendence'" (Goodenough and Deacon, "Sacred Emergence of Nature," 867–68). But that is precisely what we do not mean by transcendence, which specifically refers to a qualitatively different level. Formal theories or sequences like that of Fibonacci may "emerge" from numbers, and the sequence may have properties not found in the constituent numbers, but the sequence does not "transcend" the numbers; the mathematician transcends both the numbers and the sequence. As Pope Francis said, "We are losing our attitude of wonder, of contemplation, of listening to creation and thus we no longer manage to interpret in it what Benedict

is ultimately to be astonished at—if nothing transcends, nothing unites our disparate feelings of gratitude. If we enter a welcoming home, are we grateful to the oven where the bread is baking, to the fireplace that gives us such festive warmth—or to the persons who provided these things and who are immanent in them in the most meaningful way precisely because they transcend them as givers? A nebulous gratitude to an amorphous totality is better than indifference, but first, we have not grasped the totality at all,[45] and second, the gratitude is not yet true thanksgiving (*eucharistia*), a topic to which we shall return.

These ecologists say that their perspective on what is unexpected and novel in nature, rejected as capricious and hence irrelevant by positivist science, "opens countless opportunities to encounter and celebrate the magical while remaining mindful of the fully natural basis of each encounter";[46] this occurs through the vicissitudes of each entity's individual history, and the introduction of contingency:

> Whereas contingent is often understood to mean accidental or fortuitous, its etymology (*contingere*, to touch, meet) carries the sense of dependency, of something being conditional on something else, and this certainly maps on to the core understanding of the emergentist perspective.[47]

While contingency does include depending upon some prior condition, state, or thing, most importantly for our purposes, "contingency . . . is the condition of any essence logically distinct from its own existence—which is to say, the failure of a thing's proper description to provide any intrinsic rationale for that thing's existence."[48] Ecologists generally adopt Heidegger's critique of the supposed Christian view of creation as the fabrication of products by a kind of Supreme Being or Demiurge, with the things of nature as the resultant disenchanted factory output, but their own substitutions are no better, even if the pictures they invoke

---

XVI calls 'the rhythm of the love-story between God and man.' Why does this happen? Why do we think and live horizontally? We have drifted away from God, we no longer read his signs" (Francis, "General Audience"). The horizontal "must be integrated into the vertical since the latter gives it both meaning and form" (Balthasar, *Theo-Drama*, 5:29–30).

45. "What 'enters into our understanding' is in relation to that totality of meaning like some forlorn sounds of a symphony which are carried a long distance by the wind until they finally reach our ear" (Stein, *Finite and Eternal Being*, 113).

46. Goodenough and Deacon, "Sacred Emergence of Nature," 867.

47. Goodenough and Deacon, "Sacred Emergence of Nature," 866.

48. Hart, *Experience of God*, 100.

seem more sophisticated. There is a loss of *true* "enchantment," a childlike, metaphysical wonder at the gratuitous gift of being that lies at the heart of each created thing and all of them together; there is, as Balthasar says, no "space for wonder at the fact that there is *something rather than nothing*, but only for admiration that everything appears so wonderfully and 'beautifully' ordered within the necessity of Being."[49] And so this redefined contingency is not radical enough; it does not reach to the contingency of the whole that is at issue.[50] An entire contingent horizontal chain of events, or quantum fluctuations, or anything else, cannot explain itself. The questions of origin, newness, and surprise are not answered but merely postponed.

3. A third group, the eco-phenomenologists—influenced by Goethe, Heidegger, Levinas, Merleau-Ponty, and Hans Jonas—believe it is necessary to unmask the assumptions of modernity, which lay the "conceptual groundwork for the modern worldview in which an intrinsically meaningless objective realm ('nature') is separated epistemically from—and so needs to be mastered through the activities of—isolated, self-certain subjects."[51] A volume of collected essays entitled *Eco-Phenomenology: Back to the Earth Itself* deliberately echoes the rallying call of Husserlian phenomenology, "Back to the things themselves."[52] It takes as a starting point the phenomenological fact of living beings in their full concrete experience, pursuing relationality, and as David Woods says, "There is no richer dimension of relationality than time."[53] The tension between time and eternity opens up another tension, between finite and infinite—"an invisible in the heart of the visible to the extent that the temporal articulateness of things is not itself obviously presented in their immediate appearance."[54] In other words, there is more to things than meets the eye, a "sense of the infinite in the finite," an "intensification of the concrete" in which each moment is given "depth."[55] The consideration of these

---

49. Balthasar, *Glory of the Lord*, 5:613–14. See discussion from 619–27. They tend to resort to magical explanations—like the famous New Yorker cartoon showing a blackboard with a mathematical equation, numerical premises on one side and a conclusion on the other, and in the middle the words "Here a miracle occurs."

50. "The contingency of individual things is indisputable, but the contingency of the world as a whole is not accepted" (Ratzinger, *"In the Beginning,"* 83).

51. Thomson, "Ontology and Ethics," 382.

52. Brown and Toadvine, *Eco-Phenomenology*, xi.

53. Wood, "What Is Eco-Phenomenology?," 213.

54. Wood, "What Is Eco-Phenomenology?," 215.

55. Wood, "What Is Eco-Phenomenology?," 216.

polar tensions, made concrete in the regular rhythms of nature such as the synchronicity of fireflies lighting up at the end of the evening or the periodicity of the hatching of cicadas, interrupted by the breakthroughs of the unexpected, preserves us "against a premature holism, an overenthusiastic drive to integration . . . . *We need a model of the whole as something that will inevitably escape our model of it.*"[56]

Assuredly it is true that there is an ever-greater that always escapes our attempts to contain reality, to capture it in a totality or meta-narrative, and much eco-phenomenological thought is, to an extent, compatible with a Catholic understanding of nature, and with some Catholic language.[57] But it is not sufficient for a Catholic apologetics; there is a falling short: the depth is not yet ontological, time is not yet the fullness of time, and many phenomenologists themselves say that the key trouble is with an inability to rightfully deal with persons. Philosophical phenomenology itself is far more sophisticated than the popular form, later adopted by many non-philosophically trained ecologists. John Paul II, himself an expert in phenomenology, stressed the need for its completion by an adequate metaphysics. In our experience of nature, he said:

> We face a great challenge . . . to move from *phenomenon* to *foundation*, a step as necessary as it is urgent. We cannot stop short at experience alone; . . . speculative thinking must penetrate to the spiritual core and the ground from which it rises.[58]

What is common to positivistic environmentalism, "deep ecology," emergent ecology, secular eco-phenomenology, and even, too often, to Christian ecology, and what causes persons and the rest of the created order to be so radically misunderstood, is that the act of creation

---

56. Wood, "What Is Eco-Phenomenology?," 217, emphasis added.

57. The creature is constituted to receive others within itself, and at the same time is always open to "an other who is always already 'beyond' the self. . . . Each creature bears *within itself* as gift an *excess* signifying the presence of a transcendent other-giver. This excess we may term mystery" (David L. Schindler, "Given as Gift," 83).

58. John Paul II, *Fides et Ratio*, §83. We see the same movement in Edith Stein. What Aidan Nichols says of John Paul II and Balthasar is true also of Stein—that they "aimed so to use phenomenology as to ground phenomena in real ontology" (Nichols, *Say It Is Pentecost*, 211). In *Knowledge and Faith*, Stein says that phenomenology stresses receptivity—its mode of inquiry differs from "trends of modern philosophy wherein thinking means 'constructing' and knowledge a 'creation' of the inquiring understanding" (Stein, *Knowledge and Faith*, 46). "It has been apparent that she broke out of the limiting confines of Husserlian phenomenology to explore the unlimited horizon of metaphysical inquiry—inquiry which was off-limits for Husserl's 'rigorous science'" (Baseheart, *Person in the World*, 110).

itself is misconceived. Primary and secondary causality are mingled into one. True creation, creation *ex nihilo* ("being-called-forth-from-nothingness"),[59] is the communication of being itself, of existence, and so speaks of an ontological contingency and dependence operative at every instant rather than an event in the distant past. What is so odd is how very difficult it is to get people to see the ontological distinction, to see that the question concerns the very conditions of existence itself, of the very possibility of laws, of anything existing at all. This is a pandemic problem, and neither native intelligence nor advanced education inoculates one against it. It requires something like the shift in aspect necessary for seeing an optical illusion, rather than the addition of new material to the picture; it does not give us more information but qualifies, like the play of light, the manner in which we see. When the act is misunderstood, so is the entire created order. Creation *ex nihilo* means that created things, in their composite nature of essence and existence, are both intelligible and at the same time inexhaustible; and an abyss of mystery lies at the heart of every created thing. And only when the act of creation *ex nihilo* is grasped does one grasp the true meaning of "contingency" and "dependence" and the paradigmatic meaning of the Child for creation, for "to be a child," says Balthasar, is to "owe one's existence to another."[60]

4. Kenneth Schmitz says that "the expansion of our glance beyond the postmodern horizon is already under way, not so much through postmodern criticism as through the efficacy of environmental concern."[61] It is telling that ecological postmodern criticism itself has sought to expand beyond its own limits and has adapted language that escalates to a near-theological level. This fourth group of secular philosophers says that in considering nature, perhaps we need not dualism, not dialectic, but something "trialectical" or "triadic."[62] Ecologist David Abrams speaks

---

59. Stein, *Finite and Eternal Being*, 170.

60. Balthasar, *Unless You Become*, 49.

61. Schmitz, *Recovery of Wonder*, xi–xii. When apologists turn to environmental thought, it is generally to "deep ecology" or related versions of "holism," which privilege a purely horizontal relationality: entities become processes, temporary phenomenal constructs in an endless flow, dissolving any ontological or axiological differences between persons and other created beings. Though "deep ecology" still lives on in the popular press, these philosophies of identity were quickly rejected by postmodern eco-philosophers, who saw in it a reverse image of the univocity and linguistic naïveté of modernity. They opted instead for equivocity in emergence and the tensions of ambiguity.

62. Ivakhiv, "Thinking Through Threes."

of the "embeddedness" of the flesh in the world, an "incarnate" dimension.[63] Postmodern ecologist Romand Coles, borrowing heavily from Adorno, says that we need "reconciliation" as "togetherness in diversity," "a reciprocal gift giving," "the humility to recognize that we are beings that receive more than we can return in this encounter."[64] Even in regard to the non-human other, we need "an imaginative generosity that seeks to enter the other's voice into the dialogue through which one's actions emerge."[65] Perhaps most revealing, ecologist Barry Lopez says we need to borrow "*agape*" as "an expression of intense spiritual affinity with the mystery . . . a humble, impassioned embrace of something outside the self."[66]

Yet however amenable the language of gift, generosity, and humility is in these postmodern ecologists (as St. Paul pointed out to the men of Athens, they have it partly right), their terms "trialectic," "togetherness-in-diversity," an "incarnate dimension," and especially "*agape*," are asymptotes, forever straining toward but never reaching the deepest heart of the mystery of creation: the interpersonal life of the Trinity. It is a truth of revelation that creation is a gift of the triune God of love. "To create means to give," says John Paul II, "and he who gives, loves."[67] Every created thing receives its being and life as a participation in the generous and overflowing love of the Persons of the Trinity.

> The revelation of God in His Son Jesus Christ, and with it, the deepest revelation of the nature and the end of all the reality, ratifies that logical and teleological sense of the non-human environment. It offers the final and deepest explanation of its meaning: in the beginning was the Logos and through Him all was created. In this way, finite reality, once understood as a "*physis*" enclosed upon itself, is now known as "creation." The windows are opened.[68]

---

63. Abrams, *Spell of the Sensuous*. See, for example, 63.
64. Coles, "Ecotones and Environmental Ethics," 233, 239.
65. Coles "Ecotones and Environmental Ethics," 236.
66. Lopez, *Arctic Dreams*, 250.
67. John Paul II, "Udienza Generale," §2: "Creare significa donare . . . E colui che dona, ama."
68. Quesada, "Nature, Culture."

Edith Stein's Valley

Where then does an apologetics of creation start, if creation itself is so often obscured by too-shallow ecological philosophies? Again we must return to the child, specifically, Hans Urs von Balthasar's image of the mother's smile—a relationship also hymned by Péguy—that reveals the original unity in which consciousness awakens. An ellipse of love with two irreducible, interacting poles, one prior to the other, this embracing smile is also an image of God and the created order, for this dramatic encounter opens into wonder at all being, extending beyond the interpersonal to include the entire natural world: the things of nature attract by their Beauty; are bearers of *logos*, of meaning coextensive with Truth; and bring about both awareness of and response to the Good. The smile of the mother reverberates in the "smile" of created things—as Dante writes, "what I saw seemed to me a smile of the universe"[69]—which reaches, without deduction or interpretation, to the depth of being and to God, for "although it derives from a concrete encounter and thus does not at all communicate an abstract concept of being, this intuition is wholly unbounded and reaches to the ultimate, to the Divine."[70]

A mark of the saints is the humility of a spiritual childlikeness that retains the original receptivity to creation. Edith Stein was a great intellectual and a philosopher not usually thought of as "childlike," but who approaches reality with the openness of a child. We turn now to an experience Stein describes, to borrow the words of Balthasar, "of which all one knows to begin with is just that it exists," yet which ultimately reveals God's presence. While there are poets and writers who make us feel the numinous awe of childhood wonder—think of the chapter "The Piper at the Gates of Dawn" in *The Wind in the Willows*—Stein does something rare. She both shows and tells, reveals and explains, God's presence in creation. At the same time, in her encounter "our most ultimate discoveries and our most basic starting assumptions reciprocally illuminate each other, and through simultaneous ascent and descent reason penetrates ever more profoundly into its object."[71] Stein's luminous example is one of encountering transcendence within the immanence of a concrete experience of beauty in creation, and she witnesses both to the catholicity of reason and to the possibility of seeing creation as an apologetics for itself.

---

69. Dante, *Paradiso*, 27.4–5 (301): "Ciò ch'io vedeva me sembiava un riso de l'universo" (300).

70. Balthasar, *Unless You Become*, 18.

71. D. C. Schindler, *Catholicity of Reason*, 289.

We opened with the beauty of the stars and now return to them in a concrete encounter in which Edith Stein deepens the metaphysics of creation from a consideration of "existence" to the depths of trinitarian love and relationship in a trajectory that follows Balthasar and Dante. This moment, perhaps drawn from her hikes in the Black Forest, unfolds creation as its own apologetics. Deliberately choosing an inanimate example to make her point clear, she describes

> A valley, enclosed by pale walls of rock, not very high, bathed in moonlight, vaulted by a sky of sparkling stars, against which the contours of the rocks clearly emerge, though without any sharpness. It is a picture of indescribably clear, gentle, and peaceful beauty.[72]

She takes pains to say that the term "indescribable" is in the strict sense; the beauty is quite literally indescribable, not because it is unintelligible, but because it will be revealed as inexhaustible: "The fullness of the world we perceive with our senses holds more than we can understand through the methods of natural science.... [it is] nature revealing itself to us as a whole and in each of its parts, yet ever remaining a mystery."[73] It is apparent that the beauty is not material, "though the whole form to which it adheres is constructed of material things, and material qualities essentially determine the impression of the whole,"[74] for as we drink in this lovely scene in an attitude of receptive openness, something of its clarity, gentleness, and peace is communicated to us, and we perceive the resulting disposition of the soul as "spiritual."[75] One might argue that the feeling of peace is merely our own subjective state projected onto the landscape, but this contradicts our experience of clarity and gentleness "as characteristics of the valley itself, even if we ourselves are internally distraught and without peace, and perceive our inner opposition to the character of the landscape as something painful."[76] And should we be transformed interiorly—brought into harmony with what we behold—we experience this harmony as a gift, as something coming from the landscape itself.[77] The saint's vision of

---

72. Stein, *Aufbau*, 114. There is no English translation; all translations are by the author.

73. Stein, *Knowledge and Faith*, 99.

74. Stein, *Aufbau*, 114. I am indebted to Miguel Salazar of the Sodalitium Christianae Vitae for first pointing out these passages to me.

75. Stein, *Aufbau*, 114.

76. Stein, *Aufbau*, 114–15.

77. Stein, *Aufbau*, 115.

nature is that of a shared community of being, pregnant with meaning, and not of a collection of objects or a malevolent power against which our nature revolts in an antagonistic superiority; compare, for example, Kant's experience of rock cliffs and the heavens.[78]

Our experience—the connection between the structural properties of natural things and the meaning we perceive—is not arbitrary but organic: in the person, the concrete sense and the symbolic meaning are "linked internally, correspond to each other."[79] Among Stein's examples are a moonlit night, in which "everything harsh, sharp and glaring is muted and soothed," leading to a "gentle lucidity of the spirit . . . . a deep, grateful repose,"[80] and granite, so fitting for monuments that will outlast the human race, striking our senses as strong and massive, and also quite naturally speaking to us of unwavering reliability and sheltering care.[81] These powerful symbolic correlations are not found in the glare of the desert at noon, or with clay or sand.[82]

Stein draws on an analogy with persons, who are also present to us as material forms. Clearly the inner impressions that arise in us are not our own subjective projection.[83] The human spirit "speaks" through a whole,

78. "Bold, overhanging, as it were threatening cliffs, thunder clouds towering up into the heavens, bringing with them flashes of lightning and crashes of thunder . . . etc., make our capacity to resist into an insignificant trifle in comparison with their power. But . . . [we] found in our own faculty of reason . . . a superiority over nature itself even in its immeasurability: likewise the irresistibility of its power certainly makes us, considered as natural beings, recognize our physical powerlessness, but at the same time reveals a capacity for judging ourselves as independent to it and a superiority over nature" (Kant, *Critique of the Power*, 144–45).

79. Stein, *Aufbau*, 116. The nature of created, material things is "not exhausted in their spatial being." Not just "external analogies" for "linguistic metaphors often express an inner relationship that exists between different genera of existents as well as between finite existents and the divine archetypal reality . . . . it is of the essence of everything material and spatial to be a symbol of something immaterial or spiritual. This is its mysterious meaning and its hidden inwardness . . . . And so we see that in its essence each and every thing bears within itself its own mystery and thereby points beyond itself" (Stein, *Finite and Eternal Being*, 244). See also her discussion in Stein, "Difference in the Character."

80. Stein, *Science of the Cross*, 40. There is a particularly beautiful passage on pages 39–40 on night as symbol.

81. Stein, *Aufbau*, 116.

82. Stein, *Aufbau*, 116.

83. This isn't animism, Stein says. The things of nature do not become persons, and "we have no right to award them a soul (that would indeed be 'projection')" (Stein, *Aufbau*, 116). See also Robert Spaemann: "Beyond such analogy, any attempt to say what animal life 'really' is, leads into fantasy, of which materialistic reductionism is the most irresponsible form" (Spaemann, *Happiness and Benevolence*, 117).

a structural form rich in meaning. Analogously, in nature, "color and spatial forms, light and darkness, rigidity and strength, the form of the whole—all have meaning, through them something spiritual speaks."[84]

The spiritual meaning of nature is something we can share in, something nature gives us while at the same time preserving it,[85] as the diffusiveness of the Good does not diminish the Good, but rather unites with creaturely being while at the same time remaining distinct from it. And so "precisely what makes the material and spatial a symbol of the spiritual makes it likewise a symbol of the eternal."[86] The meanings we perceive in nature, concrete and symbolic:

> both point beyond themselves to suggest a personal spirit which is behind the visible world, who has given every entity its meaning, has shaped it according to the place that was intended for it in the structure of the whole, who wrote this "great book of nature" and thus speaks to the human spirit.[87]

Who is this spirit that speaks to the human spirit, who enters and decisively breaks open what would otherwise be what Benedict XVI calls our windowless bunker ("*in seinen Lebenszusammenhang eingreifend*"[88])? Using Heidegger's language, Stein says that if we find ourselves, as *Dasein*, "thrown" into existence, "the question concerning the thrower cannot be suppressed."[89] The eternal spirit continuously present in all of creation is personal, a Person, present as Love: the mysterious interplay of the *esse*/existence distinction, the key ontological insight of Aquinas into the act of creation, is analogous to love between persons. "The way of faith," says Stein, "gives us more than the way of philosophic knowledge. Faith reveals to us the God of personal nearness, the loving and merciful one, and therewith we are given a certitude which no natural knowledge can impart."[90]

---

84. Stein, *Aufbau*, 115.

85. "Es geht etwas von ihnen aus, was wir in uns aufnehmen können und was doch in ihnen bewahrt bleibt" (Stein, *Aufbau*, 115).

86. Stein, *Finite and Eternal Being*, 244.

87. Stein, *Aufbau*, 116–17. Cf. Aquinas, *Questiones Disputatae de Veritate*, which Stein translated into German: "Res ergo naturalis inter duos intellectus constituta" (q. 1, a. 2). And she continues: "So there is no structure without spirit—formed matter is permeated with spirit. The form is not a personal spirit, is not a soul, but it is meaning, coming from personal spirit and speaking to personal spirit, participating in the context of his life. So, it is objectively justified to speak of 'objective spirit.'"

88. Stein, *Aufbau*, 117.

89. Stein, *Finite and Eternal Being*, 556n34.

90. Stein, *Finite and Eternal Being*, 60.

Before looking more deeply at "the loving and merciful one," we must note that the similarities and differences between the two ways of knowing must be rightly understood. Faith does not simply pick up where reason leaves off, as if reason and faith were two separate, juxtaposed methods. The catholicity of reason is both said and shown in the encounter, which is for Stein a *Gestalt*, a whole, with movements of both ascent and descent. In natural knowledge:

> When at a later moment [the mind grasps] something in the object it has not grasped before, it must add what is given later along with what was given before. This it will be able to do only if it has already grasped in a certain way what was given before.[91]

In an analogous manner, this is true of the movement of faith to the Person of God: He was always immanent as the source, present along the way, and resplendent as the end. He is not deduced at the end of a chain of reasoning—he is not a purely *a posteriori* discovery, but neither must some irrational leap be made. While Stein acknowledges the limits of reason, it is not in the sense that reason tells us nothing at all about God; if that were the case, faith would remain an extrinsic and arbitrary imposition. Nor is it the case that whatever faith "adds" has no bearing whatsoever on what we knew before—natural knowledge is transfigured, as natural virtues are infused by grace. It would be more accurate to say that Stein speaks from the heart of reason to the heart of faith, and vice versa. These two ways of knowing mutually implicate each other, though asymmetrically; she reminds us of the Fourth Lateran Council's *"major dissimilitudo"*[92] and says, "Reason would turn into unreason if it would stubbornly content itself with what it is able to discover with its own light,

---

91. Stein, *Knowledge and Faith*, 68. Stein continues, "When the be-ing that is known in the mental life of the knowing person, the actual content is given at every now-moment by the actuality phase and the reflection falling together.... The actuality phase harks back into the past and is kept in retention. At the same time, what previously had been anticipated as potential blends with what is now actual (by fulfilling it or countering it) and is taken up into the synthetic unity which had already been anticipated at the outset of the experience...." Cf. D. C. Schindler, who says that if revelation recasts the meaning of something previously known by reason "by revealing a more profound content to it than was initially evident, reason will rejoice in the discovery precisely as reason: it will experience the disclosure as an unanticipated fulfillment, that is, as a genuine novelty (*a posteriori*) that is what it always wanted (*a priori*) without knowing it" (D. C. Schindler, *Catholicity of Reason*, 297).

92. See for example Stein, *Knowledge and Faith*, 89; Stein, *Finite and Eternal Being*, 554n11.

barring out everything which is made visible to it by a brighter and more sublime light."[93]

If an apologetics of creation were simply about looking at the things of nature, we could still end up with seeing it as a mechanism. What Stein shows is not a "what" but a "way" of seeing; as John Paul II said:

> We need first of all to foster . . . a contemplative outlook. . . . It is the outlook of those who see life in its deeper meaning, who grasp its utter gratuitousness, its beauty and its invitation to freedom and responsibility. It is the outlook of those who do not presume to take possession of reality but instead accept it as a gift, discovering in all things the reflection of the Creator and seeing in every person his living image.[94]

Stein has unfolded the meaning of contemplation as beginning with receptivity to objective reality.[95] This receptivity is not merely passive but an active reaching out in desire (*eros*) beyond ourselves and beyond any closed system of nature.[96] In the person's encounter with the valley, a

---

93. Stein, *Finite and Eternal Being*, 22. Cf. *Fides et Ratio*: "Revelation endows these truths with their fullest meaning, directing them towards the richness of the revealed mystery in which they find their ultimate purpose. . . . Reason needs to be reinforced by faith, in order to discover horizons it cannot reach on its own" (John Paul II, *Fides et Ratio*, §67).

94. John Paul II, *Evangelium Vitae*, §83. Stein echoes John Paul II's "invitation to freedom": "God wishes to let himself be found by those who seek him. Hence he wishes first to be sought. So we can see why natural revelation is not absolutely clear and unambiguous, but is rather an incentive to seek. . . . faith is a gift that must be accepted. In faith divine and human freedom meet. But it is a gift that bids us ask for more" (Stein, *Knowledge and Faith*, 113–14).

95. Stein, *Knowledge and Faith*, 46: "Receiving," being "led by the objective ratio" rather than modern philosophy where "thinking means 'constructing' and knowledge means a 'creation' of the inquiring understanding." For an account of why a contemplative attitude is needed for a fuller and truer science than the reduction to a mechanistic ontology proposed by Dawkins et al., see Hanby:

> The very act which establishes the novel identity of every [concrete, intelligible universal and incommunicable particular] *ens* and differentiates it substantially from every other binds it into an antecedent order of actuality shared by every other. This is true not only of the objects of knowledge, but its subjects as well, whose acts of being and knowing implicate this antecedent order in their substantial identity. This antecedent order confirmed in the act of being and the mutual actuality of knower and known means that there is a priority of contemplative receptivity in all knowledge of the world, as indeed there must be if it is to be knowledge of the world . . . . My every action is therefore preceded, ontologically if not temporally, by an act of contemplative receptivity. (Hanby, *No God, No Science?*, 390)

96. It is also not a merely psychological "disposition" but rather includes the

"third" is revealed: all things, Stein says, stand together (*con-stare*) in the *Logos*,[97] for the *logos* of the world—all the meanings in the encounter—converge beyond our horizon in Christ, the *Logos* who is the Word, the archetype of all finite units of meaning.[98] As Benedict XVI says, we live in "an open parabola" with our center or focus lying outside of us[99]—we are "ec-centric" beings—and so the *con-stare*, standing together, is at the same time ec-stasy, standing forth.

> The creaturely act is first *contemplative* . . . The creaturely act first "lets the other be" in its givenness as such. This letting be, as a response to being which, as created, is good and beautiful, is an act of wonder.[100]

Balthasar notes that the "child is a master of contemplation," the "humbling gaze" before reality, and that the masters among the fathers of the church were all "lovers of childhood." Theirs is a contemplation that "sees in the childlikeness of the Son ultimately the reflection of the eternal newness of the whole Trinitarian life."[101]

We have now returned to the "loving and merciful one." While the "New Atheists" and postmodern ecologists often speak about God—usually negatively—the truth of the Trinity, that the "one" is the "three-in-one," is utterly opaque to them. For Stein, by contrast, the metaphysics of creation, rooted in the gift of being, flowers in the Trinity:

> We have ascended to the divine being by starting out from creaturely being . . . . We have also crossed that borderline which is indicative of what can be learned about the creator from creatures and of what God himself has revealed concerning his own nature. Without crossing this borderline, it would be impossible to learn anything about creaturely being as viewed from the perspective of the divine being. We thus look in the Triune Deity for the archetype of what in the realm of creaturely being we have designated as meaning and fullness of life.[102]

---

objective priority of object to subject.

97. Stein, *Finite and Eternal Being*, 112.

98. Stein, *Finite and Eternal Being*, 112–13.

99. Ratzinger, *Dogma and Preaching*, 386.

100. David L. Schindler, "Given as Gift," 83.

101. Balthasar, *Man in History*, 254–55, 257. "This total poverty is the way and condition of true contemplation."

102. Stein, *Finite and Eternal Being*, 418.

A shared participation and grounding in a common source, a clear distinction of beings who are bound together in love, is the *imago trinitatis* in the created order. Against positivistic science, to distinguish is to unite, not divide, at the deepest level. The relationality of all existents is not only biological and social, but ontological, and beyond this, they are seen also in their most profound beauty, "because they are now seen from the vantage point of the foundational and transcendent reality of God . . . . via a Logos who is a Person in a Trinitarian communion of Persons, who create, within this communal dynamic, in an overabundance of love which explains the logical and teleological sense that can be perceived in creation."[103]

The Eternal Child

If Stein embodies the open receptivity of the child, she also embodies another characteristic of the child: trust. "Sustained in existence from moment to moment" we are each a "nothinged being" (*ein nichtiges Sein*).[104] From the perspective of Heidegger, this should occasion anxiety; for Stein, only under pathological conditions would we live in such dread. This is not because we are deluding ourselves, but because the knowledge of our nothingness is counterbalanced by the "equally undeniable fact that . . . being holds me, I rest securely. This security, however, is not the self-assurance of one who under her own power stands on firm ground, but rather the sweet and blissful security of a child that is lifted up and carried by a strong arm."[105] Péguy speaks of the child sleeping in his mother's arms, "laughing secretly because of his confidence in his mother."[106]

The image of the child in his mother's arms opens a dimension that ecological philosophy never confronts and without which creation can never be fully understood. "In theological language," said Stein, "the coherence of meaning of all existents in the Logos is called the divine plan

---

103. Quesada, "Nature, Culture."

104. "A nothinged being" is Baseheart's translation (Baseheart, *Person in the World*, 116).

105. Stein, *Finite and Eternal Being*, 58. She continues, "If a child were living in the constant fear that its mother might let it fall, we should hardly call this a 'rational' attitude."

106. Péguy, *Portal of the Mystery*, 128.

of creation."[107] Christ the *Logos*, the "image of the invisible God,"[108] "the glory of God" who "bears the very stamp of his nature,"[109] the "coherence of meaning" through whom all was created, has entered his creation:

> The novelty of Christian proclamation does not consist in a thought, but in a deed: God has revealed himself. . . . Yet this is no blind deed, but one which is itself Logos—the presence of eternal reason in our flesh. *Verbum caro factum est*: just so, amid what is made (*factum*) there is now Logos, Logos is among us. Creation (*factum*) is rational. Naturally, the humility of reason is always needed, in order to accept it: man's humility, which responds to God's humility.[110]

Creation, where the plan of God is made visible, is inseparable from the Incarnation. And because Christ was born as a child, and remains—in humility, receptiveness, obedience, and trust—a child of the Father, then he reveals, redeems, and transfigures the very meaning of childhood. Christ calls us to "turn and become like children," whose "angels always behold the face of my Father"; "whoever does not receive the kingdom of God like a child shall not enter it."[111] And in the face of the near-contempt for children in some philosophies, he reminds us that whoever welcomes a child, welcomes him.[112]

Being childlike in the Christian sense is not at odds with being a mature Christian; in fact one who does so is "the greatest in the kingdom of heaven."[113] To become childlike in the sense we are called to is not to return to infantilism or to a sentimentalized Romantic version of innocence, lost in the past: in Christ, through the waters of baptism, the forgiveness of sin, and the life of grace, the "longing for a lost innocence and oneness with God that Jesus and Mary never lost . . . always lies

---

107. Stein, *Finite and Eternal Being*, 114. "The Logos . . . shows, as it were, a double countenance, the one mirroring the one and simple divine nature, the other mirroring the manifold of finite existents. The Logos is the divine nature (as object of divine knowledge), and it is the manifold of meaningful existence of created things as encompassed by the divine intelligence and as reflecting the divine nature in images and likenesses" (Stein, *Finite and Eternal Being*, 119).

108. Col 1:15.

109. Heb 1:3.

110. Benedict XVI, "Meeting with Representatives," para. 12.

111. Matt 18:3; Matt 18:10; Mark 10:15.

112. Matt 18:5.

113. Matt 18:4.

before us."[114] Through Christ, the windows of the "concrete bunker" are opened: "the ways of the child, long since sealed off for the adult, open up in an original dimension in which everything unfolds within the bounds of the right, the true, the good . . . a sphere of original wholeness and health and . . . holiness."[115] The rupture with reality could be said to be a *felix culpa* if it is followed by a new immediacy, an immediacy after reflection,[116] after suffering, after repentance.

The childlike stance embodies a stereoscopic vision, seeing each thing in creation—each star and stone and sparrow and flower—as something beautiful in itself and at the same time as a gift in and from another. Balthasar's "smile of the mother" and Stein's encounter with the valley—from the concrete beauty to the "indescribable mystery" to the "personal spirit"—retrace the path of Christ's experience, the paradigm of all human experience:

> We can be sure that the human Child Jesus was in amazement over everything: beginning with the existence of his loving mother, then passing on to his own existence, finally going from both to all the forms offered by the surrounding world, from the tiniest flower to the boundless skies. But this amazement derives from the much deeper amazement of the eternal Child who, in the absolute Spirit of Love, marvels at Love itself as it permeates and transcends all that is . . . . Through all ages of life the interpersonal thou abides as an unmasterable reality . . . . Now the Christian task lies in trying to deepen the erotic faculty from the surface of the senses into the depths of the heart . . . . "The Father is greater than I" lies hidden in all human experiences.[117]

This knowledge, spoken from the depths of reality to the depths of the human heart, points to the ontological foundation of the "gratitude" that confounded the emergent philosophers, and to the childlike thankfulness of the person, acting in community with the church:

> This has a second direct consequence: the elemental thanksgiving, the model for which we again see in the eternal Child Jesus. Thanksgiving, in Greek *eucharistia*, is the quintessence of Jesus' stance toward the Father.[118]

---

114. Balthasar, *Man in History*, 257.
115. Balthasar, *Unless You Become*, 12.
116. The phrase is from Kierkegaard, *Papers and Journals*, 299.
117. Balthasar, *Unless You Become*, 45–47.
118. Balthasar, *Unless You Become*, 45–47.

Eucharistia is the liturgy of the church, the sphere of receptivity and mediator of the sacraments.[119] Through those sacraments, the work of the Incarnation will culminate in the assumption—prefigured by Mary—of the whole of creation into the trinitarian life, for creation is also inseparable from the Redemption:

> In the bread and wine that we bring to the altar, all creation is taken up by Christ the Redeemer to be transformed and presented to the Father . . . . The substantial conversion of bread and wine into his body and blood introduces within creation the principle of a radical change, a sort of "nuclear fission" . . . which penetrates to the heart of all being, a change meant to set off a process which transforms reality, a process leading ultimately to the transfiguration of the entire world, to the point where God will be all in all.[120]

Through the eyes of the child, creation is resplendent. Perhaps more than any other poet, Péguy opens up the fruitfulness of childhood—"the spring that . . . pours from the eternal mystery of the Childhood of God through the eternal mystery of the childhood of Christ into the eternal childhood which is given to men: eternal hope."[121] If we would but become like children and see as through the eyes of Jesus, the incomparable Child, faith would indeed be obvious. "And the gaze of children is purer than the blue of the sky, than the milky sky, and than a star's rays in the peaceful night."[122]

Bibliography

Abrams, David. *The Spell of the Sensuous*. New York: Vintage Books, 1997.

Aquinas, Thomas. *Questiones Disputatae de Veritate*. Translated by Robert W. Mulligan. Chicago: Henry Regnery Company, 1952. https://isidore.co/aquinas/QDdeVer.htm.

———. *Summa contra Gentiles II: Creation*. Translated by James F. Anderson. Notre Dame: University of Notre Dame Press, 1975.

---

119. "Anyone acceding to a sacrament is a pure childlike receiver, even if he must contribute something of his own, but this something is nothing other than the perfect readiness of the child" (Balthasar, *Unless You Become*, 52).

120. Benedict XVI, *Sacramentum Caritatis*, §47, §11.

121. Balthasar, *Man in History*, 256.

122. Péguy, *Portal of the Mystery*, 3–4.

Augustine. "Sermo 117." In *Sancti Aurelii Augustini, Hipponensis Episcopi, Opera Omnia*, edited by J. P. Migne, 661–71. Patrologia Latina 38. Paris: Bibliothecae Cleri Universae, 1845.

Balthasar, Hans Urs von. *The Glory of the Lord.* Vol. 1, *Seeing the Form.* 2nd ed. San Francisco: Ignatius, 2009.

———. *The Glory of the Lord.* Vol. 5, *The Realm of Metaphysics in the Modern Age.* San Francisco: Ignatius, 1990.

———. *Man in History: A Theological Study.* London: Sheed and Ward, 1968.

———. *Theo-Drama.* Vol. 5, *The Last Act.* San Francisco: Ignatius, 1998.

———. *Unless You Become Like This Child.* Translated by Erasmo Leiva-Merikakis. San Francisco: Ignatius, 1991.

Baseheart, Mary Catharine. *Person in the World: Introduction to the Philosophy of Edith Stein.* Dordrecht: Kluwer Academic, 2010.

Benedict XVI. *Caritas in Veritate.* Encyclical Letter, June 29, 2009. https://www.vatican.va/content/benedict-xvi/en/encyclicals/documents/hf_ben-xvi_enc_20090629_caritas-in-veritate.html.

———. "Easter Vigil: Homily of His Holiness Pope Benedict XVI." Homily, Apr. 23, 2011. https://www.vatican.va/content/benedict-xvi/en/homilies/2011/documents/hf_ben-xvi_hom_20110423_veglia-pasquale.html.

———. "The Listening Heart: Reflections on the Foundations of Law." Address, Sept. 22, 2011. https://www.vatican.va/content/benedict-xvi/en/speeches/2011/september/documents/hf_ben-xvi_spe_20110922_reichstag-berlin.html.

———. "Meeting with Representatives from the World of Culture." Address, Sept. 12, 2008. https://www.vatican.va/content/benedict-xvi/en/speeches/2008/september/documents/hf_ben-xvi_spe_20080912_parigi-cultura.html.

———. *Sacramentum Caritatis.* Apostolic Exhortation, Feb. 22, 2007. https://www.vatican.va/content/benedict-xvi/en/apost_exhortations/documents/hf_ben-xvi_exh_20070222_sacramentum-caritatis.html.

Brown, Charles S., and Ted Toadvine, eds. *Eco-Phenomenology: Back to the Earth Itself.* Albany: SUNY Press, 2003.

Coles, Romand. "Ecotones and Environmental Ethics." In *In the Nature of Things: Language, Politics, and the Environment*, edited by Jane Bennett and William Chaloupka, 227–49. Minneapolis: University of Minneapolis Press, 1993.

Crutchfield, James P., et al. "Chaos." *Scientific American* 255 (Dec. 1986) 46–57.

Cunningham, Conor. *Darwin's Pious Idea: Why the Ultra-Darwinists and Creationists Both Get It Wrong.* Grand Rapids: Eerdmans, 2010.

Dante Alighieri. *Inferno.* Translated by Charles S. Singleton. Princeton: Princeton University Press, 1970.

———. *Paradiso.* Translated by Charles S. Singleton. Princeton: Princeton University Press, 1975.

———. *Purgatorio.* Translated by Charles S. Singleton. Princeton: Princeton University Press, 1973.

Francis. "General Audience." June 5, 2013. https://www.vatican.va/content/francesco/en/audiences/2013/documents/papa-francesco_20130605_udienza-generale.html.

Goodenough, Ursula, and Terrence W. Deacon. "The Sacred Emergence of Nature." In *The Oxford Handbook of Religion and Science*, edited by Philip Clayton and Zachary Simpson, 853–71. Oxford: Oxford University Press, 2006.

Hanby, Michael. *No God, No Science? Theology, Cosmology, Biology.* Chichester: Wiley-Blackwell, 2013.
Hargrove, Eugene C. *Foundations of Environmental Ethics.* New York: Prentice-Hall, 1989.
Hart, David Bentley. *The Experience of God: Being, Consciousness, Bliss.* New Haven: Yale University Press, 2013.
Heidegger, Martin. "The Question concerning Technology." In *The Question concerning Technology and Other Essays,* translated by William Lovitt, 3–35. New York: Harper & Row, 1977.
Ivakhiv, Adrian J. "Thinking Through Threes (and Deities)." Immanence (blog), Mar. 3, 2012. http://blog.uvm.edu/aivakhiv/2012/03/14/thinking-through-threes-deities/.
John Paul II. *Centesimus Annus.* Encyclical Letter, May 1, 1991. https://www.vatican.va/content/john-paul-ii/en/encyclicals/documents/hf_jp-ii_enc_01051991_centesimus-annus.html.
———. *Evangelium Vitae.* Encyclical, Mar. 25, 1995. https://www.vatican.va/content/john-paul-ii/en/encyclicals/documents/hf_jp-ii_enc_25031995_evangelium-vitae.html.
———. *Fides et Ratio.* Encyclical, Sept. 14, 1998. https://www.vatican.va/content/john-paul-ii/en/encyclicals/documents/hf_jp-ii_enc_14091998_fides-et-ratio.html.
———. *Reconciliatio et Paenitentia.* Apostolic Exhortation, Dec. 2, 1984. https://www.vatican.va/content/john-paul-ii/en/apost_exhortations/documents/hf_jp-ii_exh_02121984_reconciliatio-et-paenitentia.html.
———. "Udienza Generale." Mar. 5, 1986. https://www.vatican.va/content/john-paul-ii/it/audiences/1986/documents/hf_jp-ii_aud_19860305.html.
Kant, Immanuel. *Critique of the Power of Judgment.* Translated by Paul Guyer. Cambridge: Cambridge University Press, 2001.
Kierkegaard, Søren. *Papers and Journals: A Selection.* Translated by Alastair Hannay. London: Penguin, 1996.
Lopez, Barry. *Arctic Dreams.* New York: Vintage Books, 2001.
Nichols, Aidan. *Say It Is Pentecost: A Guide through Balthasar's Logic.* Washington, DC: Catholic University of America Press, 2001.
Paul VI. *Gaudium et Spes.* Pastoral Constitution, Dec. 7, 1965. https://www.vatican.va/archive/hist_councils/ii_vatican_council/documents/vat-ii_const_19651207_gaudium-et-spes_en.html.
Péguy, Charles. *The Portal of the Mystery of Hope.* Grand Rapids: Eerdmans, 2005.
Quesada, Alfredo Garcia. "Nature, Culture, and the Theology of Reconciliation." Unpublished paper, 2013.
Ratzinger, Joseph. *Dogma and Preaching.* San Francisco: Ignatius, 2011.
———. *"In the Beginning": A Catholic Understanding of the Story of Creation and the Fall.* Grand Rapids: Eerdmans, 1995.
Schindler, David L. "The Given as Gift: Creation and Disciplinary Abstraction in Science." *Communio* 38.1 (Spring 2011) 52–102.
Schindler, D. C. *The Catholicity of Reason.* Grand Rapids: Eerdmans, 2013.
Schmitz, Kenneth L. *The Recovery of Wonder: The New Freedom and the Asceticism of Power.* Montreal: McGill-Queen's University Press, 2005.
Sheed, Frank. *Theology and Sanity.* San Francisco: Ignatius, 1993.
Spaemann, Robert. *Happiness and Benevolence.* Notre Dame, IN: University of Notre Dame Press, 2000.

Stein, Edith. *Der Aufbau der Menschliche Person.* Freiburg: Herder, 1994.

———. "Difference in the Character of the Symbol: 'Emblem' and 'Cosmic Expression.'" In *Science of the Cross*, translated by Josephine Koeppel, 38–42. Washington, DC: ICS Publications, 2003.

———. *Finite and Eternal Being: An Attempt at an Ascent to the Meaning of Being.* Translated by Kurt F. Reinhardt. Washington DC: ICS Publications, 2002.

———. *Knowledge and Faith.* Washington DC: ICS Publications, 2000.

———. *Life in a Jewish Family.* Washington, DC: ICS Publications, 1999.

———. *Science of the Cross.* Translated by Josephine Koeppel. Washington, DC: ICS Publications, 2003.

Taylor, Mary. "'Faith Is Obvious': The Apologetics of Creation." *Communio* 41.1 (Spring 2014) 61–91.

Thompson, Judith Jarvis. "A Defense of Abortion." *Philosophy and Public Affairs* 1.1 (Fall 1971) 47–66.

Thomson, Iain. "Ontology and Ethics at the Intersection of Phenomenology and Environmental Philosophy." *Inquiry* 47.4 (2004) 380–412.

Wood, David. "What Is Eco-Phenomenology?" In *Eco-Phenomenology: Back to the Earth Itself*, edited by Charles S. Brown and Ted Toadvine, 211–34. Albany: SUNY Press, 2003.

Zimmerman, Michael. *Contesting Earth's Future: Radical Ecology and Postmodernity.* Berkeley: UCLA Press, 1994.

2

Rhetorical Style as Real Substance

Interpreting the Work of Creation and the
Novels of David Adams Richards

Norm Klassen

Our general title, "The Gift of Creation," makes me think of two things.[1] The first is that the created order is itself a gift from God; the second is that we have ourselves been given the gift of creativity. Many of the other chapters make excellent observations related to both. My own title is meant to point to both aspects, but I suppose it is focused more on our creativity, our styles. I see ecology in general, and Pope Francis's phrase "car[ing] for our common home" in particular, as implying the need for responsiveness, interpretation, and creativity.[2] By "rhetorical style," I mean our creative responses to the challenge to care for this home of ours. My first point will be that it's good to think about something like ecology in rhetorical or poetic terms because to do so connects us

---

1. Thank you to Mátyás Szalay and the whole gang at the Instituto de Filosofía Edith Stein for organizing "The Gift of Creation" International Symposium and Summer School, a terrific and seamless online event. It was a pleasure to join everyone from Hamilton, Ontario, Canada.

2. Francis, *Laudato Si'*. By "ecology," I have in mind standard definitions like Pimm and Smith's "study of the relationships between organisms and their environment," and Ernst Haeckel's originary "'relation of the animal both to its organic as well as its inorganic environment'" (cited in Pimm and Smith, "Ecology"). The authors themselves imply the importance of responsiveness in the basic meaning of ecology when they immediately go on to say: "Some of the most pressing problems in human affairs—expanding populations, food scarcities, environmental pollution including global warming, extinctions of plant and animal species, and all the attendant sociological and political problems—are to a great degree ecological" (Pimm and Smith, "Ecology," para. 1).

with the Christian tradition in important ways. I also want to posit a good ecological style and a bad one. These will be my second and third points. A good ecological style will be poetic: that is, it will be revelatory. A bad ecological style will be bureaucratic: these days, I am especially concerned about bureaucracy, which is a general and primordial evil.

When ecology and poetry are linked, as we are doing here, one might reasonably expect to look at poetry that raises ecological issues or that meditates on natural beauty. But we can do other things too. Poetry always accentuates a relationship between form and content, or style and substance. What do we mean by "form" or "style"? As an example, the phrase "rhetorical style as real substance" repeats a pattern of /r/ . . . /s/ sounds. The repetition (or alliteration), even apart from the meaning of the words involved, itself suggests a relationship of some kind. Form is bound up with content in this way. I'll come back to the idea of relationship in a moment. But please notice that in poetry and rhetoric our actual words, sounds, and verbal patterns matter.

In referring to "real substance," I mean to gesture to the analogy of being and participatory theology. Only God is truly substantive or subsistent.[3] All other being is merely a participation in his being. So we might already anticipate how notions of repetition and resonance are relevant. They make sense in a participatory environment. But the title refers to rhetorical style as real substance. Style, which seems idiosyncratic and perhaps ephemeral, is of the same order as substance. We must, in the first instance, be talking about divine rhetoric, the divine Word of God revealed in the person of Jesus Christ. Style really does matter. All of creation participates in this trinitarian reality, in which difference and

3. Of created *esse* Thomas writes, "*being [esse]* denotes something complete and simple, yet non-subsistent" (Aquinas, *De Potentia Dei*, q.1, a.1.18). Of the act of creation itself he says, "creare autem est dare esse"—to create is to give *esse* (Aquinas, *Scriptum Super Sententiis I*, d.37, q. 1, a.1, cited in Bieler, "Consummation of the World," 370). Martin Bieler points out that for Thomas, "Subsistent being is absolute freedom; it is God himself, who turns toward us and grants us friendship" (Bieler, "Consummation of the World," 371). In phrasing entirely relevant to our theme, he goes onto write, "The giver is . . . the other and the not-other at the same time, the one who remains different from his gift and yet is entirely present in it" (Bieler, "Consummation of the World," 374). Similarly, Mary Taylor observes that part of the gift of creation is that the act of creation involves a "holding nothing back, that accounts for the autonomy and positivity of creation, a true 'other . . .'" even while "all of creation participates in *esse*, in God's love and generosity" (Taylor, "'Sparkling of the Holy Ghost,'" 542). The Taylor article is part of an issue of *Communio* dedicated to the theme of "Nature in Theology." Readers of this volume may also be interested to consult that journal's special issue on "Integral Ecology" (*Communio* 42.4 [2015]).

particularity are as native as unity, wholeness, and oneness. Every created thing shines with the beauty of the wholeness of divine life which gives it being. Paradoxically, its participation is the source of its vivid particularity. All human rhetoric is caught up in a participatory way in this reality and it too can be revelatory.

The affirmation of divine rhetoric and our participation in it is well established by both Augustine and Aquinas. If you have ever read *On the Trinity* books 8–15, you will have noticed how fascinated Augustine is with what he knows: things in the world; the body and its senses; things in the mind like memory and self-reflection; experiences like having faith in your friends. You may have noticed that he talks increasingly about the inner word of the things he knows, for instance at 8.6.9 and at 9.7.12. *On the Trinity* builds to a crescendo in which Augustine explains what it is that we know when we know anything at all. Where does the inner word come from? It comes from the thing that we know. Here is what Augustine says in book 15, just before he finishes this great work by inviting us to respond with praise and worship:[4]

> Whoever, then, can understand the word, not only before it sounds, but even before the images of its sound are contemplated in thought—such a word belongs to no language . . .—whoever, I say, can understand this, can already see through this mirror and in this enigma some likeness of that Word of whom it was said, "In the beginning was the Word, and the Word was with God; and the Word was God" . . . . For the thought formed from that thing which we know is the word which we speak in our heart, and it is neither Greek, nor Latin, nor of any other language, but when we have to bring it to the knowledge of those to whom we are speaking, then some sign is assumed by which it may be made known.[5]

Augustine's notion of the inner word sets us up to think properly about the nature of our knowledge of the world and what it means to respond. When we know something, we really know it. A medieval writer would say the knower participates in the thing known. It may not seem this way because Augustine says the inner word does not belong to any language. Make no mistake: the inner word is not *dis*-incarnational! It is exactly

---

4. I have lectured on the important role Augustine plays in the development of pre-modern rhetoric in Klassen, "RR5b. Rhetoric and Reality." See also Klassen, *Fellowship of the Beatific Vision*, 173–92.

5. Augustine, *On the Trinity*, 15.10.19 [186–87], quoting John 1:1.

the opposite. Augustine goes on to say that the inner word assumes signs and thoughts of signs just as Christ the Word assumed flesh but was not turned into flesh. For Augustine, the Incarnation is how we know that we have meaningful knowledge of things. Conversely, knowing we know things can encourage us to seek "that Word of whom it was said, 'In the beginning was the Word, and the Word was with God; and the Word was God.'" Ecology begins with this recognition of our actual situation.

Aquinas says much the same thing. As Josef Pieper reminds us in the pages of *The Silence of St. Thomas*, Aquinas says that we know the *logos*.[6] Because all things derive their being from their participation in the divine being, we do not know them in a way that gives us mastery over them. Any such pretense to mastery is an illusion. Rather, things are infinitely knowable. We really do know them, but in the words of Pieper, we stand on the edge of an abyss—an abyss not of darkness but of light.[7] Each of our styles is an opening onto this abyss of light: a way of bringing out hidden dimensions of what is knowable. This is something that poetry helps us to see, and ecological description can too.[8]

If there is a relationship between style and substance, and all being is a participation in divine being, can there be such a thing as a bad style? In absolute terms, probably not. However, style is affected when participation is unacknowledged.

Now let's talk about poor ecological style. To understand and interpret creation poorly is to bureaucratize. What does the word "bureaucracy" mean? Most importantly, bureaucracy is the opposite of poetry and art. Near the end of her essay on "Man: The Creating Creature," Dorothy Sayers says the following about the relationship between artistry and bureaucracy:

> It is for the sacrilegious hand laid on the major premise that the artist is crucified by tyrannies and quietly smothered by bureaucracies.[9]

---

6. Pieper, *Silence of St. Thomas*, 96. For Thomas on the *logos*, see especially Aquinas, *Commentary on St. John*. For an excellent analysis of that commentary, see Ramos, "Metaphysics of the *Logos*." See also Aquinas, *Summa Theologica*, 3.1–49 (2019–287), in which Thomas works out his Christology. Rowan Williams discusses this portion of the *Summa* in Williams, *Christ the Heart of Creation*, 12–40.

7. Pieper, *Silence of St. Thomas*, 96.

8. I offer a longer discussion of the knowability of creation and the abyss of light in an online lecture: Klassen, "Dr. Keith Cassidy Lecture 2021."

9. Sayers, "Man," 128.

"Sacrilegious" in this context does *not* refer to the way artists sometimes try to shock gratuitously or literally blaspheme sacred things. The major premise is that efficiency and stable power structures are most important. This is what the artist lays a hand on. She speaks truth to power and so she is "crucified" or "quietly smothered." Secondly, please note that Sayers effectively equates tyranny and bureaucracy. Bureaucracy is a form of power, and it threatens a proper understanding or interpretation of ecology.

In some ways, bureaucracy is a very old-fashioned word. At one time, it may have conjured Nietzsche's last man or a Kafkaesque trial. These days, it has acquired a deep stain of moral probity. The earnestness of contemporary public discourse makes it harder to discern as such, but identity politics and cancel culture are forms of bureaucracy. They are legalism. Contemporary moralism appears to be divorced from dialogue and from genuine politics. Bureaucracy once implied the opposite of moral feeling, of any feeling. Old bureaucracy was cold and soulless, pseudo-scientific and objectivizing; new bureaucracy is warm and soulless, pseudo-scientific and moralizing. Ecology mustn't be simply a bureaucratic discourse, a discourse of manipulation and non-transcendence, however moralizing.

For the rest of the way, I want to use a Canadian writer to serve as a good guide to artistry and bureaucracy and how ecology needs to be styled appropriately. The writer I have in mind, David Adams Richards, is a novelist as well as a poet, and technically I'll be talking about poetics rather than poetry. This is an unimportant distinction for our purposes. However, if you want a short, useful discussion about poetics specifically, some pages in an essay by Paul Ricoeur are very helpful.[10]

A regional Catholic writer, David Adams Richards (b. 1950) has written some nineteen novels as well as other books. He usually sets his stories in the province of New Brunswick on Canada's Atlantic coast, in an area called the Miramichi for the river that runs through it.[11] Richards writes about ne'er-do-well characters, blighted characters, officious, infuriating characters that make readers feel helpless. A friend of the New Brunswick author has rightly said that Richards loves all of his characters.[12] He evokes their smallness, their confrontations with fate, and the

---

10. Ricoeur, "Toward a Hermeneutic," 98–104. I discuss these pages in Klassen, *Rationality Is . . . The Essence*, 81–87.

11. A friend whose family hails from the area has gently corrected my pronunciation of this name: mir-a-mih-SHEE.

12. Johnson, "Afterword," 228.

sacred quirkiness of their glorious freedom. His style is rough, elliptical, and revelatory. It's like he writes his novels in a Tim Horton's coffee shop in typical Atlantic weather—in other words, weather that changes every fifteen minutes. (Tim Horton's, by the way, is the Canadian equivalent of McDonald's, but with donuts instead of hamburgers. I know you know about McDonald's, even if you don't want to admit it.)

Richards is an ecological writer in the wide sense. The Miramichi is an ecology, a small, seemingly self-contained world replete with powers that act on it. Sometimes that power is mysterious and healing; usually, it is some university-trained bureaucrat or someone who has been away to university and come back. The bureaucrats don't control the narratives, but they represent power and folly. Grace, meanwhile, can be seen, however glimpsingly, to have been inside Richards's fictional world all along.

This Maritime writer discerns that the moral pretensions of contemporary university education devolve into bureaucratic machinery that destroys people and threatens the local ecology. In *The Lost Highway* (2007), a loser called Alex Chapman refuses to enter the priesthood and for a while finds himself in a university. The refusal of his vocation, incidentally, turns out to be the lost highway. In the following, one can hear the author's ironic tone as he portrays the dangerous smugness of the professoriate:

> [Alex] became a protégé of one of the professors, Dr. Doug Cavanaugh. The man, not to be outdone by nostalgia or precedent, dressed in tweed and smoked a pipe, and you could see its smoke almost blue in the winter sky, and he balanced his courses on semantics with his love affair with a former colleague's wife, Fiona. For a while Alex was in their circle and believed in their circle more than any other. He loved their kind and bookish house like he loved paradise. There was no religious calendar to evoke shame, no base Christ on the wall, no bible in the corner—except an ancient one picked up at an auction. They spoke of politics and the inherent power shift that must come.[13]

Richards understands that university culture is a faith: "Alex believed in their circle"; "They spoke of . . . the . . . power shift that must come." The enlightened professoriate think that history is on their side.

Alex rides this wave into the academy:

---

13. Richards, *Lost Highway*, 75.

> Then in his ninth year at university he was assured of a tenured position. He knew this, and felt safe in assuming it. The debates within the halls of university were important and nonthreatening to a person such as himself. And he believed that his own life was set.
>
> Yet in all of this there was one salient point he did not admit to. He was, like most men who have never really stood on their own, frightened of being disapproved of, while pretending radical theory that was really the standard theory of a coddled academia. As long as they were the theories of many who never worked a day with their hands, he was in tune and safe, and being secure he could say he was radical.[14]

The so-called "radical theory" of the academy is standard, not radical. It is cowardice and conformity pretending to be morally outstanding, produced by people who "never worked a day with their hands." For Richards, their attitude poisons life. Alex, for his part, loses his safe position when he ends up on the wrong side of a case of political correctness. The bureaucracy eats him alive. He will be redeemed, but not before he returns home and his provincial life turns to squalor.

The 2016 novel *Principles to Live By* puts the focus on bureaucracy as moralism (principles).[15] It features a social worker named Melissa Sapp. Her last name says everything you need to know about her, but if you don't know about Tim Hortons, you might also not know that sap is old-fashioned North American slang for someone easily taken in. Sapp may have power in the novel, but for Richards such characters are pathetic, even though they regularly wield bureaucratic machinery.

Sapp helps to discredit the detective who takes up the case of a teenager he suspects is a powerless victim. That boy's improbable story involves his fleeing from a Hutu attack that engulfs his Canadian parents working in Rwanda in 1994. When the boy arrives in New Brunswick, the local authorities show no interest in finding out his identity or what his story might be. He seems simply to be a troubled youth who first arrived at, then vanished from, a local foster home—not worth another thought.

The ecology in question here is the international network of shared responsibility and its vulnerability to bureaucratization. Sapp's aunt, Midge Nolan Overplant, at the time works in a satellite office in New York

---

14. Richards, *Lost Highway*, 80.

15. This novel is the first in a trilogy that continues with *Mary Cyr* (2018) and *Darkness* (2021).

that has dealings with the Rwandan ambassador. In describing her government work environment, Richards pulls down everything he can that has anything to do with Canadian officialdom, including its high culture. Moral superiority and bureaucracy have replaced genuine principles:

> In 1994, Midge's office in New York was not very big. It was a place for gentle conversation, splendid imported teas and shortcakes. In it were posters of certain well-known Canadian writers—Laurence, Ondaatje and Atwood—the address Lester Pearson gave when he won the Nobel Prize for Peace. A picture of an African woman tilling soil with a child on her back. A map of Rwanda that she had been given by Rwandan ambassador Jean-Damascène Bizimana. She had travelled extensively and had the worldly air of the no-nonsense middle-aged feminist divorcee, wearing loose-fitting pant suits and large skirts. Always with a hat that made her look mischievous.[16]

Richards recognizes the weakness of official posturing and its complicity with far-reaching injustices.

Narrower forms of environmentalism can be caught up in this moralism. It can be a fashionable cause, a rhetorical style based on an understanding of reality that is at best manipulative. An early novel features another of Richards's university-trained characters, Vera Pillar. Her name of course literally means "true pillar" and she sees herself as a pillar of society. A journalist and a social worker, Vera pretends to be interested in a local man who has run into trouble with the law. She tells him she wants to write a book about him. In typical Richards fashion, she is only using the hapless man, who develops feelings for her, and as the novel reaches its climax, she abandons him:

> "Jerry, I should tell you I'm involved."
>
> "Involved—in what?" Jerry said.
>
> "I mean I have a friend—he's studying Environmental Marine Biology in Halifax . . . . He's second-generation Chinese-Canadian—so he certainly knows about stereotyping."[17]

This exchange is just plain funny. "I'm involved" . . . . "Involved—in what?" Jerry's earnest misunderstanding exposes the pseudo-sophisticated language of decorum. Meanwhile, Vera's "friend" studies environmental

---

16. Richards, *Principles to Live By*, 224–25.
17. Richards, *For Those Who Hunt*, 184.

marine biology and knows about stereotyping simply by being second-generation Chinese-Canadian. He ticks the right boxes. The word "environment" is a badge for Vera, and that's precisely the satirical work it's doing for Richards. This character doesn't understand or care about ecology: it's just another cause for her to manipulate.

A fourth novel, *The Friends of Meager Fortune*, offers a sympathetic look at the New Brunswick lumber industry in the 1940s. For cancel culture, this would be provocation enough. In 2006, when he wrote the novel, Richards probably suspected that his approach was politically incorrect. He will have relished that. For him, the physical environment is deeply meaningful as part of a local but larger ecology at once nobly tragic and redeemable. Whereas those caught up in the machinery of officialdom attempt to manipulate reality, Greek tragedy recognizes human limitations. This sensibility inflects our introduction to Will Jameson, one of the story's heroes:

> Yet once, after he had broken the jaw of a man ten years older than him with one punch, because wood had been stolen from a sled as a protest, and the sled burned, he drinking a pint of rum straight down said to his brother in boyish exuberance, "What prophecy can f[***] me" . . . .
> Not knowing that in his smile was visible all the boyish tragedy he had already managed to compile. Like the Athenians heading toward Syracuse, not knowing there would be no way back.[18]

Richards's own style in this passage invokes tragedy sympathetically. "Yet" is a word of contingency and qualification. At the start of a sentence, it conveys drama. "He drinking" does the same. An ordinary writer anxious about grammatical, if not political, correctness would put a comma after the pronoun "he" and set off the participial phrase: He, drinking a pint of rum straight down, said to his brother . . . . "He drinking" is slightly off, like a poor fit in the world, which tragedy acknowledges. Furthermore, "He drinking a pint of rum straight down said to his brother . . ." *is like* the act of drinking a pint straight down without a pause. Swearing about a prophecy is probably never a good idea: it sets the speaker up for a fall. The low-class f-bomb and the sentence fragments that follow show that genuine tragedy threatens everybody. Even the world of the Miramichi is riven by it.

---

18. Richards, *Friends of Meager Fortune*, 15.

In *The Friends of Meager Fortune*, the story of two brothers' lives (and that of a boy nicknamed Meager Fortune) plays out on Good Friday Mountain. That's the source of their lumber. There is tragedy there, but even deeper healing and hope. At the end of the novel, the narrator looks back in time and contemplates a monument built in honor of these characters:

> The woods are muted and stilled and broken and bull-dozed away, by machinery none of these men could have foreseen. Nor could they have foreseen our great skyscraper mills that turn our logs into soft toilet paper for softer arses. Our companies owned by other countries.
>
> They could not have foreseen that this monument to tenacity and courage and goodness would be the cause of such disruptive anger over the years. That some mining company would claim this tract and want to take the monuments down . . . .
>
> So these men who died, faithful to Buckler's mountain, over time became again part of a scandal. Another scandal started because of our famine. To fill up our souls with the trinkets of life, instead of with life itself.[19]

"Our famine" is caused by filling up our souls "with the trinkets of life, instead of with life itself." This is the context for a scandal about a monument (Richards is truly prescient here); it is also Richards's explanation for our being so interested in scandal generally: we are detached from "life itself." Foreign ownership of our companies reflects this detachment. A bureaucratic sleight-of-hand interposes itself between people and the real. Detachment is also evident in softer arses that don't care where their toilet paper comes from: they too contribute to the problem of "our famine."

Finally, let's turn our attention to good ecological rhetoric. Despite being "hunted down" and trapped in bad circumstances, someone in Richards's novels always encounters the charged realities of life anyway.[20] These are concentrated in the signs and symbols of Christianity. In the novel featuring Vera Pillar, the husband she long ago divorced—another pathetic figure—helps the ministers of a local church raise a new cross on it:

> Nevin looked down.
> No one knew him, and he knew none of them.

---

19. Richards, *Friends of Meager Fortune*, 360.

20. The novel discussed featuring Vera Pillar is Richards, *For Those Who Hunt the Wounded Down* (1993). It is part of a trilogy that includes *Nights Below Station Street* (1988) and *Evening Snow Will Bring Such Peace* (1990).

> When he had brought his books to the rented trailer—a most quixotic collection of books—sex manuals sat atop the environmental study of 1987, atop works by Schopenhauer and Kant near cookbooks and Andy Capp comic books—the young minister had smiled at him ruefully and had said: "You won't need none of those here."
>
> "Oh," Nevin said.
>
> "You'll find there is only one work here—the work of the Lord."[21]

After he has finished raising the cross and is back on the ground, he is given to further reflection:

> He was alone in the little churchyard. Suddenly he was depressed as he was at times when he thought of ending his life.
>
> He thought of reading Kant in his studies at university and felt he had made a great mistake in being here.
>
> "Come inside," a woman said to him. He blinked and put on his glasses and looked at her. She was standing with her little boy near the door.
>
> "Come on—you'll freeze your arse off out there," she said. She smiled and he smiled also.
>
> She was Loretta Bines.
>
> He looked up at the cross. Now that it was done it didn't seem at all an important thing to do.
>
> "You were brave to do that," she said. The little boy nodded and smiled at him.[22]

Nevin reads various kinds of books. He is confused. He doesn't know how to read the cross. Loretta Bines and her son have to interpret it for him. They do, and represent a fresh start for him within the church and within the novel's small world.

Principles to Live By likewise confronts the difference between being connected with life itself and living in a world of bureaucratic manipulation. The orphaned teenage boy's father Hugh, we discover, was a Canadian engineer who took his family to Rwanda to help with their electricity needs. Hugh and his wife Lily get caught with others in the atrocities of that genocide:

> The captain did make one more plea for the Canadians and the Irishman to come. But all of them were too stubborn. They

---

21. Richards, *For Those Who Hunt*, 218.
22. Richards, *For Those Who Hunt*, 221.

could not go. They wanted to—they desperately wanted to. But they could not.

Why were they too stubborn? Because Vanessa, the Roman Catholic nun, who was twenty-nine years old, would not leave the boys and girls; and the Irish doctor realized that Vanessa couldn't leave, even though her order had already gone back into Uganda. She would not go, so the Irish doctor would stay beside her. And Hugh looked at the great generators behind the mesh fence with the sign that said DANGER HIGH VOLTAGE and would not leave either. And Lily could not leave him. And so it came to that moment, as fruitless as it all seemed, where there were principles to live by.[23]

Again, the ecology of this novel is presented on a large scale. For Richards, the notion of "principles" within it is malleable. In this case, the principles seem to be "fruitless," but for Richards, that doesn't matter. The principles of these characters connect them with the lives of innocent boys and girls.

In the novel, though, the reader first encounters the phrase "principles to live by" as a slogan over the lintel in a home where foster parents are bilking the system. Midge Overplant and her niece Melissa Sapp are presented as people with high principles. Principles are part of the problem. The issue, to paraphrase Alasdair MacIntyre, is "Whose principles?"[24] The choice is between principles for the sake of bureaucracy and principles for their own sake, because of some inarticulable awareness of connectedness.

Richards's style in all his novels is rough-hewn. Why is it like that? One effect is that you don't feel like the author is trying it on, like a coat. Rather, the characters and the scenes emerge from this language and come into being with it. There is no sequencing, no sense that *first* the author has an idea, *then* seeks a way to express it. He plays his part in an unfolding, a revealing, and invites his readers to play theirs. Bureaucratic rhetoric in the novels, by contrast, tends toward stasis and death. Calculated to eliminate surprises, it is the language of rules—of a dominant discourse someone feels they can control. The rules that characters like Alex Chapman embrace at university seem to be the most open-ended and inclusive imaginable, but what matters most is that they form a grid nonetheless. Richards's style, by contrast, is unkempt, even forbidding.

---

23. Richards, *Principles to Live By*, 232.
24. MacIntyre, *Whose Justice? Which Rationality?*

The syntax is slightly off; the registers are mixed (Kant and arse might appear side-by-side). His heroes have glimpses of the real that are startling and precise. They arise out of some act of commitment, however arbitrary, like Nevin's. A vision of the real, in its turn, demands an intuitive response and interpretation. It is in this way that one develops a style.

Like any meaningful human undertaking, "care for our common home" is susceptible to bureaucratization. It may seem obvious that ecology means concern with life itself, but untethered from a view of the real suffused with the presence of God, it represents a simulacrum. Bureaucracy hides behind its facelessness, its unobjectionability. Wherever morality looks obvious—whether in hashtag slogans, self-righteous charges of hypocrisy, or in pronouncements to "trust the science" (without reference either to the people who actually practice it or the ends science properly serves)—you are probably in the presence of bureaucracy. It is up-to-date and shape-changing; it's also primordial, as old as Pharisaism. It leads to the denial of life itself.

The event of the cross has happened, yet our writing must continue. We must continually inscribe on the face of creation creation's true name. Pope Francis's greatest insight may be that care of our common home is as much about human trafficking as it is global warming. The Church never parses the world and human problems in such a way as to forget the whole. Against bureaucracy it speaks poetry; against wokery it writes novels. Where you and I live and read and do our painting, the issue isn't whether we are experts: it's whether we are willing to make lines in the dust of our daily lives.

To summarize, my three points in this chapter have been as follows. For one, it's helpful to think about our ecological concerns in rhetorical terms. They resonate with profound Christian teaching when we do. Secondly, moralism is a feature of modern bureaucracy, which strives against genuine ecological description, concern, and responsiveness. Finally, good ecological rhetoric is poetic; it recognizes that our common home participates in a larger reality and, like good poetry, always reveals something of that truth.

Bibliography

Aquinas, Thomas. *Commentary on the Gospel of St. John*. Translated by James A. Weisheipl and Fabian R. Larcher. Albany: Magi, 1998. https://isidore.co/aquinas/SSJohn.htm.

———. *Quaestiones Disputatae de Potentia Dei*. Translated by the English Dominican Fathers. Westminster: Newman, 1952. https://isidore.co/aquinas/QDdePotentia.htm.

———. *Scriptum Super Sententiis I*. https://aquinas.cc/la/en/~Sent.I.D37.Q1.A1.C.2.

———. *Summa Theologica*. Vol. 4. Translated by Fathers of the English Dominican Province. Westminster, MD: Christian Classics, 1981.

Augustine. *On the Trinity, Books 8–15*. Edited by Gareth B. Matthews. Translated by Stephen McKenna. Cambridge: Cambridge University Press, 2002.

Bieler, Martin. "The Consummation of the World as a Re-Capitulation." *Communio* 43.3 (2016) 365–87.

Francis. *Laudato Si'*. Encyclical, May 24, 2015. https://www.vatican.va/content/francesco/en/encyclicals/documents/papa-francesco_20150524_enciclica-laudato-si.html.

Johnson, Wayne. "Afterword." In *Evening Snow Will Bring Such Peace*, by David Adams Richards, 227–30. Toronto: McClelland and Stewart, 2003.

Klassen, Norm. "Dr. Keith Cassidy Lecture 2021: Is Reality Knowable? with Dr. Norm Klassen." Mar. 5, 2021. YouTube video. https://www.youtube.com/watch?v=q9ZleAXGU2w.

———. *The Fellowship of the Beatific Vision: Chaucer on Overcoming Tyranny and Becoming Ourselves*. Eugene, OR: Cascade, 2016.

———. *Rationality Is . . . The Essence of Literary Theory*. Eugene, OR: Cascade, 2022.

———. "RR5b. Rhetoric and Reality: Augustine DT Bks 14–15." May 27, 2021. YouTube video. https://www.youtube.com/watch?v=v-K2WrLMXdc.

MacIntyre, Alasdair. *Whose Justice? Which Rationality?* Notre Dame: Notre Dame University Press, 1988.

Pieper, Josef. *The Silence of St. Thomas*. Translated by John Murray and Daniel O'Connor. South Bend, IN: St. Augustine's Press, 1999.

Pimm, Stuart L., and Robert Leo Smith. "Ecology." *Britannica*. Last updated Aug. 9, 2024. https://www.britannica.com/science/ecology.

Ramos, Alice. "A Metaphysics of the *Logos* in St. Thomas Aquinas: Creation and Knowledge." *Cauriensia* 9 (2014) 95–111.

Richards, David Adams. *For Those Who Hunt the Wounded Down*. Toronto: McClelland and Stewart, 1993.

———. *The Friends of Meager Fortune*. Toronto: Doubleday, 2006.

———. *The Lost Highway*. Toronto: Anchor, 2008.

———. *Principles to Live By*. Toronto: Doubleday, 2016.

Ricoeur, Paul. "Toward a Hermeneutic of the Idea of Revelation." In *Essays on Biblical Interpretation*, edited by Lewis S. Mudge, 73–118. Philadelphia: Fortress, 1980.

Sayers, Dorothy. "Man: The Creating Creature." In *Christian Letters to a Post-Christian World*, 67–129. Grand Rapids: Eerdmans, 1969.

Taylor, Mary. "'The Sparkling of the Holy Ghost': The Metaphysics of Nature and Grace in Dante's *Paradiso*." *Communio* 46.3–4 (2019) 520–65.

Williams, Rowan. *Christ the Heart of Creation*. London: Bloomsbury Continuum, 2018.

3

Re-Homing the Human

Reflections Arising from *Laudato Si': On Care for Our Common Home*

Jeffrey Dirk Wilson

The Problem: Humans Are Not at Home in the World

In 1977, Wendell Berry first published his jeremiad and manifesto, *The Unsettling of America: Culture and Agriculture*.[1] The presenting issues that he addresses have to do with the state of farmland in America. The problems that he discusses have only become more serious. There are now even fewer farmers today than there were then. Farmland becomes concentrated in the hands of fewer people, and many of those themselves investors rather than farmers, and the processing of food is controlled by a half-dozen transnational corporations. Berry situated the farm crisis in the context of the ecological crisis, and the ecological crisis he identified as a fundamentally cultural crisis. Berry was humble enough to let someone else formulate the problem to which he addressed his book. David Budbill of Wolcott, Vermont wrote a letter to Berry. The letter is quoted at length, but Budbill had a gift for concision and precision. He summed up the problem as "a syndrome I call the Terrarium View of the World: nature always at a distance, under glass."[2] He continued, "In *Audubon* magazine"—Budbill was an Audubon Society member—"almost always the beautiful pictures are without man; the ugly ones with him. Such self hatred! I keep wanting to write to them and say, 'Look! My name is David Budbill and I

---

1. Berry, *Unsettling of America*.
2. Berry, *Unsettling of America*, 28.

belong to the chain of being too, as a participant not an observer (nature is not television!)."[3] The human being is defined as "other" than the natural world, and thus Planet Earth is viewed and experienced as a foreign realm to be plundered or preserved, but not lived in. Humans are not at home in the world, but are rather outside it, looking in.

An Autobiographical Excursus

I, with my family, am a farm owner. It is a small holding, 135 acres (56 hectares). I like to say that our farm is preserved and conserved. My parents agreed to place our property under perpetual easement so that it would never be developed residentially, commercially, or industrially. We have a tenant for the arable ground. He is a wonderful farmer and human being. For example, he has practiced carbon sequestration since before he began renting our place fifteen years ago. When the residue of a crop is left on the ground, it decomposes and releases carbon into the atmosphere. By employing best practices, this carbon can be fixed in the soil, thereby both preventing air pollution and enriching the soil. Because he is recognized as a practitioner of responsible farming, he is invited to give talks to other farmers across the United States of America. I cannot imagine having a better tenant. That having been said, however, the crop fields are "green deserts." They are sprayed with both herbicides and insecticides to prevent weeds and pests from growing in the fields. To the degree that the spraying is unsuccessful, the harvest is reduced and the value of the land is diminished. Over the course of my lifetime, these state-of-the-art farming practices have meant loss of habitat for pheasant, quail, mourning dove, and other wildlife. Even with the best-possible tenant, the cropland is partially removed from the realm of nature. Meeting global food and energy needs depends on the practices described.

We also have thirty-four acres in a conservation program with the US federal government. The land is planted with trees, shrubs, and warm and cold-season grasses, with a view both to conservation of the land and providing cover for wildlife. The government pays us annually an amount as rent and for maintenance of the conservation practices. The government also regulates the management of the practices in a highly bureaucratized way, such that compliance is often onerous. For example, we are not supposed to enter the acres under conservation from April 15 to August 15

---

3. Berry, *Unsettling of America*, 29.

because that is the primary nesting season for birds. At the same time, we are not allowed to permit noxious weeds—certain weeds are deemed noxious by law—to go to seed. These two rules are often in conflict. In order to enter the conserved fields during the primary nesting season in order to spray the noxious weeds, we must apply to a government agency for permission to enter the fields for that purpose. When a weed is a clear problem, but not noxious by law, the agency is likely to refuse permission to spray. One especially problematic weed became so widespread that it has been removed from the official list, presumably because preventing its spread was deemed hopeless. That is to say, the pertinent agency could actually refuse permission to spray for that weed, not because it posed no threat, but rather because it posed so great a threat. I sometimes consider selling the farm and becoming a writer of absurdist plays.

Has my experience with government agencies always been this negative? No! So, what has changed? Bureaucracy is necessary for civil society. It is a mediating mechanism between large policy goals (ends) and actions on the ground (means to those ends). As long as those large policy goals are good and as long as bureaucracy does mediate those ends, then bureaucracy is, in fact, good. When, however, those ends are themselves evil (e.g., genocide, oppression), then the bureaucracy—insofar as it is a mediating mechanism—is evil. The ends of the conservation programs in which our farm is enrolled are good. How is it that the bureaucracy as the mediating mechanism has become not evil, but surely less successful in achieving the announced ends? The difference is the decline of prudential judgment—and I mean Aristotelian *phronēsis*—by the agents of the government working with local farmers and landowners. Sometimes that decline is because government officials above the local-office level have dictated that prudential judgment shall not be exercised, but rather that regulations shall be applied categorically. Other times, the decline in prudential judgment is because the agent on the ground does not possess prudential judgment (or possesses it very inadequately). A decade or more ago, I remember sitting at the table with the representatives of all the pertinent agencies, and I asked a question about how to handle something. One of the officials leaned across the table and said to me, "Jeffrey, do whatever you need to do to make this work!" I told this story to an official a few weeks ago—someone who does possess prudential judgment and who has been around the system for decades. He responded, "Those days are over." Without prudential judgment, ends become totalized and, therefore, destructive of the ends themselves as well as oppressive of those to whom the regulations are categorically applied. The restoration of prudential judgment—both its capacity and the freedom of its application—is imperative as one criterion for transcendence of the status of human alienation from the earth, both in plunder and preservation/conservation.

The government program has been successful in that the acres under conservation contracts have become a habitat for abundant wildlife. Those acres surround my home. As I write these words, I can hear a choir of birdsong. There are two kinds of hawks that nest on the farm. Bald eagles sometimes hunt here. We have rabbits, foxes, raccoons, opossums, and other abundant animal life. When I was a boy, it was a rarity to see deer. Now they are overpopulated. Last year, my gamekeeper took eight deer, which is only helping to keep the population healthy. In fact, we have so many deer that they reduce the tenant farmer's crops to the extent we may need to apply for crop damage permits to take deer above the established limits and outside the established seasons.

In short, on our farm, we have two competing models—agricultural production and preservation/conservation—that are in conflict with each other. In the former, both plant and animal wildlife are problems. In the latter, the human being is the problem. For me, personally, I experience cognitive dissonance that can be disorienting. I also have practical and potentially legal problems in managing the property for my family. The irony is that the human being is a stranger in both the agricultural production and the conservation. We are invaders in the first model, doing what we do, then leaving, re-entering to spray or to harvest. We are strangers or interlopers in the second model. That we have to enter the conserved acres at all seems a kind of embarrassment to the environmental designers of the program. They would prefer to leave nature to itself, which is to say that humans are not considered part of nature. In short, humans are not at home in either model. I have two terrariums, one for production, the other for conservation. I am supposed to live outside of both. As a human agent (not to mention as the landowner), I am exceedingly uncomfortable with my not-at-homeness on the property that a piece of paper says I own. I do not make my living by farming. Continuing to engage in the farm at all is, frankly, a professional inconvenience. I am here because my grandfather and father farmed here, and because I hope there will be future generations of our family who will farm here. I am here because I live here, and I mean to make this place my home. As a philosopher, I ask, "How did we come to this state of not-at-homeness with our farmland?"

Martin Heidegger's Theory of Not-at-Homeness

Whether the thought of Heidegger was a catalyst to this sense of human "not-at-homeness" in the world or it merely describes a phenomenon he observed—or some combination of the two—is not a question to be resolved here. That he does describe this "not-at-homeness" is a fact. In his *Introduction to Metaphysics*—based on a set of lectures given in 1935 after he had resigned the Freiburg University rectorate and lightly revised in 1953[4]—he offers an exposition of "the first choral ode from Sophocles's *Antigone* (lines 332–75)" by way of giving an account of human not-at-homeness. That choral ode begins, in Heidegger's translation, "Manifold is the uncanny [*polla ta deina*], yet nothing / uncannier than man bestirs itself, rising up beyond him."[5] The original Greek word here—translated from Heidegger's German translation into English as "uncanny"—is *deinon*. Liddell, Scott, and Jones offer the following translations: (1) "fearful, terrible"; (2) "marvelously strong, powerful . . . wondrous, marvelous, strange"; (3) "clever, skillful." There are other subsidiary definitions, but these give a fair sense of the range in meaning.[6] Heidegger's German translation of *deinon* is *unheimlich*,[7] which literally means "without a home." It has other resonances, however. It can mean "paranormal." Ghostly apparitions would be *unheimlich*. In this sense, Fried and Polt offer "uncanny" as their standard translation. The sense of déjà vu is uncanny. The feeling of having been somewhere or experienced something before is unsettling, and therefore gives a sense that one is not at home in the world. *Unheimlich* also can be used as an emphatic in the way that "awful" can be used in English. *Unheimlich gut* becomes "awfully good." Both *unheimlich* and "awful" have a sense of uncanniness at their roots, but that sense is altogether lost when using the locution *unheimlich gut* to describe a pepperoni pizza. I suggest that all these varied meanings are at play in both the original Greek *deinon* and the German *unheimlich*. Berry's term "unsettling" fits well into the range of meanings for *unheimlich*. Berry means a literal unsettling, as in "displacing," but he is poet enough

---

4. Heidegger, *Introduction to Metaphysics*, vii–viii, xiii.

5. Heidegger, *Introduction to Metaphysics*, 163n112. It is likely that Heidegger gleaned the beginning of his insight from Rudolf Otto in his *Idea of the Holy*, the first German edition published in 1917. Otto begins his brief discussion with a reference to the *Antigone* of Sophocles, even quoting the same line with which Heidegger begins his discussion, *polla ta deina*. See Otto, *Idea of the Holy*, x, 39–40.

6. Liddell et al., *Greek-English Lexicon*, q.v. *deinos*, 374–75.

7. Heidegger, *Introduction to Metaphysics*, 269.

that we can suppose he also means "unsettled" in the sense that bad news can unsettle someone. I suggest that Berry and Heidegger both point to the same basic human phenomenon of not being at home in the world.

Dasein—literally, "there-being" or "being there" as in "being in that place," a fundamental "point-to-ability"—is, famously, Heidegger's term for human being. *Dasein* is the uncanniest (*deinontaton*)—the most not-at-home—thing in the world.[8] Everything else has its fixed nature and place, but there is an indeterminacy about humans that makes it difficult to point to the human, to name the human, as one can point to and name in the case of gods, animals, plants, and objects.[9] There is, then, a contradiction to be closed: humans are inherently indeterminate, but to be authentically human one must achieve the determinacy, the point-to-ability of *Dasein*, and yet even then the indeterminacy persists.[10] According to Heidegger, the closing of the contradiction is through violence. This is not the violence of the wild beast, for they are violent according to their fixed natures. The human is decisively violent, violent in this way and not that, in this place and not another, as Heidegger says: "*Deinon* means the violent in the sense of one who needs to use violence—and does not just have violence at his disposal, but is violent-doing, insofar as using violence is the basic trait not just of his doing, but of his Dasein."[11] This is violence in the Heraclitean sense—as Heidegger understands it—of *polemos* in Greek, in English "war, strife, or struggle."[12] If violence is the essential means, how or where does the human—as understood by Aristotle or Aquinas—become *Dasein*, that is, "human" in the Heideggerian sense? Heidegger's answer is the *polis*, "the political community." He writes, "Not all the routes into the domains of beings are named, but the ground and place of human Dasein itself, the spot where all these routes cross, [is] the *polis*."[13] How does violence transform and transport the human from inauthenticity to authentic *Dasein* in political community?

---

8. "The saying 'the human being is the uncanniest' provides the authentic *Greek* definition of humanity" (Heidegger, *Introduction to Metaphysics*, 168–69n116).

9. This human indeterminacy can be traced back to Pico della Mirandola's *Oration on the Dignity of Man* and is one of the most basic claims and principles of modernity.

10. Here is an example of this persistent indeterminacy: "The *logos* is what human beings are continually amidst and what they are away from all the same, absently present" (Heidegger, *Introduction to Metaphysics*, 144n99).

11. Heidegger, *Introduction to Metaphysics*, 167n115.

12. Heidegger, *Introduction to Metaphysics*, 67n47, n4.

13. Heidegger, *Introduction to Metaphysics*, 169n117.

Whenever someone tried to explain Heidegger—during his lifetime—in terms other than his specific formulations, he usually said that the other person had gotten him all wrong (e.g., famously Sartre). I am sure that Heidegger or a Heideggerian or even an anti-Heideggerian might say that I have Heidegger wrong, but I shall try to say simply, perhaps even simplistically, how being-under-way to *Dasein* takes place. For this purpose, I shall leave behind the Greek and the German terms. The decisive violence of the human is technology in relation to nature. If the human applies technology fittingly, then that will be just; if unfittingly, then unjust.[14] To be fair to Heidegger, he is trying to answer Hume's challenge of whether there be any justice in nature. After all, the sun shines on the just and unjust. Heidegger's reply is that the unfitting, and therefore unjust, application of technology will bring swift retribution from nature—Anaximander B1 is strongly in the background here.[15] To use a contemporary example, if we release too much carbon into the atmosphere, then hundred-year floods will come twice a decade. To explain technology that is fitting—going beyond this text—Heidegger loved the example of the woodcutter who sharpened his ax with exquisite care and practiced using it until it became an extension of him. One could contrast that image with the use of chainsaws to clear-cut a forest. One sees his point, and many in the twentieth-century environmental movement have seen the point and have built extensively on it.[16]

One problem with Heidegger's paradigm of finding the fitting technology is that it supposes the fittingness of technology *qua* technology is both necessary and sufficient as a condition for justice. That is to say, all that one needs to do is determine which technology is fitting, and no other determination needs to be made. For Heidegger, there are no Aristotelian ends. As Clare Pearson Geiman puts it: "Human Being in its temporality is given only in and through possibilities and potentialities."[17] Being "under way" is primary for Heidegger; thus, the end to which technology is put is secondary—at most—to the technology itself as the means. Part of the reason for putting consideration of technology before consideration of the human being is that humans are not "animals having

---

14. For Heidegger's circuitous account of what I have summarized, see Heidegger, *Introduction to Metaphysics*, 177–89nn121–29.

15. Heidegger, *Introduction to Metaphysics*, 185n127.

16. "Heidegger is one of the most referenced philosophers in environmental ethics" (Paul, "Import of Heidegger's Philosophy," 79).

17. Pearson Geiman, "Heidegger's *Antigones*," 166.

reason," but rather—contra Aristotle—nature is *logos* having the human ("*phusis = logos anthrōpon echon*").[18] In other words, the human is under destiny and without that freedom which is concomitant with reason. In the context of a lecture, Heidegger likened the mass murder of the Jews with the mass production of food.[19] I should like to ask Heidegger, or someone who defends his theories—I am reticent about calling it "philosophy"—would Hitler have applied technology fittingly had he killed the Jews carefully with his sharpened ax, one by one—not unlike the way that Julius Caesar was responsible for the slaughter of a million Gauls? Would that have been just? And, if not, why not? Heidegger has a category of "the Ought," but he makes clear that it is not a moral "Ought" in any way that Aquinas or Hume or Kant would recognize.[20] The closest that Heidegger ever came to repudiating the Nazis comes just two pages after explaining that his "Ought" is not moral and only five pages before the end of his *Introduction to Metaphysics*: "What is peddled about

---

18. Heidegger, *Introduction to Metaphysics*, 195n134.

19. "The occasion for Heidegger's infamous remark was at a series of lectures given at the Bremen Club in 1949 where he discussed many of the themes found in 'Question Concerning Technology.' In this context, during one of the lectures, Heidegger makes a massively controversial remark. The comment has provoked extreme outrage. The common denominator running through the responses is that Heidegger's remark is shockingly inadequate and insensitive, that he grossly diminishes the horror of the Holocaust and the gas chambers by comparing them to agricultural practices" (O'Brien, *Heidegger, History and the Holocaust*, 21). O'Brien seeks to exculpate Heidegger:

> So, we must dispel the myth that Heidegger is saying that there is no difference between the mass production of crops or meat and the systematic extermination of millions of people! He insists that they are the same thing "in essence." Heidegger suggests that the essence of technology is nothing technological. He is critical of the traditional concept of essence. For Heidegger, the essence of something is what holds sway within it such that it appears *as* what it is. Heidegger believes that the mechanized food industry, the Holocaust, the splitting of the atom, nuclear bombs, have as their common feature a technological backdrop. That is, regardless of the moral status of what happens or is done, they involve a *technological way of revealing* the world, or people or energy or animals. That is not to say that Heidegger is morally equating the consumption of animals with genocide. (O'Brien, *History*, 39)

The insertion of the category of "the moral" into Heidegger's thought is unwarranted. Indeed, how can a moral right or wrong be determined independent of *per se* essence which Heidegger clearly rejects? Those who attribute categories of "the moral" or "the ethical" to Heidegger are guilty of projection. That there is hot scholarly debate about these matters is clear. It is also clear on which side of that debate I range myself.

20. "The 'good' here does not mean what is orderly in the moral sense, but the valiant, which achieves and can achieve what is proper to it" (Heidegger, *Introduction to Metaphysics*, 219n150).

nowadays as the philosophy of National Socialism [1935] . . . has not the least to do with the inner truth and greatness of this movement [what follows was added in 1953] namely, the encounter between global technology and modern humanity."[21] I ask again, had Hitler murdered Jews one at a time with a finely sharpened ax, would that have made slaughter fitting and, therefore, just? I know of no basis in Heidegger's writings by which such slaughter could be deemed wrong when the human employs a fitting tool. In a word, the measure of technology is—at a bare minimum—inadequate to assess an action. If my conclusion is correct, then how can Heidegger's thought be considered a fitting route—to use his term—for modern environmentalism? There should be no surprise that post-moderns find themselves alienated from themselves, displaced from their world, seemingly forever not-at-home. Wendell Berry falls into the Heideggerian trap when he proposes "responsible use" as the alternative to the binary choice between "intentional protection of . . . 'the environment' and its inadvertent destruction of others [i.e., other parts of the environment]."[22] By that standard alone, organic and sustainable growth of poppies for heroin would be indistinguishable from the organic and sustainable growth of beans and greens for the human diet.[23] Determining the fitting technology may well be a necessary condition for re-homing the human, but it is certainly not sufficient.

21. Heidegger, *Introduction to Metaphysics*, 222n152.
22. Berry, *Unsettling of America*, 27.
23. I acknowledge that Berry is talking about the responsible use *of the land*, which is not the same thing as finding the fitting technology. Though they are not identical, responsible use of the land—as Berry understands it—entails finding the fitting technology. His invocation of Ivan Illich (Berry, *Unsettling of America*, 19) makes that clear. Further, there is a soft idealization of the Amish (Berry, *Unsettling of America*, 210–17)—I am, myself, full of admiration for my Amish neighbors and friends—that does not account for just the sort of problem I have identified when sustainably produced poppies for heroin production meet Heidegger's test for fitting technology. The Amish depend upon the morally dubious cash crop of tobacco, which they are able to grow so profitably precisely because of their low-tech approach to farming made possible by large families working together in the fields.

Re-Homing the Human

The Creation in the Bible

In the second creation account,[24] God makes man and *settles* him in a garden. *Contra* Heidegger and using his terms, God gives the human precisely that point-to-ability, that determinacy of nature which Heidegger (and most moderns since Pico della Mirandola) denies. God gives the human both being (*sein*) and a place (*da*). The place of the human's most basic thereness is not in a political community (*polis*), but rather in a garden. God observes, however, "it is not good that the man should be alone; I will make him a helper fit for him.'"[25] To that end, God makes all the species of animal and presents each species to the man "to see what he would call them."[26] The man names all the animals but does not find among them a suitable "helper." God, then, performs surgery on the man and forms woman from a rib taken from the man. The man deems woman a suitable helpmate, his completion. Here is the biblical authority for heterosexual monogamy as the standard for marital vocation, but it is more the relation of the man—and also of the woman as man's completion—to the garden and animals that interests us here. The first human vocation is to be the gardener in the plant world as garden. The second human vocation is that of naming the animal world in relation to his need to not be alone. Though the man found none of the animals a suitable "helper," nevertheless God offers them to the man as companions. Here, then, is the paradigm of the human relation to plants and animals according to the order of creation: man and woman are gardeners in a garden in companionship with animals. The messianic vision of Isa 11 is further instructive on the human relation to animals:

> The wolf shall dwell with the lamb,
>   and the leopard shall lie down with the kid,
> and the calf and the lion and the fatling together,
>   and a little child shall lead them.
> The cow and the bear shall feed;
>   their young shall lie down together;
>   and the lion shall eat straw like the ox.
> The sucking child shall play over the hole of the asp,
>   and the weaned child shall put his hand on the adder's den.

---

24. Gen 2:5–25.
25. Gen 2:18.
26. Gen 2:19.

> They shall not hurt or destroy
> in all my holy mountain;
> for the earth shall be full of the knowledge of the Lord
> as the waters cover the sea.[27]

Even in the disorder of the Fall, there remains implicitly the human companionship with sheep, goat, and cow as distinguished from the wild beasts—wolf, panther, lion, bear, and poisonous snakes—which are at odds with both humans and domestic animals alike. In the age of the Messiah, the initial companionship of all animals with each other and with humans shall be restored.[28]

The human being, then, on this account has primary human vocations in relation to plants and animals and is very much at home in the world. In fact, one might ask whether humans can fulfill their human nature without gardening and without some companionable relationships with animals. At the same time, it can be said that the natural world relies on human stewardship for the fulfillment of its nature. A garden is only a garden with a gardener. There is that splendid moment of irony in the resurrection account of John 20 when Mary Magdalene mistakes the risen Christ for the gardener, but—of course—in the deepest sense, he was and is supremely the gardener. Further, naming in biblical theology is powerful. There is a level of being called into existence through naming. Whether the infant at the baptismal font or the stray rescued from the pound, naming lifts the named to a higher level. The baby becomes Julio or Julia. The stray dog becomes Evan or Boofer. Perhaps this likeness of human babies and stray dogs will rankle some, but can you imagine going through life without a name? Part of the tragedy of Victor Hugo's Jean Valjean is that his humanity was reduced to a number, "24601"—a tragedy that Hitler multiplied by millions. The human is doubly co-creator with God. God made the world as a garden, but he charged the human to go on creating a garden out of the world. The human—man and woman as completion of each other—is clearly co-creator with God in the generation of human beings. St. Paul makes the fine chiastic formulation: "for as woman was made from man, so man is now born of woman. And all things are from God."[29] As namer, the human is co-creator with God, lifting an animal to a higher level of being. The human being is the

---

27. Isa 11:6–9.

28. C. S. Lewis plays with questions of the remnant and restored relationships of humans and animals in his *Chronicles of Narnia*.

29. 1 Cor 11:12.

gardener that makes the world into a garden and is the namer of companions, and even of potential or eventual companions in the garden.

Can this conclusion stand, however, in light of 1 Pet 2:11 where Christians are admonished "as aliens and exiles to abstain from the passions of the flesh that wage war against your soul"?[30] The clear context is political. From the time of Nero, the church was an illegal institution and Christians were *ipso facto* "wrongdoers."[31] The guidance that follows has to do with how Christians were to comport themselves in a state where Christians were outlaws.[32] More interesting is Heb 11:13–16. The author of Hebrews was influenced by middle-Platonism, and we see ideas here that will come to philosophical fruition in the *Enneads* of Plotinus:

> These all died in faith, not having received what was promised, but having seen it and greeted it from afar, and having acknowledged that they were strangers and exiles on the earth. For people who speak thus make it clear that they are seeking a homeland. If they had been thinking of that land from which they had gone out, they would have had opportunity to return. But as it is, they desire a better country, that is, a heavenly one. Therefore God is not ashamed to be called their God, for he has prepared for them a city.[33]

If read in a literalistic and de-contextualized way, that passage seems to dichotomize the life in this world and the life in the city of God. One could regard the human life on earth as the uncanniest of all. A first principle of exegesis is that a text is its own best interpreter. Hebrews 11 must be read with Gen 2. The sense of being "strangers and exiles" must be read with being "gardeners and namers." It is the Platonism that influenced the author of Hebrews that brings the two passages together. The "Promised Land" is both Canaan and the eternal city of God—thus, St. Augustine, a close reader of Plotinus, read the story.[34] St. Paul provides another

---

30. 1 Pet 2:11. The Greek here is *paroikos* (someone who is elsewhere than home) and *parepidēmos* (someone with nowhere to live). "Strangers and refugees" might be the most accurate translation. Liddell et al., *Greek-English Lexicon*, q.v. *paroikos* and *parepidēmos*, 1337, 1342. See Aland et al., *Greek New Testament*, 795.

31. 1 Pet 2:12.

32. 1 Pet 2:13–17.

33. Heb 11:13–16. Regarding verse 13: "These all" refers to those from Abel to Jacob; for "strangers and exiles" see Ps 39:12. The Greek here is *xenos* (foreigner) and *parepidēmos* again. See Liddell et al., *Greek-English Lexicon*, q.v. *xenos*, 1189.

34. Augustine, *City of God*, 541. Indeed, though he does not say so, Augustine seems to be offering a commentary on Heb 11 in 16.12–43.

perspective from which to see the connecting link of Gen 2 and Heb 11. He writes, "We know that the whole creation has been groaning in travail together until now; and not only the creation, but we ourselves, who have the first fruits of the Spirit, groan inwardly as we wait for adoption as sons, the redemption of our bodies."[35] I have only once had the privilege of being in the labor hall. I remember not groans but screams of pain with blood and other body fluid we call "water" all across the floor. That is what St. Paul evokes here. In other words, the whole creation shares in fallenness and in longing for redemption. Christians of every stripe and hue explain the Fall too anthropocentrically. This is another example of seeing humans as separate and apart from the natural world, of human not-at-homeness. In fact, all creation, not just humans, fell with the disobedience of Adam and Eve. Something was let loose in the world that has been defeated, but not yet eliminated. The metaphysical cataclysm of the Fall has ecological as well as moral consequences. Fallen creation is alienated from itself as well as from us, humans. There was darkness[36] and an earthquake[37] as our Blessed Savior died. The natural world wept at the death of the Savior, though all the humans who watched it did not. It is not only we, humans, who are strangers and pilgrims, but the whole of the natural world. Even so-called inanimate nature in some sense recognizes how great the distance is between her and her maker. The new heaven and earth are not just for us, humans. We are too anthropocentric about redemption just as we are about the Fall. The new heaven and earth are for the old heaven and earth. The old heaven and earth are passed away—as are we: "And he who sat upon the throne said, 'Behold, I make all things new.'"[38]

Plotinus and Odysseus

Plotinus, under the guise of merely interpreting Plato, synthesized the thought of Plato and Aristotle in his system of The One, the Divine Intellect, the Cosmic Soul, and the World. Plotinus describes a world of matter-form composites that participate in the Forms or Ideas of the Divine Intellect. Every material thing is, therefore, a window into the

---

35. Rom 8:22–23.
36. Matt 27:45; Mark 15:33.
37. Matt 27:51.
38. Rev 21:5.

Divine Intellect. Ultimately, we come from The One, but it is the Divine Intellect that is the creator of the world of material beings.[39] Thus, all material beings in the world are icons of the Forms or Ideas in the Divine Intellect. We come from The One and the Divine Intellect (procession), but how do we get back there (return)? Though antecedents of this principle, "procession and return" (*prohodos* and *epistrophē*), can be found in the thought of Plato and Aristotle, and—before them—in the thought of Heraclitus, it is Plotinus who develops this rich principle for understanding the differentiated unity of all reality. In *Ennead* 5. 9. (5), he addresses exactly the problem of how we return to The One. All human beings live by their five senses to some degree, but some never go beyond those five senses. Another class of humans begins there, but they have wings and ascend above the material to recognize purely intelligible realities; however, they then fall back to earth. He continues, and this is the passage that I think we ought to read with Heb 11:

> But there is a third kind of godlike men who by their greater power and the sharpness of their eyes as if by a special keen-sightedness see the glory above and are raised to it as if above the clouds and the mist of this lower world and remain there, overlooking all things here below and delighting in the true region which is their own, like a man who came home after long wandering to his well-ordered country.[40]

The last referenced "man who came home after wandering to his well-ordered country" was Odysseus. He went to Troy with the other Achaeans where he fought for ten years, and then it took him another ten years and overcoming many obstacles to arrive home in Ithaca. For the contemporaries of Plotinus, that tagline would have implicitly loaded into Plotinus's text the entire story of Odysseus's homegoing. For the purpose of this paper, I want to focus on just two portions of that homegoing: first, the encounter between Odysseus and his wife Penelope, and second, the encounter between Odysseus and his father Laertes.

While Odysseus made his way home, Penelope had been busy fending off suitors who wanted to marry her and become king in Odysseus's stead. Faced with the stranger—as Odysseus is styled in the text, and people can change over two decades—she protests that she does not

---

39. For a thorough treatment of Plotinus on creation and for an exhaustive review of secondary literature on the subject, see Zimmerman, "Does Plotinus."

40. Plotinus, *Ennead V*, 286–89 (5. 9. [5], 16–22).

want to sacrifice her chastity to a wily scoundrel in case the man standing before her is just one more pretender to her hand and the throne. At the same time, she does not want to deny Odysseus the right to sleep in his own bed, if he genuinely be her husband, so she commands her servants to move the master's bed into the hallway where he can sleep in it alone. At this Odysseus loses his cool composure:

> Woman, by heaven you've stung me now!
> Who dared to move my bed?
> No builder had the skill for that—unless
> a god came down to turn the trick. No mortal
> in his best days could budge it with a crowbar.
> There is our pact and pledge, our secret sign,
> built into that bed—my handiwork
> and no one else's!
>   An old trunk of olive
> grew like a pillar on the building plot,
> and I laid out our bedroom round that tree,
> lined up the stone walls, built the walls and roof,
> gave it a doorway and smooth-fitting doors.
> Then I lopped off the silvery leaves and branches,
> hewed and shaped that stump from the roots up
> into a bedpost, drilled it, let it serve
> as model for the rest. I planed them all,
> inlaid them all with silver, gold and ivory,
> and stretched a bed between—a pliant web
> of oxhide thongs dyed crimson.
>   There's our sign![41]

Wendell Berry comments on the estrangement of modern marriage and modern agriculture: "It may be argued that these two estrangements are very close to being one, both of them having been caused by the disintegration of the household, which was the formal bond between marriage and the earth, between human sexuality and its sources in the sexuality of Creation." He finds "one of the best examples" of that bond in the scene from the *Odyssey* of Odysseus declaring the sign, the pact and pledge between himself and Penelope.[42] I affirm all that Berry says in his analysis, but I want to add a few points. First, from Homeric times to today, the olive tree has been one of the most important crops for the Mediterranean culture and economy. Odysseus built his bed into more than a mere tree,

---

41. Homer, *Odyssey*, 401, 23.182–202.
42. Berry, *Unsettling of America*, 124, 123–30.

for the olive tree was emblematic of his world. His bed—the most private place—was built into a most public reality. That is one of the reasons that, as Berry observes, "In the renewal of his marriage . . . the restoration of order [is] complete." This realization helps to make sense of why the Achaeans would fight a war in the first place over the rupture in the marriage of Menelaus to Helen. The most private institution was also the most public institution. In that Menelaus and Odysseus were kings, the restoration or renewal of marriage was a righting of the political order. Second, the bed was a human artifact, while the tree was a natural object. For Odysseus—and presumably for the pre-philosophical Mediterranean world—there was a fluidity of being between human artifact and natural object. Aristotle will make this distinction centuries later, and we take the distinction for granted today, but it was not a distinction observed by Odysseus. It was not only Odysseus's marriage that was rooted in the earth—as Berry observes—but also his house and furniture. This growing a house from the earth has been a phenomenon until recent decades. In my home area, even the humblest of buildings was roofed in slate because the local quarries made slate so cheap. In another community, a dozen miles away to the east, the houses are all built with granite because of the quarries behind the town. Heading west, the red brick houses and outbuildings evidence the red clay soil of that region. Today, all houses come from building supply companies. I have seen exactly the same housing development a thousand miles away in Florida as in my Maryland county, with even the same name.

 Wendell Berry and I are only recent noticers of Odysseus's homegoing as paradigmatic. Plotinus noticed as well, and he found in that homegoing an icon for the philosophical return of human beings in the material world to the intelligible realms of the Cosmic Soul and Divine Intellect—and even beyond the intelligible realms to The One. The fluidity of being—tree, bed, house, marriage, politics, everything—is essential to the homegoing of Odysseus as icon of Plotinus's "glory above." Plotinus says, in effect, "If you want to know how to escape this material world and to ascend to the highest order of reality, then follow the example of Odysseus in his homegoing. Though he was no philosopher, Odysseus recognized the unity and fluidity of being, the rootedness of human relations in the order of the created material world." This reading of Homer through Plotinus (and Berry) is a corrective to Heidegger. It is not through and because of the human's not-at-homeness in the natural world that the human forms the political community, but rather precisely because the human has found his way home in the natural world that true politics is possible at all. The king's bed is built into the natural world. Not only is the king part of the natural world, but his bed is part of it as well. And all of that is an icon for ascent to the highest of all realities.

The second point to notice in Odysseus's homegoing is his encounter with his father in book 24. This final book of the forty-eight in the two principle works attributed to Homer has a strange pedigree. The shape of the *Iliad* and *Odyssey* as we have the epic poems today was determined by the Alexandrian editors of the third and second centuries BC. Aristarchus (d. 146 BC), one of the two most important of those editors, denied the authenticity of *Odyssey* 24 entirely.[43] There are so many inconsistencies with the rest of the *Odyssey*'s narrative. Even taken by itself, there are problems. In short, it is difficult to know how to read *Odyssey* 24. The first two hundred lines give an account of how the souls of the slain suitors went down to the House of Hades and there gave an account of Odysseus's arrival home and triumph. That breaks off abruptly, and there is an account of Odysseus in the present making a journey to "Laertes' garden lands / long since won by his toil from the wilderness."[44] Odysseus finds his father alone, "spading the earth around a young fruit tree. He wore a tunic, patched, and soiled."[45] Berry comments briefly upon this meeting and points out that Laertes, working in an orchard, "is a king" though he is dressed as a peasant.[46] Odysseus does say that his father's appearance is "kingly,"[47] but is Laertes a king? If so, why did he not go to the Trojan War? Yes, now—twenty years later—he is an old man, but there was at least one old king—Nestor—who did go to Troy. But twenty years earlier, Laertes would not have been so old. Odysseus is the king of Ithaca. If Laertes is a king, then why is Odysseus king? Is it possible that Laertes is, in fact, dead? That is certainly not said in the text, but again, the two hundred lines prior to the description of this meeting take place in the House of Hades. Clearly, however, Laertes is not in the House of Hades. The House of Hades was not the only possibility as a place for dead souls; there were also the Elysian Fields. Could the "garden lands" of Laertes be the Elysian Fields? It seems, however, that Laertes cannot be dead because the suitors in the House of Hades tell of Penelope weaving the

43. Murray, *Rise of the Greek Epic*, 283–96.
44. Homer, *Odyssey*, 415; 24.205–7.
45. Homer, *Odyssey*, 416; 24.226–28.
46. Berry, *Unsettling of America*, 128.
47. Homer, *Odyssey*, 416; 24.253.

shroud for Laertes. Every proposed resolution to the problem of Laertes's status runs quickly into counter-factual problems in the text itself. I suggest that there is—at very least—a quality of liminality to the encounter between Odysseus and his father. The "garden lands" are distant from the town and from the political crisis that will occupy the balance of *Odyssey* 24 after the narrative of the reunion of father and son is complete. They are also not in the House of Hades. The garden lands of Laertes are another kind of place. They are a kind of statement about the human being making himself at home in the natural world, having been "won by his toil from wilderness." Fruit trees themselves constitute a kind of liminal status between natural object and human artifact. Trees grown from seed vary because of the ever-rolling dice of genetic makeup. In order to have a consistent variety of apple or pear, the orchardist takes cuts of wood from the tree he wants to reproduce and grafts it into the rootstock of another tree, often into a related wild cousin, e.g., a graft from a cultivated apple into crabapple rootstock. Thus, an apple or pear tree is both natural object and human artifact, evidence perhaps that we should not make too much of Aristotle's distinction. In a real way, there is fluidity of being.

Not only did Odysseus find his father working as an orchardist, but Odysseus reveals himself to his father by reciting a series of signs, the last of which is his ability to name a catalogue of fruit trees and vines that Laertes had named for Odysseus in his youth:

> I was a small boy at your heels wheedling
> amid the young trees, while you named each one.
> You gave me thirteen pear, ten apple trees,
> and forty fig trees. Fifty rows of vines
> were promised too, each one to bear in turn.[48]

Part of Odysseus's training to become king was in the arts of war, but part also—and the part that was the sign between him and his father—was in the horticultural arts possible only in peacetime. Central is the naming of the trees and vines, decades earlier by Laertes to Odysseus, and now Odysseus to Laertes. They know each other by naming the trees and vines. The scene is an alternative to the House of Hades as a destiny and destination for the dead. This is a brief idyll of two men—father and son—who transcend the question of kingship in an orchard, and—more—from which they unite to resolve the political turmoil that has been mounting

---

48. Homer, *Odyssey*, 419; 24.337–41.

in the town during their reunion.[49] Here is a vision that is beyond the household, beyond politics, beyond the House of Hades where humans are most human, at peace and most mutually knowing, and most at home naming fruit trees and vines while tending their orchard.

Odysseus was a hero who was able to travel as few epic and mythological heroes could, even beyond the boundaries of the earth to the House of Hades. His journey to his father's garden lands was a different kind of journey, to a place that does not fit into normal categories, a liminal place. We can say much more easily—from the text—what the garden lands were not than what they were. To put in terms scandalous to the rationalist philosopher, Laertes's garden lands were beyond the Principle of Non-Contradiction: neither A, nor ~A. That liminality, that beyondness fits well Plotinus's use of Odysseus's homegoing as an icon of the return to The One that is—as even Plato says of the Good—beyond being.[50] The boundary experience of Odysseus's encounter with his father, of their mutual recognition, of a place where both men were most at home in the natural world, is icon of Plotinus's journey to The One.

Laudato Si'

"Praise be to you, my Lord!" What does it mean to "praise" God? The Judeo-Christian understanding of praise is that it is a rightful and even dutiful act of creatures toward God. Aristotle raises the question of whether, in fact, humans have the right to praise God, whether we are competent to do so, whether the incommensurability of God and humans is so enormous that humans simply are unable to praise the divine, and that to do so approaches the unfitting.[51] He states:

> It seems absurd that the gods should be referred to as our standard, but this is done because praise involves a reference . . . to something else. But if praise is for things such as we have described, clearly what applies to the best things is not praise, but something greater and better, as is indeed obvious; for what we do to the gods and the most godlike men is to call them blessed and happy. And so too with good things; no one praises

---

49. Homer, *Odyssey*, 424–26; 24.491–542.
50. Plato, "Republic," 509b (1130).
51. Has anyone attempted a philosophy of praise?

happiness as he does justice, but rather calls it blessed, as being something more divine and better.[52]

The reality of the gods is not in "reference . . . to something else," but is rather *sui generis* in relation to nothing but the gods themselves. Aristotle returns to the same question as near the end of the *Ethics*, as the first quotation is near the beginning. He is discussing how contemplation is different from all other kinds of activity. The point he makes is that contemplation is supremely the act of God—to understand this passage fully, one must bring *Metaphysics* 12.7 and 9 to bear on what he says here—and the human contemplation of God is nearest of all human activities to God as "Understanding understanding Understanding."[53] On the way to his conclusion in the *Nicomachean Ethics*, however, he makes the point that it is senseless to praise the gods for their contemplative life in any way analogous to the way one praises a soldier for a brave action under fire or a businessman for justly fulfilling his contract: "Is not such praise tasteless, since they have no bad appetites?"[54] Humans may rightly bless the gods, but praising them is unfitting. The gods are beyond our praise, and we are not competent to praise them. He blesses the divine whom he is not worthy to praise and who—in any event—is entirely beyond the category of praiseworthiness. He does not discuss immovability in the *Ethics*, but we might load into what he says here what he says about God's immovability in *Metaphysics* 12.6. If a thing is moving—and thus, is in act—it still has even in the perfection of actuality the potency for not-moving. God's immovability stands beyond the question of moving or not-moving.[55] His immovability is of a category incommensurate with the categories of moving and not-moving. The praiseworthy human can also be blameworthy. The divine is beyond praise and blame. There is a beauty to Aristotle's state of wonder before the divine, taken exactly as it is.

Nevertheless, is there some way to bridge Aristotle's insights about the nature of praise and why human praise of the divine is unfitting, and the Judeo-Christian understanding of praise as what humans rightfully and dutifully offer to God? There is such a way, a way that helps us see the human's at-homeness in the world, to see a way of exploding the terrarium

52. Aristotle, "Nicomachean Ethics," 2.1740 (1.12.1101b18–28). The Greek words are *epainesis* (praise), *epainos* (praiseworthy), and *epaineō* (to praise) used throughout the cited passages; see Aristotle, *Nicomachean Ethics*, 58.

53. Aristotle, "Metaphysics," 12.9.1074b34, my translation.

54. Aristotle, "Nicomachean Ethics," 2.1864–65 (10.8.1178b8–23).

55. Aristotle, "Metaphysics," 2.1693 (12.6.1071b12–22).

view of the natural world. That way is through a philosophical principle of Aristotle's teacher, which Aristotle rejected and for which he never found an adequate replacement in his own system; that is, the principle of participation. It is here that we see the outworking of Plotinus's principle of procession and return. The Thomas Ken doxology in "Praise God from Whom All Blessings Flow" provides a starting point.[56] There we have the procession of blessings from God that enlivens the heavenly hierarchy as well as the natural world. The praise that is enjoined is a return to God as a response to the procession of all blessings from God. That praise is not only to be given by humans, but by all creatures to God as a participation in the being of God. In that doxology, humans are at home with all other creatures, from seraph to amoeba. It is their shared hymn of praise that makes them neighbors. To Aristotle's question, "What gives any of them the right to praise God?" we answer—with Plotinus, Augustine, Dionysius, and Aquinas—the procession of divine goodness lends the divine nature to all creatures of every rank. St. Thomas Aquinas says—but it is the metaphysical system of Plotinus that makes the assertion possible—that the form of any natural being is a window into the Form or Idea in the mind of God.[57] The seraph and the amoeba alike receive form from God, the one for the participation of existence, life, and understanding, the other for the participation of existence and life only, but that they participate in the being of God is alike. Man and woman, as they praise God along with their neighbors—seraph and amoeba—are at home in the world. St. Francis has this exactly right in his "Canticle of the Creatures." Humans praise God with Brother Sun, Sister Moon, Brother Wind, Sister Water, Brother Fire, Sister Earth, and even Sister Bodily Death. We might add in the spirit of Homer, Brother Tree and Sister Bed.

One of my favorite principles of Neoplatonism is its inclusivity. There are no garbage dumps in the Neoplatonic system. Everything is a jagged piece in the giant jigsaw puzzle of reality. No entity is left out. Plato has his teacher observe that Beauty is the first Form to be noticed.[58] It is irresistible. The atheist, the nihilist, the despairing are all moved by beauty.[59] Though they do not know it, though they may deny it, when

---

56. Ken, "Praise God."

57. Aquinas, *Quaestiones Disputatae de Veritate*, q. 1, art. 2, solution (2).

58. Plato, "Phaedrus," 250c7–e1 (528).

59. A memory of nearly a half-century ago bubbles up in my mind of a friend who committed suicide. My one definite memory about him is of his coming into the dining hall, bright-faced and happy. He told us of seeing a pheasant in the field that day. Beauty

they praise the beauty of a sunset or laugh at a baby's smile, they too are participating in the neighborly procession and return of all reality. Thus, a strategy emerges. Among believers—even those with only a vague belief in some higher power—the invitation to praise of that "higher power" is a step toward re-homing the human. Among unbelievers, a winsome evangelism is a pointing to beauty. One of the places where that pointing can and should begin is in the garden. Giving a garden tour is an enterprise of naming: "Those are the Brandywine tomatoes, and those the Roma paste tomatoes, and on and on." The human discovers his primary vocations and celebrates beauty by offering God continuous praise along with all creatures—animate, growing, and so-called inanimate—as companions. From such starting points, it is still a long way to changing bureaucratic regulation and finding sustainable alternatives to green deserts. The example of Odysseus reminds us that the way home is long and full of trials,[60] but—in the end and *contra* Thomas Wolfe—there is no place else to go.

Bibliography

Aland, Kurt, et al. *The Greek New Testament.* 2nd ed. Stuttgart: United Bible Societies, 1968.

Aristotle. "Metaphysics." In *The Complete Works of Aristotle: The Revised Oxford Translation*, edited by Jonathan Barnes, 2:1552–728. Princeton: Princeton University Press, 1984.

———. "Nicomachean Ethics." In *The Complete Works of Aristotle: The Revised Oxford Translation*, edited by Jonathan Barnes, 2:1729–867. Princeton: Princeton University Press, 1984.

———. *The Nicomachean Ethics with an English Translation.* Edited and translated by Harris Rackham. Cambridge, MA: Harvard University Press, 1999.

Aquinas, Thomas. *Quaestiones Disputatae de Veritate.* 9th rev. ed. Edited by Raymundi Spiazzi. Rome: Marietti, 1953.

Augustine. *The City of God.* New York: Modern Library, 1950.

Berry, Wendell. *The Unsettling of America: Culture and Agriculture.* San Francisco: Sierra Club, 1986.

Heidegger, Martin. *Introduction to Metaphysics.* 2nd ed. Translated by Gregory Fried and Richard Polt. New Haven, CT: Yale University Press, 2014.

Homer. *The Odyssey.* Translated by Robert Fitzgerald. Garden City, NY: Doubleday, 1961.

---

moved him out of his depression, if only briefly, but in his despair, it was the one aspect of reality that had the power to heal him.

60. On these trials, one might write an exposition of God's curse of Adam, Eve, and the snake, but that would be a different paper.

Ken, Thomas. "Praise God from Whom All Blessings Flow." In *The Hymnbook*, 446 (Hymn #544). Atlanta: Presbyterian Church in the United States, The United Presbyterian Church in the USA, Reformed Church in America, 1955.

Lewis, C. S. *The Chronicles of Narnia*. New York: HarperCollins, 1950–56.

Liddell, Henry George, et al. *A Greek-English Lexicon, with a Revised Supplement*. Oxford: Oxford University Press, 1996.

Murray, Gilbert. *The Rise of the Greek Epic*. Oxford: Oxford University Press, 1960.

O'Brien, Mahon. *Heidegger, History and the Holocaust*. London: Bloomsbury Academic, 2015.

Otto, Rudolf. *The Idea of the Holy: An Inquiry into the Non-Rational Factor in the Idea of the Divine and Its Relations to the Rational*. Translated by John W. Harvey. Oxford: Oxford University Press, 1958.

Paul, Kalpita Bhar. "The Import of Heidegger's Philosophy into Environmental Ethics: A Review." *Ethics and the Environment* 22.2 (2017) 79–98.

Pearson Geiman, Clare. "Heidegger's *Antigones*." In *A Companion to Heidegger's "Introduction to Metaphysics,"* edited by Richard Polt and Gregory Fried, 161–82. New Haven, CT: Yale University Press, 2001.

Pico della Mirandola, Giovanni. *Oration on the Dignity of Man*. Translated by A. Robert Gaponigri. Washington, DC: Gateway Editions, 2012.

Plato. "Phaedrus." In *Plato: Complete Works*, edited by John M. Cooper, 506–56. Indianapolis: Hackett, 1997.

———. "Republic." In *Plato: Complete Works*, edited by John M. Cooper, 971–1223. Indianapolis: Hackett, 1997.

Plotinus. *Ennead V*. Translated by A. H. Armstrong. Loeb Classical Library 444. Cambridge, MA: Harvard University Press, 1984.

Zimmerman, Brandon. "Does Plotinus Present a Philosophical Account of Creation?" *Review of Metaphysics* 67 (2013) 55–105.

4

"Nulla mortalia efflavi"

The Living Universe of Hildegard of Bingen

Miguel Escobar Torres

One of the singular achievements of modern thought is to have conceived of the physical and social world as a secular space, autonomous with respect to the supernatural. Since the invention of the secular, Western man does not notice the presence of God in creation and ends up confining himself to an ambiguous and confused transcendence whose relationship with the immanent is one of mutual exclusion. As a consequence of this split, God becomes a *Deus absconditus*, a God exiled from creation and hidden, while creation is devoid of spirit and comes to be conceived as a mere machine, the *Deus ex machina* of Descartes. This *Weltanschauung* is also nourished by two other aspects: first, by an approach to reality based on doubt and suspicion instead of wonder, from which derives the inability to recognize the mystery that lies within creation; second, by a conception of the will as indifferent—or even contrary—to *being*, which appears as a separate reality that threatens to erode, if not make impossible, human freedom and creativity, and to impose upon the subject a fatalistic determinism.

Consequently, creation—conceived as a machine—is subjected to a new kind of limitless *dominium* whose *dominus* is capable of imagining himself as mere *res cogitans* separated from the *res extensa*, "without a body and without a world or place in which to live, . . . as a substance whose essence or nature is to think, and which, in order to exist, does not need any place nor does it depend on any material thing."[1] For such an

---

1. Descartes, *Discours de la Méthode*, 32, §25. My translation.

unlimited and despotic domain to be possible, it is therefore necessary to distinguish between the world, made of corporeality and matter, and man, identified with the immaterial soul and whose essence is thinking. Only by this process of isolating the soul can the invention of the modern subject take place: the illusory idea that man is that which is opposed to the world—the "object"—as something isolated, external, and foreign. Paradoxically, only through this *alienation* of man from the world is it possible for the modern concept of "property"—understood as an arbitrary and despotic *dominium*—to emerge. In this order of things, creation becomes subject to this *dominium* defined by transparency—everything real is accessible to a panoptic reason that no mystery can resist—and availability; its meaninglessness, fruit of the rupture of its link with the divine, invites this strange hypostatized subject to confer an artificial meaning on things based on the criteria of utility and functionality.

If the main goal of the modern subject is to free himself from the bonds of nature, first by conceiving himself as an isolated entity diametrically opposed to what he calls "nature" and then by dominating and modifying nature according to the dictates of his will, we can see that the rationality that delineated this modern subject had already taken shape as early as the twelfth century. The rise of the cathedral schools and the tradition of the *magistri* built upon the literary and scientific commentaries of the Arab world, which reached the Latin world thanks to the work of the Toledo School of Translators (especially Gerard of Cremona). The fascination with Avicenna in particular and the analytical style of these writers generated a new way of doing philosophy among thinkers in the "proto-urban" context of the emerging burghs. This marked a break with the monastic wisdom of the Middle Ages and the sapiential philosophy of the Carolingian Palatine schools, bringing about a redefinition of the concept of the liberal arts in opposition to the Benedictine "*ora et labora*."

In contrast to these cathedral schools, female monastic schools persisted in the Rhine basin. From thence would come forth the tradition of the *magistrae*, among which Hildegard of Bingen, Jutta von Sponheim, and Elisabeth of Schönau stand out.[2] These followed the Benedictine rule, devoted themselves to the study of theology and biblical exegesis as well as to the natural sciences, agriculture, and crafts.[3] The *magistri*,

2. Herrad of Landsberg of Hohenburg Abbey, who wrote the *Hortus Deliciarum*, could also be included, but her tone is slightly different, especially her optimism about the liberal arts.

3. Guibert of Gembloux, in a letter addressed to a monk called Bovo, writes: "Nam

for their part, as Jean Léclerq points out, developed a kind of philosophy whose general principles were:

1. The prioritization of intellectual activity—that which is appropriate to the human being, the liberal arts—over contemplation, thus establishing the basis for the modern redefinition of work;

2. Exorbitant attention, perhaps obsessive, to educational activity, even at the expense of the cultivation of prayer;

3. The dominance of dialectic, which was characterized by an excessive confidence in the capabilities of the *humana ratio*, regardless of faith;

4. The violation of the traditional limits of thought, submitting to rational analysis—similar to what Kant would do centuries later—that which had been exclusively a question of faith, or at minimum, inspired reason;[4] and

5. A desire for novelty that was reflected in the enthusiasm for translations that arrived from Toledo, which is why, for example, Isidore of Seville's theory of humors—a kind of sapiential medicine—was abandoned to embrace Avicenna's *Canon medicinae*, thus laying the groundwork for the modern rejection of tradition.

However, if there is something common to these five features, it is the growing inability of the *magistri* to see the mystery that lies within creation. "Theological research was approaching the dangerous point at which it might escape the limits set by faith. In trying to submit God's mysteries to reason, one could be tempted to forget their transcendency and yield to a kind of naturalism."[5] Warning of this danger, several authors of the monastic schools took up an "anti-dialectical" position against the new cathedral schools. The works of Bernard of Clairvaux against Peter Abelard stand out here, as well as the *Disputatio contra*

---

memores Domini inuitantis: *Vacate et videte, quoniam ego sum Deus*, inhibitis ab opere feriis in claustro decenter cum silentio sedentes lectioni et discendo cantu suo student; et obedientes apostolo dicenti: *Qui non laborat, nec manducet*, priuatis diebus per officinas competentes uel scribendis libris, uel aliis manuum operibus intendunt. Ita ex studio lectionis illuminatio diuine agnitionis et gratia compunctionis acquiritur, et per otiosos conuentus ex multiplicium leuitate uerborum oriri posset, compescitur" (Guibertus Gemblacensis, cited in Rabassó, "*Sapientia docet me*," 9).

4. An example of this is the rationalization that Berengarius of Tours tried to carry out regarding the mystery of the Eucharist.

5. Léclerq, *Love of Learning*, 208.

Petrum Abelardum and the *De erroribus Guillelmi de Conchis* by William of St-Thierry, in which respect for tradition, concern about novelties, and the primacy of faith over reason are revendicated.[6]

Hildegard, together with Bernard of Clairvaux and William of St-Thierry, stands out among those in opposition to the dialecticians for her critique of the analytical methods developed by the *magistri*, her adherence to Isidorian medicine, and her approach to the study of reality consisting of reading in simplicity ("*scio in simplicitate legere*") rather than isolation and division.[7] Hildegard accuses the *magistri* of seeing creation with "mortal eyes" (*mortalis oculi*), incapable of admiring the *viriditas* and miracles of God, which can only be seen through "living eyes" (*viventis oculi*).[8] Hildegard diagnosed this "enlightenment" of reason as arising from suspicion and the inability to acknowledge the *viriditas* of the world. She saw that what was lacking was an *obumbratio*—an "overshadowing"—of the *humana ratio* by the greater brilliance of the *vox de caelo*, of the *Sapientia*, which begins with wonder and seeing "in simplicity."[9] Only from a "sensitivity" like that of the *magistri*, incapable of noticing the life that impregnates all created things and bound to the urban context in which it was born, could the analytical way of approaching the knowledge of reality be conceived, given that the living—and, therefore, the sacred—cannot suffer division without becoming a corpse. In other words, if the living is not susceptible to division, then the consideration of analysis as the ideal way of knowing the world requires a sensitivity incapable of perceiving life in creation, a sensitivity that preconceives the world as a juxtaposition of things, inert and devoid of the sacred, a world subject to availability and transparency in the face of a reason that stands as a despotic *dominus*. It is a paradigm that provokes what Hildegard called *tristitia seculi*.[10]

---

6. Stover, "Hildegard, the Schools," 130.

7. Hildegard of Bingen, *Epistolarium*, letter 1, 4, 1, 20–22.

8. "For mortal eyes cannot see Me, but I show My miracles in the shadows to those I choose" (Hildegard of Bingen, *Scivias*, 3.11; translation from Stoudt, "Medical, the Magical," 271. References to the *Scivias* correspond to the 1978 version cited, unless otherwise noted).

9. Newman echoes the Hildegardian concept of *obumbratio*: "Taking her own experience as a model, Hildegard understood *obumbratio* paradoxically as illumination: the prophet, a 'mere shadow,' is overshadowed by the divine light, which enables her to see that light in which all being is foreshadowed" (Newman, *Sister of Wisdom*, 53–54).

10. Stoudt, "Medical, the Magical," 262–63.

Analysis consists in the division of the divisible. A machine can be broken down into numerous parts and be successfully rebuilt, that is, returned to being a useful, working thing. The living thing, for its part, is indivisible, and though mere logical division does not kill the thing, it does lay the foundations for this to happen; therefore, it eloquently reflects the paradigm that precedes this type of "knowledge." In effect, the analytical method—the *humana scientia*—of the *magistri* entails a triple isolation:

1. An isolation of the thing from the Creator that becomes explicit several centuries later in the philosophy of *natura pura*, according to which the knowledge of created things is closed within the thing itself, without the need to refer to its connection with the divine;

2. An isolation of the thing with respect to its created environment, understanding it as a "monad" that is not part of a world of relationality and interconnection with other created things, but is juxtaposed and whose meaning does not depend, therefore, on its integration in the universe; and

3. An isolation of the knowing subject from the world, since it is only possible to isolate the thing by placing it in a subjective isolation that precedes it.

Hildegard, for her part, not only presents her reading in simplicity, but also openly criticizes the analytical method of the *magistri*, since it is not possible to know through division what is indivisible by nature.

For example, in letter 39R to Master Odo of Soissons, and letter 40 to Master Odo of Paris, Hildegard addresses the question of the distinction between the paternity and divinity of God, a subject investigated by Bernard of Clairvaux and Gilbert of Poitiers. Here the Abbess of Bingen maintains that God is complete and whole (*plenus est et integer*) and that it is not possible to know through division what is indivisible, reflecting its simplicity with the words, "*Ego sum qui sum*."[11] In letter 39R, she writes, "Those who have the day of good knowledge whither if they look away to the useless inquiries of others and to the varieties of shadows, which do not seek help in reason but are vain. They have no *viriditas* in God."[12] Hildegard distinguishes between the misguided light of the *humana ratio*—having lost the *diem bone scientie*—and the overshadowing

---

11. Exod 3:14.
12. Hildegard of Bingen, *Epistolarium*, I, 39R, 101.

(*obumbratio*) of the *vox de caelo*, maintaining that in the former there is no vitality (*viriditas*). However, in the *Ordo virtutum* Hildegard goes further in her criticism, comparing the *magistri* to the *Diabolus*, which "uses subtle and fine-tuned rational arguments in order to seduce the Soul and challenge the Virtues."[13] In the same work, Hildegard opposes "living eyes" to "dead eyes," since the latter lead to the sadness of the world, while the former perceives and venerates the mystery and light of God that inhabits creation.

Today, faced with an obsolete modern paradigm based on an illusory secular autonomy, Hildegard's world, permeated with *viriditas* and full of God, offers a powerful contrast and refreshing reference for understanding the real world in all its richness. This is precisely because Hildegard sees a world that is very different from the one analyzed by modern science. Therefore, any apology that seeks to praise Hildegard as a modern "scientist" *avant la lettre*—as an author whose writings have historical value (usually associated with her *status* as a woman), but who remains obsolete in the light of the scientific advances of modern times—will only veil, rather than reveal, the relevance of her thought.

The Living Universe of Hildegard of Bingen

Unlike the philosophy of *natura pura*, Hildegard's thought contains no cosmology without theology, nor theology without cosmology. In other words, for Hildegard, you cannot talk about the world without talking about God, nor can you talk about God without talking about the world. There is no division or mutual isolation or exclusion, but a double-sided mirror between the divine and the creaturely, between the superior and the inferior. Although Hildegard knew of the hermetic writings, the idea of an analogical relationship between the superior and inferior does not come

---

13. Rabassó, "*Sapientia docet me*," 33n91. She also reserves the concept of "magic" to dark magic, associating it with the practices of the *magistri* and their fascination with hermetic writings. However, a study based on mere terminology would not shed sufficient light on the complex relationship between Hildegard's thought and magic, as Stoudt made manifest in "Medical, the Magical," noting that Hildegard added the application of amulets and the use of formulaic words to the herbology, diet, and surgical procedures provided by Isidorian medicine. Thus, it is possible to find thirty-one enchantments in the *Physica*: fourteen in the *lapidarium*, nine in the *bestiarium*, and six in the *herbarium*, although Hildegard is careful not to include them under the category of "magic," but more in relation to the *miracula*; see Hildegard of Bingen, "*Physica*"; for an English translation, Hildegard of Bingen, *Hildegard von Bingen's Physica*.

from these works, but more likely from the Carolingian Neoplatonism of authors such as John Scotus Eriugena. In any case, despite the fact that Hildegard associates the hermetic writings with the devil in the *Scivias*, the truth is that in the same work she formulates a very similar principle, although with certain differences, to the one that would be the second point of the *Tabula Smaragdina* ("*quod est inferius est sicut quod est superius, et quod est superius est sicut quod est inferius*").[14] Hildegard writes:

> For the heavenly Word, which is above all creatures, shows the virtue of its strength in founding creation, which is subject to Him; from this matter He forged the different species of creatures, luminous at the dawn of his birth, as a craftsman skillfully extracts figures from bronze; until the entire Creation shone in the beauty of its fullness: what is above and what is below, all filled with the brilliance and firmness of its perfect foundation, because the upper illuminates the lower, and the lower the higher [*quia superiora resplenduerunt ab inferioribus et inferiora a superioribus*].[15]

Although this text seems to allude to the inferior and superior as two categories that are situated within the limits of created being, such reflective interplay is not restricted to the cosmic order, but also to the most fundamental relationship between the created and the Uncreated. In this sense, Hildegard comprehends a living universe because God, who illuminates it, is the Living One. The conception of God is not separable or independent from the conception of the world, and *vice versa*, as Thomas Aquinas properly argued:

> The consideration of creatures is likewise necessary not only for the building up of faith, but also for the destruction of errors. For errors about creatures sometimes lead one astray from the truth of faith, insofar as they disagree with true knowledge of God.[16]

On the other hand, errors about God distance us from the true knowledge of creatures: just as God is conceived, so the world will be conceived. If God is an engineer, the world will be a machine created by him; if God is a craftsman, the world will be a magnificent work of craftsmanship; if God is an artist, the world will be conceived as a fantastic work of art, etc.

---

14. Quoted in *Meditations on the Tarot*, 21–22.
15. Hildegard of Bingen, *Scivias*, II.I.VI, 209–10.
16. Aquinas, *Summa Contra Gentiles*, II, c. 3.

Hildegard's God is more like Blaise Pascal's personal God—the God of Abraham, Isaac, and Jacob—than the Cartesian *Deus ex machina*.

However, what is peculiar about Hildegardian theology is its distinct vital character. Her descriptions of divinity are always accompanied by epithets that point to life and images that reflect great exuberance. In the first vision of the second part of the *Scivias*, expressions such as "the living God" (*vivens Deus*) or the "living fire" (*vivens ignis*) are recurrent.[17] When developing the vision of the "most lucid unfathomable fire, inextinguishable, living everything and all life [*lucidissimum ignem incomprehensibilem, inexstinguibilem, totum uiuentem, totumque uitam exsistentem*]," she writes:

> *This blazing fire* that you see symbolizes Omnipotent and Living God, Who in His most glorious serenity was never darkened by any iniquity; *incomprehensible*, because He cannot be divided by any division or known as He is by any part of any of His creatures' knowledge; *inextinguishable*, because He is that Fullness that no limit ever touched; *wholly living*, for there is nothing that is hidden from Him or that He does not know; and *wholly Life*, for everything that lives takes its life from Him.[18]

God is, therefore, "everything alive" (*totum uiuentem*) because nothing is hidden from him—or, it could well be said, there is nothing absent from him, because God "lives everything" and "everything lives" (*totus vita exsistens*) from him, who is its source. Likewise, when the creature is not only the image, but also the likeness of the Creator, it acquires by grace its vital and exuberant features: thus, Abraham, Isaac, and Jacob are described as "three immense stars" that twinkle with "vivid brilliance."[19]

Creation, therefore, illuminated by God, is also described in categories that reflect the vital exuberance of its Creator. In Hildegard's skillful and creative terminology,[20] *viriditas* appears as the divine life that permeates everything, and which can be translated figuratively as "verdure." This *viriditas* is present in all creation; there is nothing that does not carry the vital energy of its Creator. In the first vision of the

---

17. "Et audiui ex praefato uiuente igne uocem dicentem mihi" (Hildegard of Bingen, *Scivias*, II.III.Intro, 89–90).

18. Hildegard of Bingen, *Scivias*, II.I.I, 112–21; translation from Hart and Bishop, *Creation and Christ*, 44, emphasis in original.

19. Hildegard of Bingen, *Scivias*, II.I.IX, 261–64.

20. Let us recall that she invented the *lingua ignota*, a language with an alphabet of twenty-three letters and about a thousand words, for which she created a glossary.

first part of the *Liber Divinorum Operum*, God appears through a human figure—identified as *Caritas*—whose winged body is reddish, and the *vox de caelo* introduces itself and instructs Hildegard:

> I am the supreme and fiery energy, I am the one who has ignited the spark of all living beings, nothing mortal flows from me [*nulla mortalia efflavi*], and I judge all things.[21]

In the second point of the same vision, the *vox de caelo* reveals to Hildegard:

> All things in their essence are alive and have not been created in death, because I am life [*Haec omnia in essentia sua vivunt, nec in norte inventa sunt, quoniam ego vita sum*]. I am also the ability to reason, because I have the breath of the sonorous word, by which every creature has been generated. And in the Creation of all things, I have introduced my breath in such a way that no being of Creation is ephemeral in its species, because I am life. I am complete and perfect life, which has not flowed from stones, nor bloomed from branches nor has its origin thanks to the seed of a male, but rather everything that is vital has sprouted from Me.[22]

Barbara Newman, in her classic *Sister of Wisdom*, declares that "nothing is more distinctively Hildegardian than this sense of universal life, of a world aflame with vitality."[23] Indeed, this vital character is one of the most outstanding features of Hildegard's thought, since all her work is permeated with allusions to life, many of which express the exuberance of nature. Creation is full of life, and life is God. Creation is therefore full of God.

God-in-Creation: Hildegard of Bingen's Trinitarian Ontology

The proto-modern tendency—already found in late antiquity and in the early medieval period—to think of the Trinity without any reference to the cosmos was foreign to Hildegard. Her *altior philosophia* does not leave creation behind since—as can be deduced from her vision of the "cosmic egg" presented in the *Scivias*[24]—the universe is in God, but God himself is also present within created being, and present with "true

---

21. Hildegard of Bingen, "Liber Divinorum Operum," I.I.II, 743B.
22. Hildegard of Bingen, "Liber Divinorum Operum," I.I.II, 743D.
23. Newman, *Sister of Wisdom*, 67.
24. Hildegard of Bingen, *Scivias*, I.III.Intro, 40.

presence" (*veraci ostensione*).²⁵ God is not, in this sense, an engineer who designs a machine, nor is he a mere craftsman or artist who creates his work and then abandons it. Thus, Hildegard could have exclaimed, like Angela of Foligno, that "the world is pregnant with God,"²⁶ and that presence, which reflects the exuberance of life, is real and *true*:

> Thus I too, the Father, am present in every creature [*ego Pater omni creaturae adsum*] and I am absent from none as you are absent, oh man, when you look at yourself in the water, your face appears in it, but devoid of strength, and when you walk away, it is erased. On the other hand, I do not appear to creatures with that inconstancy, but I am in them with true presence [*sed adsum ei veraci ostensione*], and I do not separate my power from them; rather, I exercise in them the force of My will, as I please.²⁷

The presence of God in creation is not, therefore, a mere reflection or a simple trace, but a true presence. The powerful image that Hildegard presents here of the relationship between God and his creation goes beyond the metaphor of the craftsman or the artist: divinity rests in the very heart of creation, nurturing it. God nurtures creation from within, from his own heart. This "visible" God is also *viriditas*, a concept that has been understood as a sophianic intuition by Michael Martin²⁸ and Barbara Newman.²⁹ Hildegardian *Sapientia* is, Newman maintains, "an ambience enfolding [the world] and quickening it from within."³⁰ Her presence is, however, mysterious, secret—just like the *vox de caelo*, which

---

25. Hildegard of Bingen, *Scivias*, II.VI.XXXVII, 265.

26. Angela of Foligno, *Complete Works*, 169–70.

27. Hildegard of Bingen, *Scivias*, II.VI.XXXVII, 265. The use of the verb "adsum" already alludes to a "being present," "presenting oneself," "appearing" in a physical or bodily sense, as a "being *in corpore*"; the term "ostensione" indicates that such a presence is not completely hidden, but that it manifests itself, unfolds by becoming visible, "exteriorizes."

28. "Nowhere is this sophiological intuition found in Hildegard more than in her notion of *viriditas*, or what might be translated as 'greeningness'" (Martin, *Submerged Reality*, 176). "Sophianic" is a concept used by Sergei Bulgakov (1871–1944), father of Sophiology, to refer to God-in-creation, to his manifestation and presence of the immanent God who occupies the intermediate space (*metaxu*) between God and the world.

29. Newman likewise relates this immanence of God to the feminine figure of *Sapientia*: "As creatrix, Hildegard's Sapientia is no unmoved mover, ordering the universe from on high or even . . . molding the nascent world in almighty hands. On the contrary, she creates the cosmos by existing within it, her ubiquity expressed through the image of ceaseless or circular motion" (Newman, *Sister of Wisdom*, 64).

30. Newman, *Sister of Wisdom*, 65.

presents itself as *Caritas*, declares: "I, igneous power, *hide myself in them* [all creatures],"[31] being "beautiful in the choice and admirable in the gifts of the *secrets* of the Heavenly Father."[32] The sophianic immanence of God in Hildegard is therefore *admirable*, but it remains veiled, like a mysterious treasure amassed in the world. Man is called to admire these "secrets," as *Caritas* exhorts a little later in the same vision: "You who adore and venerate God with good will, look at the secrets of God and examine the reward of his gifts that shine day and night before God."[33]

It is precisely in this vision, the first of the first part of the *Liber Divinorum Operum*, where the "sophianicity" of Hildegard's theocosmic thought is presented with greater force: Hildegard describes a suggestive vision of God "with human appearance, beautiful and magnificent in his mystery,"[34] a human figure—with a decidedly feminine air[35]—whose aureole rested on the head of an old and bearded man. The image is, without a doubt, striking; it seems to pose a kind of duality in God similar to the theology of the orthodox Palamite tradition: a transcendence, which is presented through the head of the old man, and an immanence, represented through the igneous figure identified as *Caritas*.[36]

Although there are similarities between the formulations of the *anima mundi* of Bernardus Silvestris and Peter Abelard and the Hildegardian *Caritas*, Hildegard's suspicion regarding Plato's *Timaeus* and the *Corpus Hermeticum* distances her from her contemporaries. Hildegard, in fact, develops rather an "Augustinian version of a spiritual force that lives within all things."[37] In any case, in the *Liber Vitae Meritorum*,

---

31. "Ego itaque vis ignea in his lateo" (Hildegard of Bingen, "*Liber Divinorum Operum*," I.I.II, 743D).

32. "Pulchra in electione, et mirifica in donis secretorum superni Patris charitas est" (Hildegard of Bingen, "*Liber Divinorum Operum*," I.I.III, 744D).

33. Hildegard of Bingen, "*Liber Divinorum Operum*," I.I.XVI, 750AB.

34. Hildegard of Bingen, "*Liber Divinorum Operum*," I.I.I, 741D.

35. It is a controversial statement, however. Indeed, the figure is later described as containing the prescience of all creatures, in the way that the *Logos*, identified with *Sapientia*, usually appears in tradition (Hildegard of Bingen, "*Liber Divinorum Operum*," I.I.XIII; I.I.VI; and I.I.I). The figure of *Caritas*, although it may present certain christological reminiscences, is not identified with it, and rather seems to point to a different reality, albeit with an equally personal character. The fact that Hildegard describes both *Caritas* and *Sapientia* as a consort of God seems to support this.

36. "Imaginem quasi hominis formam . . . charitas est" (Hildegard of Bingen, "*Liber Divinorum Operum*," I.I.III, 744D). See Hildegard of Bingen, *Book of Divine Works*, figure 1.1: Theophany of Divine Love, 32.

37. Góngora, "Introducción," 49.

Caritas—despite being included among the virtues—defines herself as a divine agent that acts in the cosmos:

> I am the air, I who nourish all green and growing life, I who bring ripe fruit from the flower. For I am skilled in every breath of the spirit of God, so I pour out the most limpid streams. From good sighing I bring weeping, from tears a sweet fragrance through holy actions.[38]

The figure of *Caritas* is related to the concept, more aesthetic than ethical, of *viriditas*, and is *nutrix*, a God-who-nourishes from within each one of the beings of creation. *Caritas* penetrates all the elements of creation through *materia* (earth), *vigor* (air), *anima* (water), and *rationalitas* (stars). Through *rationalitas*, the stars and planets become the privileged places of the manifestation of uncreated *Caritas*, since *rationalitas* is "the root, the resounding word flourishes in her."[39] This rationality is likewise contained in "the resounding wind with which every word was made."[40] The winds themselves seem to be described by Hildegard as operations of divine Charity, as columns that encompass the entire orb: as soft winds, associated with corporeality, which "have their wings placed under them,"[41] and strong winds, associated with the soul, contained by the gentle winds as the body contains the soul. On the other hand, *Caritas* makes the invisible Creator visible, presenting itself as Light and Life: "I am the radiance of life in eternity . . . and life itself is God."[42] *Caritas* is, therefore, a sophianic figure that nourishes and clothes the universe and everything in it.

This sophianic presence of God in creation is not only expressed through *Caritas*, but also through *Sapientia*, suggesting a quasi-identification of the two figures. Hildegard herself affirms that "*Sapientia* and *Caritas* are one,"[43] and both figures are defined as a "consort of God." In the *Liber Vitae Meritorum*, *Caritas* presents herself as such when she cries out: "I am the most loving consort of the throne of God, and God hides

38. Hildegard of Bingen, "*Liber Vitae Meritorum*," III.VI, 107; translation from Newman, *Sister of Wisdom*, 66–67.

39. Hildegard of Bingen, "*Liber Divinorum Operum*," I.I.II, 743D.

40. Hildegard of Bingen, "*Liber Divinorum Operum*," I.I.II, 743D.

41. Hildegard of Bingen, "*Liber Divinorum Operum*," I.I.II, 743C.

42. Hildegard of Bingen, "*Liber Divinorum Operum*," I.I.II, 744A.

43. "Sic namque homo in carne et anima velut de misericordia et charitate amabilis est, quemadmodum sapientia et charitas unum sunt" (Hildegard of Bingen, "*Explanatio Symboli Sancti Athanasii*," 1067BC).

no counsel from me. I keep the royal marriage bed, and all that is God's is mine as well."[44] For her part, *Sapientia* is defined in the same work as "a most loving mistress in [God's] lovely embrace."[45] This identification will go beyond the community of attributes, both also sharing a kind of immanent triadic reflection of the transcendent Trinity.

This *Caritas/Sapientia* is not, however, a spirit of the world (*anima mundi*) as in Bernardus Silvestris's theory;[46] there is not, in Hildegard, a kind of goddess "*Natura*" apart from God, nor the uncreated energies that the Palamite theologians posit as a god distinct from the divine essence. The Hildegardian *Caritas* is not a goddess apart from the Trinity but represents the immanence of the transcendent God. On the other hand, just as the transcendent God is triune, so his presence in the world, expressed through the concepts of *Caritas*, *Sapientia*, and *Viriditas*, has a triune character. In this sense, Hildegard's trinitarian ontology is necessarily sophianic.[47]

Where the Hildegardian trinitarian ontology is reflected with greater clarity—albeit a poetic clarity—is in the hymn to the virtue of Wisdom ("*O virtus Sapientie*") included in the *Symphonia*.[48] Therein Wisdom, despite being a virtue, is described more in cosmic and ontological terms than ethical ones: *Sapientia* embraces everything, surrounding it with life ("*O virtus Sapientie, que circuiens circuisti, comprehendendo omnia in una via que habet vitam*"). In this sense, it is a divine agent that operates in the cosmos through everything, but this figure also has a triadic structure present in its three wings ("*tres alas habens*"). The first flies in the heights ("*quarum una in altum volat*"), the second is transpired from the earth ("*et altera de terra sudat*"), and the third is everywhere ("*et tertia undique volat*"), leaving no room for the secular.

That same trinitarian structure, although not with the same clarity, can also be traced in other passages of her work. Of these, the most

44. Hildegard of Bingen, "*Liber Vitae Meritorum*," III.VI, 108.

45. Hildegard of Bingen, "*Liber Vitae Meritorum*," I.XXXIV, 23.

46. As Góngora explains, Bernardus Silvestris considers that the existence of a world/soul distinct from God, which operates in the realm of the stars, follows necessarily from the idea of a living cosmos (Góngora, "Introducción," 48).

47. It would be possible to see a parallel between the sophianic trinity of Love, Wisdom, and Glory (corresponding to Father, Son, and Holy Spirit)—which Bulgakov develops in chapter 2 of *Sophia: The Wisdom of God* on the divine Sophia and the Persons of the Holy Trinity (see Bulgakov, *Sophia*, 37–53)—and the Hildegardian figures of *Caritas*, *Sapientia*, and *viriditas*.

48. Hildegard of Bingen, *Symphonia*, 100.

noteworthy is the aforementioned beginning of the first vision in the *Liber Divinorum Operum,* in which the *vox de caelo,* who is later identified with *Caritas,* is presented as a resplendent fiery figure.[49] Although there is no exact correspondence with the hymn to Wisdom, it can be pointed out that the wing that flies in the heights "flies over the circle of the earth and, covering it with her wisdom, orders it righteously." The second wing could well correspond to the operation of the "scorching life of the divine substance" that "burns on the beauty of the fields, glitters in the waters and burns in the sun, in the moon and in the stars." For its part, the third could correspond to the "celestial breath" that "incites life in all beings, vivifying them with the invisible life that sustains everything."[50]

Hildegard's trinitarian ontology is therefore sophianic since the presence of God in the world is described through the figure of *Caritas/Sapientia.* Thus, the three-winged *Sapientia* is the very immanence of God, a real reflection of the transcendent Trinity.

The Unity of the Living Universe: The Great Cosmic Liturgy

Hildegard of Bingen's living universe constitutes an immense cosmic liturgy.[51] The meaning of this expression applied to Hildegard's thought is twofold. In the first place, praise is the vital operation of created being, since everything that exists lives, everything that lives is in God, everything that is in God also conveys God, and everything that bears God in its heart praises God, as Ps 19 proclaims: "The heavens are telling the

---

49. Hildegard of Bingen, "*Liber Divinorum Operum,*" I.I.II, 743B–744B.
50. Hildegard of Bingen, "*Liber Divinorum Operum,*" I.I.II, 743BC.
51. The first to use the term was Hans Urs von Balthasar, who—in his monographic work on Maximus the Confessor, *Cosmic Liturgy*—explains what he means by this expression and why he considers it to perfectly define the cosmology of the seventh-century monk:

> Maximus presents the Church, and the sign that she imprints on the world, in the largest and most open terms possible. The Church lies in the midst of the natural and the supernatural cosmos like a source of light that sets all things revolving around itself; in that she represents everything symbolically she also is an effective guarantee of the transformation of the whole universe. The liturgy is, for Maximus, more than a mere symbol; it is, in modern terms, an *opus operatum,* an effective transformation of the world into transfigured, divinized existence. For that reason, in Maximus' view . . . the liturgy is ultimately always "cosmic liturgy": a way of drawing the entire world into the hypostatic union, because both world and liturgy share a Christological foundation. (Balthasar, *Cosmic Liturgy,* 322)

glory of God."[52] Thus, the heart of reality is doxological and the foundations of the earth tremble in praise: "The creatures of the Lord, hearing the wonders of their Creator, embrace one another, so that their wonder is linked to the wonder in the great clamor of words."[53] Second, the cosmos is not indifferent to the liturgy, the sacraments, or the history of salvation. In other words, liturgical events have a real effect on the universe.

For Hildegard, the non-indifference of creation to history's liturgical and salvific events is mediated by the presence of God in the world, which maintains the unity of all creation through the action of Wisdom. It is evident at this point that the Hildegardian universe does not constitute a kind of fortuitous agglomeration of juxtaposed Leibnizian monads, but rather, due to the action of Wisdom that orders everything correctly and with meaning (*rationalitas*), contains created beings that are woven together by the elements. Interconnection and relationality are essential properties of each created being.

The vision of the cosmic egg suggests this unity, which will be consolidated more than two decades later in the second vision[54] of the first part of the *Liber Divinorum Operum*, which contemplates the universe as a wheel contained in the chest of *Caritas*—the same igneous figure described in the first vision. Indeed, Hildegard emphasizes that the vision of the universe as a wheel expresses with greater clarity the interconnection of everything real: "The wheel refers to the action of turning, to the exact balance of the elements of the world."[55] This idea of interconnection reaches even greater expressiveness in the hymn "*O ignis Spiritus Paracliti*":

> O mightiest way,
> in which penetrating all things,
> in the heavens,

---

52. Ps 19:1.

53. Hildegard of Bingen, *Scivias*, I.III.XVIII, 49.

54. See Hildegard of Bingen, *Book of Divine Works*, figure 1.2: The Cosmic Spheres and Human Being, 47.

55. Hildegard of Bingen, "Liber Divinorum Operum," I.II.III, 155D–756A. In fact, the circular turn constitutes an image that has always been used to explain the harmonic and dynamic unity of the multiple. An example of this is the Greek concept of *perikhoresis*, which was first used by Maximus the Confessor to help conceive how the *communicatio idiomatum* of the divine and human natures took place in Christ, and which was later used to reflect the circular dance in which each hypostasis of the Trinity gives up its space and offers itself, strengthening the trinitarian unity not only in nature but also in love.

> and on the earth,
> and in every depth,
> all You compose and bind together.[56]

The last verse of the hymn is significant, as it points to the reconciling action of the Holy Spirit, who gathers, connects, joins all things. The Spirit saturates everything, gathering and connecting all created beings, in such a way that there is no dispersion or isolation, but a real harmonic unity.

The unity and order that prevail in the Hildegardian universe are the condition that enables the diffusion of liturgical and sacramental action, spreading its effects throughout the world. God nourishes creation from his heart through the elements, and this action of nurturing acquires a meaning that goes beyond merely sustaining the thing in health and life. There is something divine in the heat, for the bright fire and layer of darkness is God-in-creation, who "scorches everywhere with the fire of his vengeance all who are outside the true faith; and those who remain in the bosom of the Catholic faith, everywhere he purifies with the fire of his consolation."[57] In this sense, the notion of divine action in creation is not mere symbolism or metaphor, but has a physical character. The aforementioned ubiquity—which leaves no room for a secular space of autonomy—is not exclusive to fire since air is also ubiquitous.

Air also spreads to all spheres, carrying the effects of the events of salvation history throughout the world. The same ontological continuity that unites all beings is the fruit of air's divine action, which appears in the form of wind and whirlwinds in the vision of the cosmic egg.[58] It is precisely the air that spreads throughout the universe the radiant light and heat of the brilliant fire that surrounds and comprises the cosmic egg. The first gust and its eddies, which come from the fire, carry the words that spread the truth throughout the universe.[59] The second gust and its eddies, which proceed from the layer of darkness under the blazing fire, "spread everywhere in the instrument" the "diabolical fury" that "exhales the disastrous infamy with wicked flames."[60] The third gust and

---

56. "O iter fortissimum, / quod penetravit omnia, / in altissimis et in terrenis et in omnibus abyssis, Tu omnes componis et colligis" (Hildegard of Bingen, *Symphonia*, 148). My translation.

57. Hildegard of Bingen, *Scivias*, I.III.III, 42.

58. For Mother Placid Dempsey's copy of the vision, cf. Hildegard of Bingen, *Scivias* (1990), The Universe, 91.

59. Hildegard of Bingen, *Scivias*, I.III.VIII, 44.

60. Hildegard of Bingen, *Scivias*, I.III.IX, 45.

its eddies, arising from the purest ether, "spread everywhere throughout the instrument," carrying the "unity of faith" and the "good news with words of truth and fullness that quickly move to the ends of the world."[61]

Water, meanwhile, possessing a sphere of its own, a circle of "aqueous air and white skin," symbolizes "baptism in the Church for the salvation of the faithful . . . and spreads everywhere, thanks to the divine inspiration, bringing to the universe orb the spring that provides health to believers."[62] Hildegard poses a universal baptism, whose spring spreads throughout the world thanks to the diffusing action of the fourth gust and its eddies.[63] There is no place in the universe that remains indifferent to the sacraments or unscathed by sin.

Hildegard's cosmic liturgy, with its aspects of harmonic unity and divine action in the world, is most apparent in this passage from the *Liber Divinorum Operum*:

> The sky houses the light; the light, the air; and the air, the birds; the earth nourishes the *viriditas*; the *viriditas*, the fruits; the fruits, the animals; and all this testifies that it has been made by a strong hand: the supreme power of the whole world, which, in the strength of its virtue, has made everything that exists so that nothing lacks for its benefit, and this forger has in its omnipotence the movement of every living being: those who go after the earthly, like the beasts, to which God has not breathed reason; and the breath of those who inhabit the flesh of man, and who possess reason, discernment, wisdom.[64]

Man, Crucible of Cosmic Forces

As can be deduced from the vision of the wheel of the universe, the ontological place of the human being is the center of the universe, traversed by the elements and all the cosmic forces. Hildegardian anthropology is thus radically opposed to the Cartesian or Kantian (in which human reason is hypostatized and placed before the cosmos and outside of it), and it constitutes a real alternative to the modern paradigm. This central

---

61. Hildegard of Bingen, *Scivias*, I.III.XIII, 47.
62. Hildegard of Bingen, *Scivias*, I.III.XIV, 14.
63. Hildegard of Bingen, *Scivias*, I.III.XV, 48.
64. Hildegard of Bingen, *Scivias*, II.I.II, 113.

position of man in the cosmos is presented in a precise way in the vision of the cosmic egg:

> The man, imbued with deep understanding, who dwells in the midst of the forces of divine Creation, made of the mud of the earth with great glory and so united to the energies of Creation, that he cannot separate himself from them [*nullo modo separari valet*]; because the elements of the world, founded to serve man, render vassalage to him, and he is seated in the midst of them, governing them by divine design.[65]

Later, in the vision of the wheel of the universe, which delves into the cosmological reflection of the cosmic egg, she describes it in these terms:

> God, who for the glory of his name arranged the world with the elements, consolidated it with the winds, illuminated it by intertwining it with the stars, completed it with the rest of the creatures, and placed man in it, surrounding it with all these things and fortifying it with the greatest strength, so that they assist him in all things and help him in his works, so that he works with them; because man without them cannot live nor subsist.[66]

These two passages underline various aspects of Hildegard's vision of man. In the first place, man is a rational being, "imbued with deep understanding," possessing reason (*rationalitas*), discernment (*discretio*), and wisdom (*sapientia*), which explains the ontic preeminence of man over the rest of the created beings. Secondly, his place is the center of the "sandy globe," dwelling in the midst of cosmic forces, manifested in the winds and the elements of the world. The elements are key in the cosmic nature of the human being, beginning with the earth, of whose maternal nature Hildegard gives an account when she affirms that "the earth is the carnal matter of men, and with its sap it nourishes them like a mother breastfeeds her children."[67] The elements also acquire a central relevance in Hildegard's healing practice due to their correspondence with the humors (according to Isidorian theory). Thus, water corresponds to humidity, air to dryness, fire to warmth, and earth to cold. Hildegardian medicine is based on this anthropology, since what is unknown cannot

---

65. Hildegard of Bingen, *Scivias*, I.III.XVI, 48.

66. Hildegard of Bingen, "*Liber Divinorum Operum*," I.II.II, 755B.

67. "Quoniam terra est carnalis materia hominis, nutriens eum suco suo sicut mater lactat filios suos" (Hildegard of Bingen, *Scivias*, II.I.VII, 116).

be healed, and the human being is made up of the four elements that constitute the universe.

Man's dwelling in the middle of creation not only implies that he is nurtured by the elements, but also places him at the center of a web of wind lines that cross the globe from different origins: "In this way, this image had been intertwined and surrounded by these forms."[68] Thus, in the vision of the wheel of the universe, cosmic unity is manifested through the breath exhaled from the head of a leopard in the north, a wolf in the south, a lion in the east, and a bear in the west. The leopard and the wolf are likewise surrounded by two heads, one of a deer and the other of a crab; the lion and the bear are surrounded by the heads of a lamb and a serpent; from all originate a breath that passes through the universe and is directed especially to the human being. The human being is, therefore, a crucible in which all the cosmic forces and elements converge.

Man, who constitutes the very heart of creation, therefore has a preeminence over the rest of the creatures. However, the lordship of man in the universe should not be understood as a despotic and arbitrary domain, since it is impossible for man to be conceived as an entity separate from the world ("*nullo modo separari valet*"[69]), and his existence depends on other creatures, because "man without them cannot live nor subsist [*quia homo absque illis nec vivere, nec etiam subsistere potest*]."[70] His lordship is that of one who, from the center of the universe, reigns *with* the creatures, as a guarantor of the balance of creation. In this sense, Hildegard intuits a humanized nature, an ecosystem marked by the action of man, whose mission is to fulfill the "divine plan," making order and beauty possible in creation.

Man is not only traversed by the elements, which work at the service of *Caritas*, and by the wind lines originating from the heads surrounding the created spheres, but also by rays in the form of golden threads that arise from the mouth of the igneous figure identified with *Caritas*:

> I also saw that from the mouth of the aforementioned image, in whose chest the wheel appeared, a light came out that was clearer than daylight in the likeness of threads, by which the shapes of the circles and the shapes of the other figures, which they had been distinguished on this same wheel, and each of the forms of the members of the figure of man, namely, those of

---

68. Hildegard of Bingen, "*Liber Divinorum Operum*," I.II.I, 755A.
69. Hildegard of Bingen, *Scivias*, I.III.XVI, 48.
70. Hildegard of Bingen, "*Liber Divinorum Operum*," I.II.II, 755B.

this same image, which also appeared on the same wheel, were measured with straight and clear measure.[71]

Thus, although *Caritas* nourishes man through the elements and cosmic breath, it also does so directly and immediately, with breath that originates in the very mouth of the immanent God, and that infuses the body with life and beauty, reaching each of its members. In this sense, the body, nourished by the cosmos, and the soul, nourished by God, cannot be divided; rather, the whole man is nourished both directly and indirectly by the same divinity.

In Hildegard's living universe, man cannot separate himself from creation, nor can he subsist without the other creatures. This relationality is also manifested in the influence of the stars.[72] In the second vision of the first part of the *Liber Divinorum Operum*,[73] the stars are placed over the man's head, between the human figure and the head of the divine *Caritas*. In fact, the rays in the form of threads of light issue forth from the mouth of *Caritas* and reach the head of man through the seven planets, which multiply these rays. In this sense, the planets occupy an intermediate cosmic place between the mouth of *Caritas* and man. Three of these planets are located in the circle of brilliant fire, the first of the elements, which encompasses and illuminates the other three elements and sheds its light on all creatures, signifying "the power of God [*potentia Dei*]."[74] The sun, for its part, is located in "the innermost circle of black fire,"[75] being the herald of God who, when rising in summer, exerts God's vengeance, and when descending in winter, causes frost and plagues by divine design. Three other stars are located in the circle of pure ether, including the moon, the star closest to man.

---

71. Hildegard of Bingen, "*Liber Divinorum Operum*," I.II.I, 755A.

72. It is not the purpose of this essay to study Hildegard's position on astrology. However, although it is true that in the *Scivias* she writes against astrology, the object of her condemnation is the belief that each man has a star in which his destiny is written and that justifies the practice of divination. However, Hildegard's Catholic vision of the universe legitimizes the connection of the human being with the action of the planets, in addition to the fact that she explicitly admits that the stars emit signals by God's command (citing scripture: "'And there will be signs in sun and moon and stars, and upon the earth distress of nations in perplexity at the roaring of the sea and the waves'" [Luke 21:25]); see Hildegard of Bingen, *Scivias*, I.III.XXI, 51–52.

73. See Hildegard of Bingen, *Book of Divine Works*, figure 1.2: The Cosmic Spheres and Human Being, 47.

74. Hildegard of Bingen, "*Liber Divinorum Operum*," I.II.IV, 756A.

75. Hildegard of Bingen, "*Liber Divinorum Operum*," I.II.I, 753D.

Man's position of cosmic preeminence is owed to the fact that he represents the created being that contains in himself all of creation. The human being is not only a cosmic crucible but also the repository of the sacred, of the divine energies that emanate from the mouth of the divine *Caritas*. God is present in the world and man is called to bring together in himself this *Deus visibilis*, this *viriditas*. It is the Virgin Mary, Mother of God, the greenest branch of the tree of creation, in whom *viriditas* is most concentrated. Allusions to *viriditas* abound in Hildegard's descriptions of the Virgin, always through natural elements: Mary is the most verdant branch ("*viridissima virga*"), the mediating branch ("*virga mediatrix*"), the crowned branch ("*virga ac diadema*"), the leafy branch ("*frondens virga*"), the softest branch ("*suavissima virga*"), and the most splendid gem ("*splendidissima gemma*"). The poetic expressiveness of Hildegard's hymns more appropriately reflects the way in which *viriditas* reaches its greatest expression in Mary:

> O flower, thou didst not bud forth from the dew,
> nor from drops of rain,
> nor did the air swirl above thee,
> but the divine brightness brought thee forth
> into the noblest branch.
>
> God foresaw thy flowering,
> O branch, on the first day
> of his creation.
>
> And with his Word, God made thee
> into a matrix of gold, O praiseworthy Virgin.
>
> O how mighty the vigor of man's side
> from whom God shaped the form of woman,
> whom He made
> the mirror of all his ornaments
> and the embrace of all his creatures.
>
> Since then, the heavenly choirs sing
> and the whole earth marvels,
> O praiseworthy Mary,
> for God loved thee so much.[76]

---

76. My translation. The original Latin reads:

> O flos, tu non germinasti de rore / nec de guttis pluvie / nec aer desuper te volavit sed divina / claritas in nobilissima virga te produxit. / O virga,

Conclusion

Hildegard's work offers us a vision that is not only medieval or pre-scientific, but truly "catholic" in a universal sense. She opposes the illusory secularized and disenchanted world exhibited by the modern paradigm, which subjects creation to the criteria of transparency and availability, ignoring the presence of God in all things. Faced with this deviant system—which emerged as a parody of the liturgical order and is today disintegrating in spite of its growing aggressiveness—Hildegardian philosophy gives us the key to rediscovering the divine presence in the cosmos through a clearly sophianic trinitarian ontology. *Sapientia* is the true presence of God in the natural world, and it shines through with the splendor of *viriditas*. Catholic philosophy is based on *wonder* at being, and not on *critica*. The transfiguration of the gaze, seeing in simplicity, allows us to intuit and revere the divine mystery that nourishes creation from its depths; it also drives us to rediscover the place that the human being occupies in the cosmos. Indeed, if man is not an isolated subject who looks at creation from outside but constitutes a crucible of creation in which all cosmic forces converge, his mission is no longer to impose the designs of instrumental reason subjected to a blind will; rather, he is called to be the guarantor of cosmic order and beauty in a humanized ecosystem, in which he reigns *with* the other creatures. Only in this way will man shine with the divine exuberance of *viriditas*. Only in this way will man be able to resemble the sophianic mirror of humanity: the holy Virgin Mary, the most verdant branch of creation.

Bibliography

Angela of Foligno. *Complete Works*. Translated by Paul Lachance. New York: Paulist, 1993.

Aquinas, Thomas. *Summa contra Gentiles*. Translated by Laurence Shapcote. Edited and revised by The Aquinas Institute. https://aquinas.cc/la/en/~SCG2.C3.

Balthasar, Hans Urs von. *Cosmic Liturgy: The Universe according to Maximus the Confessor*. Translated by Brian E. Daley. San Francisco: Ignatius, 1988.

Bulgakov, Sergei. *Sophia: The Wisdom of God*. Hudson: Lindisfarne, 1993.

---

floriditatem tuam Deus in prima die / creature sue previderat. / Et te Verbo suo auream materiam, / o laudabilis Virgo, fecit. / O quam magnum est in viribus suis latus viri, / de quo Deus formam mulieris produxit, / quam fecit speculum / omnis ornamenti sui et amplexionem / omnis creature sue. / Inde concinunt celestia organa et miratur / omnis terra, o laudabilis Maria, / quia Deus te valde amavit. (Hildegard of Bingen, *Symphonia*, 128)

Descartes, René. *Discours de la Méthode*. Edited by Étienne Gilson. Paris: Librairie Philosophique J. Vrin, 1987.

Góngora, Maria E. "Introducción." In *Libro de las Obras Divinas*, by Hildegarda de Bingen, 11–65. Barcelona: Herder, 2009.

Hart, Columba, and Jane Bishop. *Creation and Christ: The Wisdom of Hildegard of Bingen*. New York: Paulist, 1996.

Hildegard of Bingen. *The Book of Divine Works*. Translated by Nathaniel M. Campbell. Washington, DC: The Catholic University of America Press, 2018.

———. *Epistolarium. Par Prima I–XC*. Edited by L. Van Acker. Corpus Christianorum Continuatio Mediaevalis 91. Turnhout: Brepols, 1991.

———. "Explanatio Symboli Sancti Athanasii ad Congregationem Sororum Suarum." In *S. Hildegardis Abbatissae Opera Omnia*, 1065–82. Patrologia Latina 197. Paris: J. P. Migne, 1855.

———. *Hildegard von Bingen's Physica: The Complete English Translation of Her Classic Work on Health and Healing*. Translated by Priscilla Throop. Rochester: Healing Arts, 1998.

———. "Liber Divinorum Operum Simplices Hominis." In *S. Hildegardis Abbatissae Opera Omnia*, 741–1038. Patrologia Latina 197. Paris: J. P. Migne, 1855.

———. "Liber Vitae Meritorum, per Simplicem Hominem a Vivente Luce Revelatorum." In *Analecta Sanctae Hildegardis*, edited by J. B. Pitra, 7–244. Monte Cassino, 1882.

———. "Physica." In *S. Hildegardis Abbatissae Opera Omnia*, 1125–352. Patrologia Latina 197. Paris: J. P. Migne, 1855.

———. *Scivias*. Edited by Adelgundis Fükrkötter. Corpus Christianorum Continuatio Mediaevalis 43. Turnhout: Brepols, 1978.

———. *Scivias*. Translated by Columba Hart and Jane Bishop. New York: Paulist, 1990.

———. *Symphonia: A Critical Edition of the "Symphonia Armonie Celestium Revelationum" (Symphony of the Harmony of Celestial Revelations)*. Introduction, translations, and commentary by Barbara Newman. Ithaca: Cornell University Press, 1988.

Léclerq, Jean. *The Love of Learning and the Desire for God: A Study of Monastic Culture*. New York: Fordham University Press, 1982.

Martin, Michael. *The Submerged Reality: Sophiology and the Turn to a Poetic Metaphysics*. Kettering: Angelico, 2015.

Meditations on the Tarot: A Journey into Christian Hermeticism. Translated by Robert Powell. Putnam, NY: Jeremy P. Tarcher, 2002.

Newman, Barbara. *Sister of Wisdom: St. Hildegard's Theology of the Feminine*. Aldershot: Scolar, 1987.

Rabassó, Georgina. "'Sapientia docet me': Hildegarda de Bingen y la Filosofía." *Mediaevalia. Textos e Estudos* 35 (2016) 7–50.

Stoudt, Debra L. "The Medical, the Magical, and the Miraculous in the Healing Arts of Hildegard of Bingen." In *A Companion to Hildegard of Bingen*, edited by Beverly Mayne Kienzle et al., 249–72. Brill's Companion to the Christian Tradition 45. Leiden: Brill, 2014.

Stover, Justin A. "Hildegard, the Schools, and Their Critics." In *A Companion to Hildegard of Bingen*, edited by Beverly Mayne Kienzle et al., 109–35. Brill's Companion to the Christian Tradition 45. Leiden: Brill, 2014.

5

Ordinatissima Pulchritudo Huius Mundi

St. Augustine's Image of Creation

Salvador Antuñano Alea

Introduction

This chapter intends, after a general overview, to consider St. Augustine's image of creation to see how it can help us renew our Christian worldview. This is all the more necessary in a time when a religious interpretation of reality often seems to be marginal or supposedly outdated.

General Framework

Shortly after his conversion and while awaiting his baptism, Augustine put forth the two great topics to which he wished to devote his research:

> A.—Deum et animam scire cupio.
> R.—Nihilne plus?
> A.—Nihil omnino.[1]

If we take into account his body of work—his theology of the Trinity and of grace, his biblical commentaries, and his abundant work and preaching—we might very easily get the impression that in the course of his life he more than completed his program of studying God and the soul. As a result, it might seem strange to inquire into the Bishop of Hippo's view of creation as this could be seen as an insignificant topic, a mere curiosity or diversion.

---

1. Augustine, "Soliloquiorum," I, 7.

However, if we dig deeper, we find that—precisely because of the essential nature of God and the soul—Augustine had to consider the Christian worldview in some depth. This is not just because creation is where humans undertake their pilgrimage to the kingdom, but also because—for that very reason—God speaks to us through it. From it, he claims us for himself, and we are directed to "a new heaven and a new earth"[2] by faith. Consequently, the pole of the world is not only present in Augustine's reflections, but it is interwoven in his meditations on man and God, thus suggesting the full meaning that the cosmos may have.[3]

Augustine wrote on creation throughout his life, mainly in his debates against pagans and Manichaeans but also in some of his major works, such as the *Confessiones* or *De Civitate Dei*; additionally, his image of the world is in the background of his discussions with Pelagians and Donatists.[4]

Furthermore, like many of his major philosophical and theological ideas, Augustine develops his image of creation based on and in contrast to his experience of the world, first as a pagan and then as a Manichaean. He bases it on the information offered to him by his Christian faith—fundamentally on the doctrines of creation, the Incarnation, and eschatology—and in contrast (and disagreement) with the implications that the Pelagian idea of freedom and Donatist exclusivism might have for the image of the world. In essence, we might expect Augustine to tell the pagans that *we are not made for this world*; to tell the Manichaeans that *we too are made for this world*; to tell the Pelagians that we must not be enslaved by this world, *but neither should we tyrannize it*; and to tell the Donatists that *this world is to be shared by everyone*.

---

2. Rev 21:1.

3. See Augustine, "Enarrationes in Psalmos," 145:13.

4. The main works of Augustine on creation include: Augustine, "De Ordine"; Augustine, "De Genesi contra Manichaeos" (book II); Augustine, "De Genesi ad Litteram Imperfectus Liber"; Augustine, "De Genesi ad Litteram" (book XII); Augustine, "Confessionum" (books XI–XII); Augustine, "Enarrationes in Psalmos" (mainly §§26, 41, 92, 99, 128, 134, 135, 144, 145); Augustine, "De Doctrina Christiana"; Augustine, "De Natura Boni"; and Augustine, "De Civitate Dei" (books XI and XII). Essential works on Augustine's image of creation include Gilson, "Contemplation de Dieu"; for an English translation see Gilson, "Contemplating God"; see also Hanby, "Christology, Cosmology"; Ortiz, *"You Made Us for Yourself"*; and Williams, "'Good for Nothing'?"

Essential Features of the *Imago Creationis*

At the risk of over-simplification, this chapter will attempt to present, succinctly and more or less organically, the main features of the view of creation given by Augustine. We will focus on three main ideas: the world is *creatio*, it is *ordinatissima*, and it is *pulcherrima*.

Creatio: Esse

Creatio is a term that in itself expresses the radical change in *imago mundi* that Augustine accepted when he converted. The words that Roman paganism used to name the world were *mundus, universus, orbis*, and *natura*. The first, *mundus*, is related to the Sanskrit root *mund*, "purified being"; by the same token it denotes the simultaneously sacred and beautiful—even divine—character of that which exists.[5] The second, *universus*, means all things together in unity.[6] The third, *orbis*—also from a Sanskrit root, *dhvar*, "bend, twist"[7]—seems to enclose all things in a circle, or rather points to the idea that they all turn constantly in an eternal wheel. The last, *natura*, derives from *nascor*, "birth," and refers to the collection of everything brought into existence;[8] thus *natura* parallels the Greek *physis*. From the Greeks, the Romans took the word κόσμος (*kosmos*).[9] This points to order in a logical, moral, and aesthetic sense; it is as though all things submit to or are governed by a law that causes them, puts them in their place, and establishes the splendor of their harmonious proportions.

Therefore, behind all of these terms is an image that the world is everything that exists—including the gods—and is the only thing that exists; thus it is sacred, harmonious, coherent, and of course determined. Humankind is part of this whole as one more element—indeed, a fairly precarious one. The subject of existence is actually the whole; the individual beings that comprise it appear briefly and then simply disappear. The dual contrasts of existence gave rise to dualism, which could be more or less radical; it could be taken so far as to exclude the opposite pole and become spiritualism (Plotinus) or materialism (Epicurus and the Stoics).

5. Logeion, "Mundus."
6. Logeion, "Universus."
7. Logeion, "Orbis."
8. Logeion, "Natura."
9. See Logeion, "κόσμος."

These names indicate that while pagan philosophy was able to develop this image in a more sophisticated way, it did not alter it substantially. If the ancient myths personified cosmic forces—physical ones like Gaia and spiritual ones like Eros—the philosophers suggested that all beings were governed, even immovably determined, by a *logos*. This *logos* could take shape in the Platonic idea of the good, in Aristotle's unmoved mover, the *lex naturalis* of the Stoics, or Plotinus's *exitus-reditus* scheme.

This entire worldview—the one that would have been held by the young Augustine—was completely uprooted when he accepted the Christian idea of *creatio*.[10] The term was rarely used in Latin before Christianity, and of course not with the meaning given to it by faith.[11] *Cerĕo*—the archaic form of the verb *creo* from which *creatio* derives—is seemingly related to the Sanskrit words *kar* and *kri*—"to make"—and means "create," "produce."[12] Through divine revelation, faith understands and uses *creatio* in opposition to a world that is immanent, self-sufficient, eternal, determined, cyclical, and ultimately tragic. In contrast with this pagan image, creation is the work of a God who exists outside and before it; it finds its foundation and origin—its ontological principle and its chronological beginning—in him. Creation is not the result of a need but of a free and loving choice; it has a development, a purpose—a *telos*, which is "end," "aim," and "goal."[13]

The idea of creation thus assumes, firstly, that the *universe has a creator*, that there is someone who is ultimately responsible for the existence of everything and is distinct from it. And if there is an author, there is also a purpose, an origin, a foundation, a development. It is true that the ancients had glimpsed something of this in their myths and the philosophers in their theories. However, in the end, both myths and theories justified the order of the cosmos on the basis of two co-principles, one active and the other passive, both mutually corresponding and integrated in the one total existing reality, a complete and self-enclosed immanence, in a very determined and fixed process. The idea of a God who is absolutely transcendent to the cosmos—who is prior to it and moreover does not need it—matures in biblical reflection and finds a high level of development in Philo of Alexandria, a Jewish rabbi and philosopher

---

10. See Logeion, "Creatio"; Logeion, "Creo."

11. Cicero uses it when speaking of the appointment of new magistrates and in the *Digest*; Ulpian uses it in relation to having children.

12. Logeion, "Creo."

13. Logeion, "τέλος."

whose influence would be essential for Neoplatonism. However, as such, it was something strange in the context of ancient paganism. Even assuming that Plotinus's One is an entity that transcends the cosmos, it is difficult not to fall into a kind of pantheism or monism if the world ultimately flows from that One and tends to dissolve and melt back into it—for the goal of Plotinus's mysticism seems precisely to be that fusion with The One. For Augustine, on the other hand, the idea of God as creator implies not only his absolute transcendence apart from the world, but that he made the world as a sovereign, loving, free decision and not as a determined process to which he was obliged.[14] This Christian idea of God naturally implies that, as creator, God is the greatest and best, the most powerful and wise being that can exist. He is so powerful and wise that—unlike the mythical gods or Plato's demiurge—he does not need any pre-existing matter to create the world, not even as a procession from himself. He displays his omnipotence through creation *ex nihilo*.[15]

On the basis offered to him by faith, Augustine develops his theology of a God who creates from nothing. According to this theology, God, who dwells in his eternity, creates the world not from himself, as suggested by Plotinus's processions,[16] nor from a pre-existing eternal matter, as claimed in Plato's *Timaeus* or the ancient myths where there is an ordering principle of the primordial chaos; instead, according to Genesis,

---

14. See Augustine, "De Diversis Quaestionibus ad Simplicianum," II, 2:8.

15. See Augustine, "De Trinitate," XV, 13:22.

16. I'm pleased to thank Prof. Jeffrey Dirk Wilson, PhD, of the Catholic University of America for his fine remarks on the transcendent character of Plotinus's "The One" and its relation with the idea of creation, and therefore his influence in this point on Augustine. Different aspects are implied in the idea of creation: origin and total dependence, identity and difference between creator and creatures, necessity or freedom in their relation—and in consequence, the kind of "love" between them—the manner of creating from a pre-existing matter or from nothing, etc. Depending on how these aspects are understood, we could see the similarities and differences in the philosophical and theological doctrines. In any case, there doesn't seem to be much trace of the idea of "*creatio*" in ancient pagan philosophy before Philo of Alexandria (20 BC–AD 45) and his commentaries on Genesis. Since then, and increasingly due to the influence of Christianity, the idea of creation overflowed the limits of Jewish and Christian thought and was, among other ideas, in the general cultural atmosphere. As for Plotinus, "An important historical question . . . is whether Plotinus's account of instrumental creation was primarily inspired by his interaction with the Jews, Christians, and Gnostics of his day or whether it arose from his development of Middle Platonic and Pythagorean speculation about the true meaning of Plato's *Timaeus*, *Parmenides*, and *Republic* and of Aristotle's reports on the One and the Dyad" (Zimmerman, "Does Plotinus Present," 105). I also thank Dr. Wilson for calling my attention to this and other papers on the question: Gerson, "Plotinus's Metaphysics"; Rist, "One of Plotinus."

God creates through his Word: he says the word and things come into being.[17] This means that our reality consists of the creative force of the divine Word and the nothingness from which we are taken.[18] Our existence therefore has an ontological connection to God that sustains us in our being. However, it does not make us identical to God. Consequently, the world is not a pantheistic universe; rather, it is a creation of something different from God but that depends entirely on him and him alone—because it is creation *a Deo ex nihilo*. Therefore, without the Word of God that pronounces us, we would be nothing. Indeed, for Augustine, this is what sin comprises: distancing oneself from God and tending toward nothingness. And, in the other direction, when creatures tend toward God and love him, because they are not made of God but by his Word, their final goal is not to fuse into him, but to live in his love; they maintain their own reality in its entirety, within the ontological distinction of creator-creature.

That the world is God's creation also means that *the world has a solid foundation* in its existence and in good because it depends on God's Wisdom. Along the same lines as Genesis—"And God saw everything that he had made, and behold, it was very good"[19]—Augustine says that, as God is the supreme Good and he created all things, *all things are originally and radically good*.[20] If they become evil, it is not because their origin is in evil, but because they have chosen badly, opting for lesser goods instead of the absolute Good.[21] The goodness of creation is guaranteed as it is God's work, but it also has a deeper root, having the trace—*vestigium*—of its maker infused within it.

With this reflection, Augustine lays the foundations for a trinitarian metaphysics of creation: the trace of God in the creature is something like its ontological structure.[22] Augustine identifies three aspects of these *vestigia*: every created thing has being, knowledge, and love. In other words,

17. See Augustine, "Acta Seu Disputatio contra Fortunatum," 13.
18. See Augustine, "De Vera Religione," 18:35–36.
19. Gen 1:31.
20. See Augustine, "De Natura Boni," 1.
21. See Augustine, "De Vera Religione," 19:37; Augustine, "De Diversis Quaestionibus ad Simplicianum," I, 1:9–10.
22.

Trinitas	Dimensions	Structure	Vestigium	Imago
Pater: *Efficient cause*	Esse	Modus/ mensura	Natura	Memoria

it is constituted in itself as a true and good existence, as the reflection and participation of God the Father, Son, and Holy Ghost—Absolute Being, Absolute Knowledge, and Absolute Love. Therefore, in every created being there is a *natura*, a *doctrina*, and a *usus* which correspond to the trinitarian divine causality: efficient, exemplary, and final. In humans, this trace—*vestigium*—is also an image: *imago*.

Furthermore, the fact that God is the creator of the world means that the world has an origin, a beginning.[23] This again involves demythifying the ancient notion of the world, specifically of a world subject to the necessary repetition of cycles. In the pagan concept of an eternal return—both mythological and philosophical—specific existence lacks meaning, and freedom is ultimately a pure illusion; this is why it is so tragic. In contrast, in a linear scheme of time like the one implicit in the idea of creation, every instant is unique, every being is unique, every act is unique and very valuable in view of their possible meaning to the fabric as a whole.

The idea of *creatio* in Augustine is directly related to *esse*, and so also to the coherence of things which truly exist: creation is real because it is based on God's act of creation.

Ordinatissima: Videre

However, creation is also inscribed in the dimension of the *videre*; it has an aspect of truth that enables it to be known, with *scientia* and *sapientia*.[24] Therefore, to know creation in this manner is to discover the order in which it is organized, the order that comprises it. In Augustine's texts, this order of creation can be understood in at least five senses or levels, which are also connected to one another.

The first sense or level in which creation is ordered is *the metaphysical structure of each created being*. On the basis of the book of Wisdom,[25]

Trinitas	Dimensions	Structure	Vestigium	Imago
Filius: *Exemplary cause*	Videre/ Intellegere	Species/ numerus	Doctrina	Intellectus
Spiritus Sanctus: *Final cause*	Diligere/ Amare	Ordo/ pondus	Usus	Voluntas/ libertas

23. See Augustine, "De Genesi contra Manichaeos," I, 2:4.
24. See Augustine, "De Trinitate," XII, 14:21–23; 15:25; XIV, 13.
25. See Wis 11:20.

Augustine continuously repeats that everything is created with "*mensura, numero et pondere.*"[26] The meaning of these terms is analogous, as they can firstly refer to the created beings themselves; secondly, in a metaphysical analysis, the expression designates the ontological structure of the created beings—the *vestigium* of God in them; finally, they also refer to God, as the measure, number, and weight are ultimately him. Thus, with these three categories Augustine can find the ontological coherence of the created beings, as well as their metaphysical structure, real proportion, and fundamental relationship with the Creator.

According to their measure, number, and weight, the different created beings are also arranged in the second meaning Augustine gives to *videre*: the "*contextio creaturarum*," the placing of each creature in its own place in a perfect network of mutual relations.[27] Created beings are arranged on a scale from the highest to the lowest and vice versa. The obvious Platonic background is also Christianized by the idea of creation, since the place that things occupy is not the result of need or a mechanical cyclical movement—one whose circle inherently excludes the notion of "high and low"—but rather of the free and provident, loving, creative act that orders all things in accordance with a different measure which is transcendent and superior to them. Also understood as *contextio*, this scale of beings refers not so much to the "static" position of some created beings above or below others, but to their mutual dynamic relationship in a shared tension toward the common good to which they aspire—which is also distinct, transcendent, and greater than them. Furthermore, this concept of the universe in height and depth implies that it is not a "circle of life," as in mythological or philosophical paganisms where each point is as insignificant as the ones before and after it; rather, it is a true hierarchy of beings in which some are more and others are less, and the position they occupy is not by chance but is given by their own ontological density in accordance with their greater or lesser proximity, by participation, to the Absolute.

As this relationship is dynamic, and as creation has a starting point (an origin) and a goal (the ultimate good), the third sense that Augustine gives to the order of creation is that of *a distentio in temporibus*:[28] creation is not yet realized, but it gradually unfolds, second by second, through the course of time. Augustine speaks not only of human life, but

---

26. See Augustine, "De Natura Boni," 3.
27. See Augustine, "De Civitate Dei," XI, 16.
28. See Augustine, "Confessionum," XI, 28:38.

of creation as a whole with the fitting and accurate metaphor of a speech or melody: created beings appear and disappear like literary elements or the notes of a song. Each one carries out its own function in due time, having a meaning both independently and through its relationship with the whole, contributing to the final meaning of the speech or song. In this way, we can understand that even dissonances, contradictions, or apparent absurdities in certain expressions are actually, if not absolutely necessary, at least useful for showing the beauty of the other parts by contrast. Similarly, evil, injustice, pain, and even sin scandalize us and try to make us lose hope, but in the history of creation they are finally reintegrated into order by the justice and mercy of God, who—as Christ shows—can turn evil into good. Through this prism, creation itself is a theology of history, and history is a history of salvation.

If the world has been created, then it has an *end*; yet, in addition to "ending," "end" can be understood as culmination, purpose, or ultimate end. Augustine refers to all these forms of comprehension. Perhaps the most basic way of understanding that creation has an end is to understand it in reference to time: *the world will come to an end*. This idea—consistent with that of creation having a beginning—is a clear belief in the Christian faith which is fully embraced by Augustine. His reflection on the end of the world intensifies, especially following the sacking of Rome in AD 410 and the devastating advance of the Vandals through north Africa. For example, in his sermons that year he explicitly stated that the world is decaying as an ailing old man and that the Lord has warned us that its end would come.[29] The image of the old man is very appropriate, not just because it accounts for Christians' painful experiences during that time of tribulation, but above all because, as it is illuminated by faith, this image makes us see that our hope cannot take root in a mortally wounded world. Augustine spoke of the decadence of the present world so that his flock could place their hearts in God, the only one who is stable, "so that your youth is renewed like the eagle's."[30] As this is not a deterministic pagan notion, but rather the Christian image of time—and therefore, a *contextio* of creation, freedom, and providence—Augustine encourages hope and effort: "*Sunt mala tempora, dicunt . . . nos sumus tempora.*"[31]

---

29. See Augustine, "Sermo 81," 8.
30. Ps 103:5.
31. See Augustine, "Sermo 80," 8.

For Christians, the idea of the end of the world *introduces us to eschatology*.[32] The end is not actually an annihilation, but rather a transfiguration of the world. Aware of the risk of millenarianism, Augustine fears entering into interpretations that are too literal or materialistic when he explains these passages, but he truly believes in the promise of "a new heaven and a new earth"[33] and accepts it with hope.[34] So, although the specific modes of this promise are maintained in the mystery of faith, the image of creation elevated to a new order—culminated and fulfilled in its maximum perfection, positioned in a permanent stability—enables Augustine to show pagans and Christians that faith frees our hope from the bonds of a decaying world. It frees our understanding of creation from an impoverished perspective and transforms it, offering an understanding of the unlimited horizon of eternity. This is a *coup de grâce*—in more than one sense—for the ancient pagan notion of *mundus* as something sacred and divine.

Such a demythification of the world suggests that the world is not something absolute in itself or for itself; rather, it is relative to something—or someone—beyond it. Therefore, the expression "end of the world" also points to another sense, in which the notion of the order of creation becomes clear: the world has a purpose, an aim, it is ordered in terms of another, "it is for something or someone."[35] In a first approach, the direct aim of the world is humankind: God created the world as a temporal home for humankind and placed them at the forefront of creation to care for and cultivate it. This idea, explicit in the text of Genesis, involves a new demythification of the pagan image of the world as a whole in which humans have no distinct function.

Augustine assumes the Christian conviction that the world is made for man, not man for the world;[36] and he further explains that if this is not always the case, it is because of original sin, which has subverted the primordial order—an order however that divine providence will eventually restore. This finality of the world with respect to man corresponds naturally to the care and responsibility that man must afford to creation—as man is put on earth to cultivate and till it . . .

This commandment can be understood either well or badly. If—like Pelagius and his followers—human freedom is overvalued, it leads

---

32. See Augustine, "De Civitate Dei," XX, 16.
33. Rev 21:1.
34. See Augustine, "De Vera Religione," 32:44.
35. See Augustine, "De Civitate Dei," XII, 5.
36. See Mark 2:27.

to a tyrannical titanism, to a will of power that can only conclude with a whimsical domination of the world. Consequently, the world would be seen—superficially and naïvely—as an arena that offers itself without any restriction to promethean freedom and therefore as something naïvely good and without nuance. But Augustine precisely rejects the Pelagian notion of freedom because he sees it as full of *amor sui* and *libido dominandi*. With this in mind, he reminds them that, if it is true that the world is originally and radically good because it is a divine creation, it is also—like man's freedom itself—wounded by original sin in such a way that it can become an idol that demands to be worshiped, but also a paradise devastated by our own pride.[37] That is why the fact that man is above creation and that he has received the commandment to cultivate it implies using creatures with a responsible freedom, always within the framework of divine law.

Precisely for this reason, the fact that the world is ordered to man also means that he must manage it in justice and charity. Following the church fathers before him and in line with biblical tradition, Augustine understands that the goods of the world are not the exclusive patrimony of a few. Rather, creation is ordered to the good of all men. For this reason, he rejects the exclusionary intolerance of the Donatists (based, moreover, on a supposed religious perfection) and exhorts them to an open solidarity, to a humble tolerance,[38] to a truly universal charity—ardent and unitive as pitch[39]—because if the world's purpose is the good of all the children of Adam, it is necessary to seek peace and harmony with heaven and earth.[40]

But that species of the "proximate end" of creation, which is man, is only an "intermediate end": the true and ultimate end of the world, the one that gives it its full meaning, is God himself, through the Incarnation of the Word. The "human" whom the world serves is, in a spiritual sense, the Son of God for whom all things have been made. Consequently, creation has imprinted in itself an order that finalizes it and puts it in tension toward the ultimate end that is God. This means that creation can only

---

37. See Augustine, "Contra Iulianum," VI, 2:3–5; Augustine, "Contra Secundam Iuliani," I, 71.

38. See Augustine, "Contra Cresconium," III, 31:35; IV, 27:34.

39. See Augustine, "Epistula ad Catholicos," V, 9; VI, 14; XIV, 35.

40. See Augustine, "Contra Cresconium," III, 41–45; 50–55; Augustine, "Contra Litteras Petiliani," II, 64–143.

come about in plenitude, can only attain its complete truth insofar as Christ takes ownership over it and submits it to his Father.[41]

The existence of creation—of man himself—is thus measured by what Ratzinger called "the principle of 'for.'"[42] But the fact that creation is made up of this principle is no more than the *vestigium* of the Son of God in it: because the existence of the Son is a gift in himself, all things bear the imprint of this character of giving and submission to something beyond themselves; according to the paradigm of the Son, only if the grain of wheat falls to the ground and dies, emptying itself, can it bear fruit.[43] The existence of all created beings is therefore directed toward this act of selfless giving.

This now leads us to the ultimate meaning of order that Augustine finds in creation: given that Christ is the one who consummates all things, he is also the criterion of order. And given that his existence is love of giving, then the criterion that orders all creation is the order of love. Augustine uses this expression in different ways—for instance, as a short definition of virtue—but the same idea is ultimately present in all of them: love is the *caritas* with which God loves. It is the very love of God who gives himself completely: the fire that comprises the trinitarian life, that spills forth from the Trinity, that has created the world and is given to us in Christ. The order of love is the relationship of all things according to this very *caritas*:[44] as love received and reciprocated. All creatures bear the mark of this love; for this very reason—despite sin—they can be integrated into the order of love. If they do so, if—far from loving themselves—they love God "*usque ad contemptum sui*,"[45] then they achieve, according to their own nature (that is to say, according to their *mensura, numerus et pondus*) the plenitude to which they have been called.

It is true that, in the face of this order, while creation is in time, there is the presence of evil—which Augustine calls "*dis-order*" and "*war*," as opposed to the "*peace*" that is "the tranquility of order."[46] Nevertheless, following Plotinus's metaphysics and the Pauline doctrine that

---

41. See Augustine, "De Genesi ad Litteram Imperfectus," 3:6; 16:61.
42. See Ratzinger, *Introduction to Christianity*, 261.
43. See John 12:24.
44. See Augustine, "De Civitate Dei," XI, 28.
45. See Augustine, De Civitate Dei," XIV, 28.
46. See Augustine, "De Civitate Dei," XIX, 13; see also XIX, 4:3; 27; 28; for translation see Augustine, "City of God."

"*diligentibus Deum omnia cooperantur in bonum*,"[47] Augustine explains that this evil has no entity of its own, but that it is in fact the absence of good, that it is not definitive and that order is restored by God, whose power and wisdom can transfigure evil into good.

Pulcherrima: Amare

Beginning from his youth in Carthage and throughout his life, the word "*species*"[48] had a powerful hold on Augustine's thoughts; it grabbed his attention in all meanings of the term: appearance, that which is seen, the face or countenance of things, their form and surface, their texture and color, their likeness, their image—and by extension their idea—the splendor with which they are shown to us, their allure, their beauty—and therefore their harmony, proportion, order.

Therefore, although the meaning he uses in each case is very different, the pagan Augustine and the Christian Augustine share an experience of the "*species mundi*": both find themselves seized by the beautiful appearance of the world. However, the term has many meanings: Augustine had learned that the beautiful appearance of the world was also ambiguous and, depending on how one looked at it, could either be treacherous and deadly or lead one to divine beauty itself.[49] In the *Confessiones*, he leaves us an intense testimony of how lost he was in the first part of his life, crashing misshapen into "*ista formosa quae fecisti*"—"the things of beauty You made."[50]

There, Augustine also says that, at the very same time, creatures spoke to him of God as creator: "My questioning was my observing of them; and their beauty was their reply"[51]—their "*species*." It is not just that the beauty of creatures is a sign of the divine Beauty: his response tells us much more than this. It speaks to us of God as creator, as the absolute source and foundation of all beauty and every being; consequently, it speaks to us of created beings as creatures in total loving dependence on God—loving, yes, because the language in which they say it is precisely

---

47. Rom 8:28.
48. See Logeion, "Species."
49. See Augustine, "De Civitate Dei," XXII, 24:5.
50. See Augustine, "Confessionum," X, 27:38; for translation see Augustine, "Confessions."
51. Augustine, "Confessionum," X, 6, 9; for translation see Augustine, "Confessions."

the beauty ("*species*") with which God has created them, the harmony he bestowed on them, the splendor of their form. Therefore, basing himself on the Psalms,[52] Augustine notes that creatures, insofar as they are beautiful, are a reflection of the divine glory, are heralds of their Maker, and carry in their existence—in their knowledge and in their love—the trace of the Father, Son, and Holy Ghost.

For Augustine, according to the order of love, the beauty of things makes us see that they are good because they reflect God's goodness and refer to it. Therefore, their goodness is relative and so is the love that they claim: they cannot be treated as absolute. In accordance with this, in our relationship with creatures, Augustine distinguishes between *uti* and *frui*:[53] If God has made us for himself and our plenitude and perfect happiness are in him, if he is our *finis*, then, strictly speaking, we can only feel joy in him and from him. All other goods—all creatures—are given to us as intermediate goods precisely so we can reach God. Because of this, we cannot treasure them in our heart definitively and fully; instead, our attitude should be to "use them" to the extent that they help us reach the absolute Good. This does not mean that we cannot take pleasure in them or rejoice in their goodness; quite the contrary: precisely because this attitude allows us to put them in their right order, we are able to use them with the joy that flows from their truth. Perhaps it might seem to us—so accustomed to utilitarianism and pragmatism—that in this way Augustine belittles creatures, "instrumentalizes" them, and uses them only in a self-serving way. But in reality, he does not propose this—quite the opposite: he seems to invite us to treat things according to the truth they express, in consonance with the original divine intention by which they were created—without divinizing them, without enslaving ourselves to them, and acknowledging all the ontological depth and meaning they have, which is that of the order of love, according to the most wise and just eternal law. If we treat them in this way, we will bring them to their fullness, and they in turn will help us reach our own. Thus the "most beautiful" character of creatures—"*pulcherrima creatio*"—leads us not only to the knowledge and contemplation of God, but to love all things as he loves them, and to love him above all things: "*Pulchritudo tam antiqua et tam nova.*"

---

52. See Augustine, "Enarrationes in Psalmos," 134.
53. See Augustine, "De Doctrina Christiana," I, 4:4.

At the end of the *City of God*, Augustine writes about the first blessing of God to his creatures and highlights two terms describing the beauty of creation: "*Conformatio et propagatio.*"[54] These two words condense an extremely optimistic and dynamic character of the beauty of creation that has a kind of Chestertonian magical exuberance. God created the world from nothing and has given it great beauty—the reflection and trace of his own. And the most admirable thing is not that God has composed this beauty in a static and fixed way from the beginning and forevermore, but that he established it under this double category of "*conformatio*" and "*propagatio*." Created beings do not just "passively" receive being and beauty; instead, they must actively adapt their own being to the order of love—make themselves in accordance with forms that are not entirely given however much their archetype existed from the beginning of time in the Mind of God—*in Dei Verbo*.

Furthermore, created beings can communicate this beauty, this dynamism, and this being to others because they possess the amazing capacity for proliferation, the innumerable and surprising fruitfulness of the seed.[55] "*Bonum est difussivum sui*"—and so are truth and beauty—and the first blessing of Genesis has infused this radiating character within the creatures, so that not just God, but God through them continues to create beauty and goodness. In this way, the "*ordinatissima pulchritudo huius mundi*"[56] is something that gradually unfolds over time with those "*rationes seminales*"[57] that allow God to carry on creating, and which he connects to his creatures in his creative activity—especially man, his image.

Application to Our Time

If we want to learn from Augustine's *imago creationis*, we could start by recognizing that the worldview of the dominant culture is more often than not a re-edited—and not exactly improved—version of the ancient pagan, Gnostic-Manichaean, Pelagian, and Donatist notions.

Like the ancient pagans, many of our contemporaries believe that their life is limited to this world and that we are part of the cycle of life of a blind evolution, where our existence ultimately is not better than

---

54. See Augustine, "De Civitate Dei," XXII, 24:2.
55. See Augustine, "De Civitate Dei," XXII, 24:2.
56. See Augustine, "Enarrationes in Psalmos," CXLIV, 13.
57. See Augustine, "De Genesi ad Litteram," VI, 5–6.

others—far from it, as if we were just sacs of DNA. They call—sometimes explicitly—for a return to the idolatrous adoration of the earth, whether under forms of radical environmentalism or nature worship.[58] With regard to them, Augustine teaches us to retrieve humankind's place in the cosmos, to recall that each one of us is worth more than the whole universe, to be aware that this world is decaying and transitory, and that our true home is "a new heaven and a new earth"[59] of which this world is but an image and—if anything—a symbol.

Like the ancient Manichaeans, many of our contemporaries believe that humans should not be subjected or bound to the material—to the body, to biology, to mortality—but that we are a conscience and have a spiritual liberty that should allow us to be separated from this material realm, which seems bad to them. Therefore, they want to bring about a transhuman technolatric future, an immaterial collective conscience, the assertion of fluid genders that involve a profound disdain for the body.[60] Regarding them, Augustine teaches us that the material world is good and exists for our use, that we are not separate from this body—which is called to resurrection—and that this world is the site of our pilgrimage and a most beautiful gift from God.

One of the consequences of the ancient Pelagian notion of liberty, based on a "*posse-velle-esse*"[61] scheme, was a voluntarist titanism that made reality dependent on a supposed absolute power enjoyed by the created being. It is not surprising that renewed forms of Pelagianism have led to such "modern" attitudes as conceiving knowledge in relation to power and mainly oriented toward pragmatic utility, to the domination of nature and society, and ultimately to the tyranny of humankind. Faced with them, Augustine teaches us that the world is a free gift from God and that human liberty reaches its culmination in a framework of *ordo amoris*, in which it is necessary to distinguish between *uti et frui* and treat reality in accordance with the divine Mind.

Like the ancient Donatists, today there are also individuals, institutions, and groups that consider themselves to be the privileged and exclusive recipients of the best goods of creation; accordingly, they exclude and exploit other human beings. With regard to them, Augustine teaches

---

58. See Augustine, "De Civitate Dei," IV, 12; X, 30.
59. Rev 21:1.
60. See Augustine, "Acta Seu Disputatio contra Fortunatum," 14, 17, 20, 21.
61. See Augustine, "De Gratia Christi," I, 4:5.

us that God "makes his sun rise on the evil and on the good"[62] and that the goods of creation are to be used by all of the children of Adam, in accordance with the original human solidarity.

Conclusion

If we consider the worldview that Augustine sets out for us, we will be able to see a multitude of magnificent works in it; we will be able to rediscover humankind's place in the cosmos; we will be able to enjoy the excellence of the good because we will discover the principle that orders everything: the love that underpins all of creation, that gives it unity, interconnection, and meaning, that leads to "a new heaven and a new earth"[63] and its plenitude. Thus we find that there cannot be any true ecology that is not a human ecology, and that the best human ecology is that which we have from divine revelation: Christian theological anthropology.

Then, as St. Augustine, we go back to "God and soul"[64] because all the magnificent beauty of creation has led us there. Its *"ordinatissima pulchritudo"*[65] "sings the glory of God"[66]: "And with a loud voice they exclaimed, He made us. My questioning was my observing of them; and their beauty was their reply."[67]

Bibliography

Augustine. "Acta Seu Disputatio contra Fortunatum Manichaeum." https://www.augustinus.it/latino/contro_fortunato/index.htm.

———. "The City of God." Translated by Marcus Dods. Moscow, ID: Roman Roads Media, 2015. https://files.romanroadsstatic.com/materials/romans/nicene-christianity/City%20of%20God.pdf.

———. "Confessions." Edited by Philip Schaff. Translated by J. G. Pilkington. In *Nicene and Post-Nicene Fathers*. Vol. 1. https://www.logicmuseum.com/wiki/Authors/Augustine/confessions/L10#10.6.9.

———. "Confessionum." https://www.augustinus.it/latino/confessioni/index2.htm.

---

62. Matt 5:45. See Augustine, "Epistola 93," 2:4; Augustine, "Sermo 4," 31; Augustine, "Sermo 45," 1, 7.

63. Rev 21:1.

64. See Augustine, "Soliloquiorum," I, 7.

65. Augustine, "Enarrationes in Psalmos," CXLIV, 13.

66. *Catechism of the Catholic Church*, §1361; cf. Ps 19:1.

67. Augustine, "Confessionum," X, 6, 9; for translation see Augustine, "Confessions."

———. "Contra Cresconium Grammaticum Donatistam." https://www.augustinus.it/latino/contro_cresconio/index2.htm.

———. "Contra Iulianum." https://www.augustinus.it/latino/contro_giuliano/index2.htm.

———. "Contra Litteras Petiliani Donatistae." https://www.augustinus.it/latino/contro_petiliano/index2.htm.

———. "Contra Secundam Iuliani Responsionem Imperfectum Opus." https://www.augustinus.it/latino/incompiuta_giuliano/index2.htm.

———. "De Civitate Dei Contra Paganos." https://www.augustinus.it/latino/cdd/index2.htm.

———. "De Diversis Quaestionibus ad Simplicianum." https://www.augustinus.it/latino/questioni_simpliciano/index2.htm.

———. "De Doctrina Christiana." https://www.augustinus.it/latino/dottrina_cristiana/index2.htm.

———. "De Genesi ad Litteram." https://www.augustinus.it/latino/genesi_lettera/index2.htm.

———. "De Genesi ad Litteram Imperfectus Liber." https://www.augustinus.it/latino/genesi_incompiuto/index.htm.

———. "De Genesi Contra Manichaeos." https://www.augustinus.it/latino/genesi_dcm/index2.htm.

———. "De Gratia Christi et de Peccato Originali." https://www.augustinus.it/latino/grazia_cristo/index2.htm.

———. "De Natura Boni contra Manichaeos." https://www.augustinus.it/latino/natura_bene/index.htm.

———. "De Ordine." https://www.augustinus.it/latino/ordine/index2.htm.

———. "De Trinitate." https://www.augustinus.it/latino/trinita/index2.htm.

———. "De Vera Religione." https://www.augustinus.it/latino/vera_religione/index.htm.

———. "Enarrationes in Psalmos." https://www.augustinus.it/latino/esposizioni_salmi/index2.htm.

———. "Epistola 93." https://www.augustinus.it/latino/lettere/index2.htm.

———. "Epistula ad Catholicos de Secta Donatistarum." https://www.augustinus.it/latino/lettera_cattolici/index.htm.

———. "Sermo 4." https://www.augustinus.it/latino/discorsi/discorso_004_testo.htm.

———. "Sermo 45." https://www.augustinus.it/latino/discorsi/discorso_056_testo.htm.

———. "Sermo 80." https://www.augustinus.it/latino/discorsi/discorso_107_testo.htm.

———. "Sermo 81." https://www.augustinus.it/latino/discorsi/discorso_108_testo.htm.

———. "Soliloquiorum Libri Duo." https://www.augustinus.it/latino/soliloqui/index2.htm.

Catechism of the Catholic Church. Vatican website. https://www.vatican.va/content/catechism/en.html.

Gerson, Lloyd P. "Plotinus's Metaphysics: Emanation or Creation?" *Review of Metaphysics* 46.3 (1993) 559–74.

Gilson, Étienne. "Contemplating God in His Works." In *The Christian Philosophy of Saint Augustine*, 269–362. Translated by L. E. M. Lynch. Providence: Cluny, 2021.

———. "La Contemplation de Dieu dans Son Oeuvre." In *Introduction à l'Étude de St. Augustin*, 246–98. Paris: Vrin, 1949.
Hanby, Michael. "Christology, Cosmology and the Mechanics of Grace." In *Augustine and Modernity*, 72–105. London: Routledge, 2003.
Logeion. "Creatio." University of Chicago. https://logeion.uchicago.edu/creatio.
———. "Creo." University of Chicago. https://logeion.uchicago.edu/creo.
———. "κόσμος." University of Chicago. https://logeion.uchicago.edu/κόσμος.
———. "Mundus." University of Chicago. https://logeion.uchicago.edu/mundus.
———. "Natura." University of Chicago. https://logeion.uchicago.edu/natura.
———. "Orbis." University of Chicago. https://logeion.uchicago.edu/orbis.
———. "Species." University of Chicago. https://logeion.uchicago.edu/species.
———. "τέλος." University of Chicago. https://logeion.uchicago.edu/τέλος.
———. "Universus." University of Chicago. https://logeion.uchicago.edu/universus.
Ortiz, Jared. *"You Made Us for Yourself": Creation in St. Augustine's Confessions*. Minneapolis: Fortress, 2016.
Ratzinger, Joseph. *Introduction to Christianity*. San Francisco: Ignatius, 2004.
Rist, John M. "The One of Plotinus and the God of Aristotle." *Review of Metaphysics* 27 (1973) 75–87.
Williams, Rowan. "'Good for Nothing'? Augustine on Creation." In *On Augustine*, 59–78. London: Bloomsbury, 2016.
Zimmerman, Brandon. "Does Plotinus Present a Philosophical Account of Creation?" *Review of Metaphysics* 67.1 (2013) 55–105.

6

Creation and the Gift-Task of the Human Person in the Thought of Ferdinand Ulrich[1]

MICHAEL DOMINIC TAYLOR

ST. JOHN PAUL II once stated, "Man [has] received the world as a gift, . . . [and] it can also be said that the world received man as a gift."[2] This paper will explore what is perhaps the most profound reason that this is true. In his magnum opus, *Homo Abyssus: The Drama of the Question of Being*, Ferdinand Ulrich describes the human person's role in creation as a "Gift-Task" (*Auf-Gabe*) that must be accepted and fulfilled.[3] According to Ulrich, because of his unique nature as a subsistent embodied spirit, the human person is the focal point of being's self-gift to creation; thus, the way in which he receives this gift will have profound consequences for all of creation. Following Thomas Aquinas, Ulrich views man as one called to "shepherd"[4] beings back to God by the path of the spoken word. Catholic philosophers tend to focus on comprehending the *exitus* of creation and restoring an understanding of its formal and final causality; however, relatively little thought is put toward understanding

---

1. A shorter version of this paper was published in *Saint Anselm Journal*: Taylor, "Gift to the World."

2. John Paul II, "Creation."

3. Ulrich, *Homo Abyssus*, 68. This tome was first published in 1961 in Germany under the title *Homo Abyssus: Das Wagnis der Seinsfrage*.

4. When Ulrich says that man "shepherds" beings, it is in opposition to the Heideggerian idea that man would "falsely . . . presume to be 'the shepherd of being'" itself (Ulrich, *Homo Abyssus*, 407, 396).

how creation is intended to return to its source, leaving this question for theology. Here Ulrich stands apart.

It should be noted from the outset that Ulrich's reflections on creation and anthropology are unavoidably integrated into his Catholic faith, but not for that less metaphysical.[5] In fact, leaving room for the religious dimension—for mystery—is a fundamental sign of healthy philosophy. Ulrich points out that to posit *a priori* theological opinions ("theologumena," as he calls them), whether they be theistic or atheistic, would amount to building one's philosophy on a theological premise. The radical giftedness of created being preserves the autonomy of both creation and philosophy while, at the same time, assuring that the barrier between theology and philosophy remains porous and mutually informing.

This chapter will explore the fundamental nature of being as "complete and simple, yet non-subsistent,"[6] particularly in relation to anthropology and the significance of the spoken word as the unification of the human person in the thought of Ulrich. As he says, "the mystery of man and the necessity of his self-understanding meet concretely and historically in the two forms of word and love, in becoming oneself by receiving oneself."[7] The fundamental thesis we will present is Ulrich's argument that, though non-human creatures cannot achieve the full return to their essences as man does, through man's word—indeed, through the names man gives to created beings—non-human creatures *do* achieve this fullness and a share in the human person's subsistence.

D. C. Schindler describes Ulrich's thought as a "'speculative Thomism,' that is . . . a 'creative retrieval' of Aquinas—whom Ulrich regards as his principal teacher from the very beginning to the end."[8] Thus, first it will be necessary to review some fundamental aspects of Aquinas's thought before we open up into Ulrich's meditation. By way

---

5. "The great temptations that man has to withstand in his self-actualization, every undergoing and overcoming of the danger of the thinking of being, every falling victim and perversion, are sealed in the word, which stands in the grace and the judgment of that Word in which in a profoundly mysterious way the thinking and loving enactment of the ontological difference is brought home with a human face to the right hand of the Father" (Ulrich, *Homo Abyssus*, 407).

6. Aquinas, *De Potentia Dei*, q. 1, a. 1, ad 1.

7. Ulrich, "Personal Unity," 558.

8. Schindler, *Companion*, 5–6. Schindler adds, "The two modern thinkers that stand out the most in *Homo Abyssus*, because the theme here is most fundamentally the meaning of being, are Hegel and Heidegger. But Ulrich engages in a serious way with Freud, Marx, Nietzsche, and Kierkegaard, among others, in his later works" (Schindler, *Companion*, 6).

of conclusion, we will present some of the consequences it holds for the way we conceive of our life on earth and our relationship with the world around us.

The Gift of Being

The modern philosophical milieu, our technocratic paradigm, and current cultural attitudes would have us believe that everything that exists was not created but is rather the consequence of a chain of physical reactions that began with the Big Bang, giving way to the world we see around us. This conception is agnostic toward the "real" noumenal world, which—if it exists at all—exists entirely hidden beyond the phenomena we experience only subjectively. The things around us and our very corporeal reality are, in this way, taken for granted as simply "given"; they are the output of physical processes that ultimately have little bearing on the existence of things that are conceived as unrelated and atomistic bodies in space that act according to the inextricable laws of physics. Without delving too deeply into the nuances, in this view human freedom is either a mere illusion born of evolutionary processes[9] or the quintessential undetermined force and identity of a human person whose mere exercise is the essence of human fulfillment.

In a strange twist, this technocratic paradigm and its postmodern offspring often blame Christianity for the ecological crises of our time—which they themselves are almost entirely responsible for—without ever suspecting the depth and beauty of Creation from a Christian perspective.

These worldviews are hopelessly trapped in their own skeptical presuppositions, which fail to grasp the essential quality of reality: the radical contingency of existence. By taking existence for granted, one is blind to the path of reflection that leads not to rationalism and nihilism,

---

9. See, for example, Goodenough and Deacon, "Sacred Emergence of Nature":
   The beauty of the emergentist approach to mind is that it suggests that to experience our experience without awareness of this underlying mechanism is exactly what we should expect from an emergent property. The outcome has been given reverent names, like spirit or soul, names that conjure up the perceived absence of materiality. But we need not interpret this as evidence of some parallel transcendental immaterial world. We can now say that the experience of soul or spirit as immaterial is simply a reflection of the way the process of emergence progressively distances each new level from the details below. We can now turn the page. (Goodenough and Deacon, "Sacred Emergence of Nature," 864)

but to self-knowledge, relationality, and fruitful human fulfillment. This path begins with the simple observation that nothing in this world is the source of its own existence, and that the existence of each thing is distinct from its own essence.[10]

The Real Distinction

It was Thomas Aquinas who first made the fundamental distinction between essence and existence. This "real distinction" present in every creature would eventually be understood as the touchstone of a fundamentally Christian worldview. Aquinas saw that being itself was to all substances as form is to matter.[11] The noteworthy exception to this rule is God, whose essence and existence correspond completely.[12] For Aquinas, the act of being, *esse*, is the fundamental aspect of every subsistent being, for a created essence does not contain in itself the reason for its existence. This radical transformation of Greek thought, uniting Platonic participation and Aristotelian act/potency, offers a resolution to the ancient tensions between transcendence and immanence through the polar relationship made possible through analogy: *esse* gives existence to creaturely essences while these give *esse* a home, for without creatures, *esse* could not subsist in the world.

Creatio ex nihilo

This real distinction between *esse* and essence allows for a deeper understanding of what it means to be a creature in this world. Because no created being is the source of its own existence, ultimately it must receive its existence from Existence itself and come into being *ex nihilo*, from nothing. As we will see in a moment, this *nihilo* is not a reference to some kind of magic trick we simply can't comprehend without theological

---

10. This is easily understood when one thinks of something with a specific form—such as a phoenix or a griffin—that has no existence in the real world. It is again evident, for example, when something dies. A rabbit, senselessly killed in traffic, ceases to be a rabbit and its accidental qualities—the warmth of its blood, the softness of its fur, the weight of its body—are now those not of a rabbit but of carrion, a pelt, or meat.

11. "In conceiving *esse* as actual in relation to the potency of essence (the formal element), Thomas in effect reverses the relation of form and act" (Healy, *Eschatology*, 43).

12. See Exod 3:14.

assistance, but rather corresponds to the simple philosophical necessity of the pure mediation of being as *non subsistens*.

It is also important here to distinguish between cosmology and ontology. Cosmology speaks to the temporal ordering of events while ontology speaks to the logical and metaphysical necessity of the source of existence. Whether all matter came into existence in the Big Bang or the universe is eternal, as Aristotle thought, is of little importance to the metaphysical question of creation. Aquinas did not agree with Aristotle but pointed out that, even if the world were eternal, it would still need a Creator, as it is evident that the world is not the source of its own existence.[13] This is the basic metaphysical principle that eludes every materialist.

Creatio ex nihilo must be understood as the constant and continuous gift of existence at the heart of reality. Creation is not a change from potency into act, but rather describes a relationship between cause and effect in which, following the maxim of Aquinas, the effect is radically new and yet always represents its cause to some degree.[14] All other forms of causation are thus dependent on this primordial causal relationship that is always actual, always happening in the *present*. The Latin *praesentem*—the present participle of *praeesse*, "to be" (*esse*) "before" (*prae-*)—reveals a unity between the present as time and the present as gift, but the ontological root of this unity is not always apparent: the continuously given gift of being—or, the gift of Creation.

The Paradox of Being

The logical necessity of *creatio ex nihilo* reveals an apparent paradox that would become the central meditation for Ulrich's *Homo Abyssus*. This paradox is Aquinas's characterization of *esse* as "*completum et simplex sed non subsistens*": the act of being is "complete and simple, yet non-subsistent."[15] Nicholas Healy describes this reality as such: "The gift of *esse* is the source of all the perfections within every created entity, and yet, paradoxically, created *esse* is itself dependent upon essence to attain subsistence."[16]

---

13. Cf. Aquinas, *De Aeternitate Mundi*.
14. Cf. Aquinas, *Summa Theologica*, I, q. 45, a. 7.
15. Aquinas, *De Potentia Dei*, q. 1, a. 1, ad 1.
16. Healy, *Eschatology*, 25.

This can be understood through analogy with the verb "to sing"; for example, "to sing" does not itself *sing*, though many other things do. In the same way, everything that exists *is*, and thus participates in being, but "to be," *esse*, does not. However, *esse* is unlike any other verb because it is the fundamental condition for reality. In order to subsist, *esse* must give itself away in the form of a true gift. This is the fundamental pattern of the cosmos. It can be seen, analogically, in the interrelatedness of organisms in the trophic webs describing ecosystems, in the bonds that unite a family, and it is ultimately a reflection of the Holy Trinity itself. Needless to say, this true gift of being has profound metaphysical implications.

Valuing Creatures

First of all, the gift of being has important implications for the value of created beings that contradict the negativity toward physical beings found in Gnosticism, modern empiricism's supposed neutrality toward physical existence, and the indifference of postmodern monist perceptions. Most dualistic conceptions of physical creatures regard physicality as a corruption of the purity of spirit, as a certain fall from grace.[17] For materialism and scientism, everything is fundamentally neutral and passive before the scientist while the human subject determines the value of things subjectively and extrinsically. Finally, while postmodern ecophilosophies claim to value all life forms equally, they comprehend all things as momentary crystallizations of the cosmic evolutionary flux, within which there is no basis for differentiating values, for we are all just stardust born of the Big Bang.

Only a comprehension of created being as an authentic participation in the primordial goodness of *Esse Subsistens* permits all creatures to be perceived as fundamentally *good* in themselves, both in their being and in their essence.[18] It is the knowledge and affirmation of this goodness that will be central to our discussion later on.

---

17. Those that would include Plato in this group forget that he designated the Good as the final cause of both being and truth. Schindler notes that "Platonism" is the name given to a dualistic "version of Plato that disregards the role of the good in his thought" (Schindler, *Plato's Critique*, 288).

18. Thus, as Schindler describes, this "allows us therefore to affirm the difference of creatures as ultimately and essentially good; and it allows us to affirm the overcoming of dualism as Plato does with his notion of participation, without depriving the material cosmos of any reality of its own" (Schindler, "What's the Difference?," 21).

The Significance of "esse non subsistens" in Ulrich's Thought

This paradox of being "designates the very core" of Ulrich's philosophical reflections.[19] It indicates the radical generosity and self-gift at the heart of being itself, which is both "poor" and infinitely "wealthy"—terminology he uses frequently. Thus, Ulrich argues, at its heart, the very meaning of being is *love*. Truly, "the whole of *Homo Abyssus* revolves around the speculative unfolding of this self-emptying mystery of being as love."[20]

However, for Ulrich, both the wealth of being's perfect simplicity and the poverty of its non-subsistence are merely two perspectives of one phenomenon that only appear to be contradictory if we forget *esse*'s radical capacity for self-gift. He describes this self-gift of being as the "movement of finitization" or "into subsistence."[21] In both cases, *esse* should be understood as a pure act of self-donation: pure mediation, whose perfection is only found in its reception by the other.[22] Thus, the non-subsistence of *esse* is not a deficiency, but the most radical of perfections.

This comprehension of being avoids the two fallacies that plague modern philosophy that originate from overemphasizing one of being's two dimensions. On the one hand, we avoid the "hypostatization" of being: the conception of being, based on an overemphasis on its complete simplicity, as a thing in and of itself, leading to onto-theology à la Hegel.[23] On the other hand, we avoid scientific positivism's suggestion, based on an overemphasis on being's non-subsistence, that being is only to be found in physical bodies, which would thus no longer be creatures at all but mere materiality to be manipulated and utilized.

This vacuous notion is at the heart of the Cartesian system that bifurcates the world into *res extensa* and *res cogitans* and goes hand-in-hand with an evolutionary conception of all existence as materiality, which is only ever influenced from the bottom up. With magical concepts like emergence that purport to explain how novel features (such as life and

---

19. Bieler, "*Analogia Entis* as an Expression," 322.
20. Gonzales, "Massive Sea Change," para. 19.
21. Cf. Ulrich, *Homo Abyssus*, 501.

22. As Schindler describes, for Ulrich, *esse*'s perfection "is always already given away, or more adequately, possessed as having been given away. Thus, the perfect wealth of *esse* is coincident with a complete poverty" (Schindler, "What's the Difference?," 19).

23. This is precisely what Hegel was guilty of when he attempted to force the absolute into finitude through reason and what Heidegger would later condemn as ontotheology; cf. Bieler, "Introduction." Ulrich describes this transcendence of *esse* beyond essence as its "superessentiality" (*Überwesenhaftigkeit*); cf. Ulrich, *Homo Abyssus*, 507.

consciousness) appear from qualitatively different material conditions, the need for the gift of being is, in their minds, dissolved.[24]

The deformations that the human person is capable of inflicting on being are not mere intellectual errors. Fundamentally, it impacts how one receives his or her own gift of being. For Ulrich, given the fact that the human person is the maximum representation of being's self-gift, the person, in a sense, co-decides the very meaning of being. This becomes clear when we consider being as a gift of love that may be received or rejected.

The Human Person as Frontier and Microcosm

The affirmation that man is the maximum representation of being's self-gift requires some unpacking. The human being is understood as the pinnacle of the created universe; not in such a way as to be isolated from it, but rather as a compendium and unity of every other manifestation of created being. In this sense, the human being is a micro-cosmos (μικρῶι κόσμῳ) who lives on the frontier of matter and spirit.[25] These notions originate from the recognition of man's spiritual soul, unique among created forms in that it continues to exist without the body after death.[26] Aquinas taught that the human soul must be understood as a form that not only confers substantiality on the body, but also possesses substantiality itself.[27] Part of the novelty of this vision is that the union between soul and body is not forced or precarious but natural. Aquinas says:

24. "'Emergence' is merely the name of some kind of magical transition between intrinsic disparate realities" (Hart, *Splendid Wickedness*, 237).

25. Aristotle, *Physics*, VIII, ch. 2, cited in Aquinas, *Commentary on Aristotle's Physics*, VIII, lectio 4. Regarding ethics, we can consider the fact that man is situated on a horizon, but he is not fixed there. Every choice he makes moves him through what Verbeke calls "a sort of ethical topography . . . either in the direction of the superior level or the inferior one" (Verbeke, "Man as a 'Frontier,'" 196). Rather than movements up or down, which reinforce the idea of a dualism, an improvement upon this image could imply a movement further inward or outward, toward or away from a deeper unity between spirit and material. This would better clarify the fact that both an overattachment to the material world and a disconnected spiritualization draw man away from his true nature.

26. "The human soul exists in its own right and is to a degree united with a matter that does not wholly capture it—this form is greater in dignity than to be a capacity for matter. Nothing prevents its having some operation or power to which matter does not attain" (Aquinas, *De Unitate Intellectus*, III, 84).

27. This also resolves the question of the resurrection of the body for Christian theology.

> The human soul is as a "horizon" and a "frontier" between the corporeal and the incorporeal because, although it is an incorporeal substance, it is nevertheless the form of the body. The resulting unity between the intellectual substance and the corporeal matter is not less than that of the form of fire and its material, but rather greater because, the more the form subdues the matter, the greater the unity between them.[28]

What is crucial here is that, in the profound integration of the human body and soul, the material and spiritual realms flow together naturally. The human person is thus revealed not only as a natural member of the cosmos, but the *most* natural—indeed, the focal point that unites the spiritual and the material effortlessly. It is from this privileged center that the human person is called to a great responsibility.

Exitus, Reditus, and Reditio Completa

Aquinas describes creation as adhering to a pattern of *exitus* and *reditus*, going out and returning, in that all creatures have both their source and final end in their Creator. Metaphysically, this pattern takes on a meaning that describes the extent to which each creature, according to the expression of their essence, can live out relationality, consciousness, and freedom.

Exitus describes the flowing out of the gift of being to each particular substance according to its essence. This gift is each substance's ability to "sub-stand," to "stand under" itself and continue to be what it is. Meanwhile, *reditus* ("return") describes the creature's ability, beyond simply sub-standing, to *subsist*, which Aquinas describes in *De Veritate*:

> . . . the return to one's own essence is called the very subsistence of a thing in itself; for non-subsistent forms are, as it were, poured out upon something other than themselves, and are not in possession of themselves. But subsistent forms reach out to other things, perfecting them and influencing them—in such a way, however, that they still retain their immanence and self-possession.[29]

Among the myriad substances of creation, only persons are capable of completing the process of *reditus*, and thus only persons are subsistent in the way Aquinas describes. For this reason, man is, as Ulrich puts it,

---

28. Aquinas, *Summa contra Gentiles*, II, 68.
29. Aquinas, *De Veritate*, q. 2, a. 2, ad. 2.

"the focal point of being's movement of finitization."[30] Joseph Ratzinger eloquently describes what this means:

> The *exitus* ... does in fact aim at *reditus*, but this does not mean that created being is revoked. Rather, it means the coming-into-its-own of the creature as an autonomous creature answers back in freedom to the love of God, accepts its creation as a command to love, so that a dialogue of love begins—that entirely new unity that only love can create. In it the being of the other is not absorbed, not annulled, but rather becomes wholly what it is precisely in giving itself.[31]

But the *reditio completa* also implies self-consciousness, self-possession, and thus freedom.[32] Therefore, for the human person, the gift of being is also a task beset by temptations to "co-determine" the meaning of being. Though this full return is only achieved by the human person, non-human creatures are not to be understood as mere passive participants in an anthropocentric drama. Man's role is not to concentrate all being *in* himself, as it were, but to "set creation free" *through* himself, in gratitude and the affirmation of being.[33] What we should appreciate here is that the hierarchy of created beings does not deny the perfection of any creature, but rather expresses an interdependence within which every creature has a meaning that is always good, true, and beautiful. Additionally, as we will see, this incompleteness in Ulrich's view is only temporary.

The Gift/Task of the Human Person

Ulrich is perhaps best known for his interpretation of being as love, which has been appreciated and adopted by others such as Balthasar and David L. Schindler. Love is the central theme of Ulrich's reflections on the thought of Aquinas and, in this sense, is also the basis for his critique of

---

30. Cf. Ulrich, *Homo Abyssus*, 105, 159, 174, 200.

31. Ratzinger, *End of Time*, 20–21.

32. "In man, consciousness attains greater interiority and so becomes self-consciousness. His inner dimension is not only luminous, as it is in the case of the animal, but is also light for itself. Man is the first entity that possesses itself and, because of this self-possession, is free. It is not just that his interior space, like that of the animal, has certain features of consciousness; he is himself substantially spirit. To the extent that man is spirit, he can dispose of himself" (Balthasar, *Theo-Logic*, 1:93).

33. "Insofar as this occurs as gratitude, it is not a usurpation of being in the ideality of spirit, but rather the setting free of the 'other,' which is 'itself' and subsists as a result of *the self-same* [*der-selben*] movement of finitization" (Ulrich, *Homo Abyssus*, 374).

modernity. This critique is not merely an intellectual critique, a problem of the failure to make proper distinctions or grasp important concepts; nor is it simply a moral critique, a problem of acts of the will that turn away from the good. The problem with modernity rather is a failure of love, understood comprehensibly to encompass both the will and the intellect, at once and inseparably. This section will focus on the intellect, of which the will is an aspect, according to Aquinas.[34] However, it is impossible to do so without considering the self-gift of Being and man as the paradigmatic locus of that gift.

The Intellect, the Will, and the Crisis of Being

In order to offer a glimpse of the depth of Ulrich's meditation on the significance of the spoken word, we must make at least a passing reference to the fundamental relationship between being, the intellect, and the will. What is at stake here can be summarized by the adage "you cannot love what you do not know": the way in which we come to know being—as mediated by the intellect, decided by the will, and expressed in the spoken word—could not be more fundamental in Ulrich's thought.

The intellect ought to be understood as the openness to being that "reads into" (*intus-legere*) created beings through the sensory experience of their outward expressions, to receive their essences into itself. In its active and passive dimensions (*intellectus agens* and *intellectus possibilis*, respectively), the intellect is simultaneously that by which all is made intelligible *and* that which can, in a sense, be made into all things.[35] In this way, the intellect possesses a simultaneous wealth and poverty that is directly analogous to the wealth and poverty of being as *complete and*

---

34. Here it is crucial to distance ourselves from the dualist, materialist, and evolutionary preconceptions that are inherent to our modern cultural *Weltanshauung* and that distort our presuppositions before we have even begun to think. Cartesian dualism would lead us to believe that the intellect is wholly other and wholly separate from the material world, the polar opposite of our physical "real-world" existence. Materialism would have us posit our intellect as the direct product of the physical processes that occur within our brains, and that its only role is to work upon the world around us—which is entirely material—by analyzing and calculating the best way to achieve our material needs. Finally, evolutionary premises would have us believe that our intellect is the fruit of bottom-up, random flukes, and that it has no higher cause or analogue to look up toward. None of these positions are consistent with reason or experience.

35. "Reason . . . is both *intellectus agens: quo est omnia facere* (light) and *intellectus possibilis: quo est omnia fieri* (night)" (Ulrich, *Homo Abyssus*, 440).

simple and *non-subsistent*.³⁶ Ulrich refers to this feature of the intellect as "the luminous night."³⁷

As we come to know the multiplicity of created beings, *esse* remains not *hidden*—shrouded in darkness—but in a sense, *too obvious* due to its superabundant intelligibility:

> . . . just as the eye does not open itself up immediately to the light of the sun and receive that light as such, but instead perceives the light "as" the actualizing power that illuminates the multiplicity of appearing essences, so too does the *intellectus possibilis* never receive the pure light of being as such. Instead, it sees the "light of being" in the *intelligibilia*.³⁸

Thus, there is an analogical relation between the light of the intellect and the light of being within which the latter is the cause of the former. However, the person discovers its source only through the experience of other created beings and, in addition, is *free* to err or to deny its origin. The proper response is to accept being as the act of acts and ever-present gift of pure mediation, and to comprehend one's own intellect as utterly dependent on, receptive to, and grateful for being. However, refusal is also an option—one that amounts to an intellectual pride that does not accept the gift of being nor the gift of creation as they are given, but imagines the light of the intellect as superior and autonomous.³⁹

Ulrich's pursuit of love at the heart of all things is a continuous critique of modern and postmodern philosophies that have abandoned this path and an attempt to bring the necessary humility back to metaphysical thinking.⁴⁰ Stefan Oster describes the virtues of this approach:

---

36. Cf. Aquinas, *De Potentia Dei*, q. 1, a. 1, ad 1.

37. Ulrich, *Homo Abyssus*, 440.

38. Ulrich, *Homo Abyssus*, 444.

39. What is at stake here, as Martin Bieler points out, is whether the intellect understands being analogously or it "collapses on the one hand into the equivocity of a fragmented reality [or] on the other hand into the univocity of a being that holds on to itself. Univocity and equivocity are simply flip sides of the same refusal to receive being" (Bieler, "Introduction," xxxi).

40. This is especially significant as Ulrich surveys the history of German philosophy—especially Hegel and Heidegger—and sees the ever-present temptation that the intellect is exposed to as it goes about knowing the world. In 1955, in the foreword to his *Being and Essence: A Speculative Unfolding of an Anthropological Ontology*, Ulrich stated, "Philosophy finds itself in a moment of decision. It is being called, in its innermost conscience, to discern the spirits in order to make the proper decision" (Ulrich, *Sein und Wesen*, quoted in Bieler, "Introduction," xviii).

On the one hand, it is unfettered by any compulsion to hypostatize being's simple completeness in order to bring being within our intellectual grasp. On the other hand, it is equally free from the constraint to pervert the poverty of being's non-subsistence by treating being as an abstract "nothing"; it resists positivism's temptation to bury being in the things-that-are, which then become the empty material out of which a loveless science forces concrete subsistence to emerge as the result of its own autonomous experiment.[41]

When the above-mentioned temptations are avoided, the will as the "intellectual appetite" represents the intellect's pursuit of the good into the heart of all things.[42] Yet, everything comes down to the way in which the will seeks to possess what the intellect places before it. It is for this reason Ulrich says that the intellect *opens up* the crisis of being, but that it is brought to completion by the will.[43] "Only in the thinking that is a thanking does the question of whether man has properly decided what he is come to legitimate expression—and in gratitude, man sets creation free insofar as he decides it *through or by himself*."[44]

Thus, the gift of being for creation becomes the gift/task (*Auf-Gabe*) of the human person. It is in the comprehension of being's unfolding *in himself*, as the focal point of being's movement of finitization, that the person will co-decide the meaning of being. Ulrich reminds us repeatedly that the act of being is the most fundamental act of love, and that the gift of being finds its fulfillment in the good. He is concerned from the outset with understanding how this love is fulfilled in the fullness of both its *exitus* (the giving away that allows the other to be) and *reditus* (the invitation back into a free and loving plenitude). In the final analysis, the *reditio completa* is also the bringing together of all of creation in the act of loving reason. Ulrich describes as the "anthropological reduction" the "leading back" (*re-ducere*) of all things through man, to their source.[45]

---

41. Oster, "Thinking Love," 691.

42. As Aquinas explains, "through willing and loving the person is, in a way, drawn *into the very things*" themselves (Aquinas, *Commentary on the Sentences*, III, d. 27, q. 1, a. 4, emphasis added).

43. Cf. Ulrich, *Homo Abyssus*, 295.

44. Ulrich, *Homo Abyssus*, 374.

45. Ulrich's use of the term "anthropological reduction" (*anthropologische Reduktion*) is not to be confused with the negative sense in which Balthasar uses it. See Ulrich, *Homo Abyssus*, 394.

Only through the proper reception of the gift of being is man's subsistence and freedom preserved, strengthened, and communicated to others. In the end, the "sameness" between being and thinking "has its original proof in thinking as thanking, in which man lovingly liberates all that is, lets it be, and contents himself with the 'little way' of being as outpoured love."[46] The human person, by receiving his freedom with love and gratitude, affirms the unification of his own *esse* and essence in the good.[47] This unification will not be truly complete, however, until the human being's embodied dimension is integrated into it through speech, which has great significance in Ulrich's thought as the very center of the "anthropological reduction."

The Spoken Word as the "Yes" of Love

The will's fundamental "yes" to the gift-character of being is not complete until it becomes a spoken expression of the unification of truth and goodness in the love of existence itself, which necessarily includes oneself amid the whole of creation:

> *In whatever manner* man undergoes the ontological difference, it is *thus* that he comes to speech, he names beings, he shepherds them. It is only in the word that he has the world, that he is in the world and the world is with man and "through" him. Man comes out of himself once again into the world "through" the word. The word is man's path: "from the knowledge which we possess, by actual thought we form an internal word; and thence break forth into love."[48]

In fact, the necessary sense of being, which is for man a gift/task, implies that man's "yes" to the gift of being is not exclusive to his *own* particular *esse creatum* but to all gifts of being. It is our own task—our vocation, in a sense—to affirm all of creation in its goodness by simply giving things a name and then calling them by their right name. In this way, we affirm that it is good that they exist.[49] This is precisely what is

---

46. Ulrich, *Homo Abyssus*, 438.

47. These three elements correspond to the three ontological moments—"bonicity," "ideality," and "reality"—that we do not have space to present here.

48. Ulrich, *Homo Abyssus*, 407, citing Aquinas, *Summa Theologica*, I, q. 93, a. 7.

49. As Ratzinger says, "it is the way of love to will the other's existence and, at the same time, to bring that existence forth again" (Ratzinger, *Principles of Catholic Theology*, 80).

captured in Ulrich's concept of the "anthropological reduction," the leading back through man into the freedom of subsistence.

However, this is not a one-sided relationship. Let us not forget that it is only through the knowledge of created beings that the person even comes to the knowledge of being itself. And in Genesis, Adam is better able to recognize Eve as "bone of my bones and flesh of my flesh" only after his encounter with the animals.[50] John Paul II commented on this reality, saying:

> Self-knowledge develops at the same rate as knowledge of the world, of all the visible creatures, of all the living beings to which man has given a name to affirm his own dissimilarity with regard to them.... With this knowledge which, in a certain way, brings him out of his own being, man at the same time reveals himself to himself in all the peculiarity of his being.[51]

In this sense, while man has the responsibility to give other creatures a name and thus a loving home in his substantiality, non-human creatures have a certain responsibility to reveal man to himself, to point him toward the gift/task of being, and to call him to fulfill his vocation.[52]

The fact that we are called to share our subsistence with non-human creatures has clear eschatological significance for the participation of creation in the kingdom of Heaven. While some Thomists are quick to point out that animals lack a rational soul, which they understand as the condition for the possibility of salvation, Ulrich's observations do not deny this point; rather, they affirm it to reveal to us our fundamental responsibility to the whole of the created world—a responsibility already carried out by Christ, but that invites our participation.[53]

In light of Ulrich's reflection, the spoken word takes on a renewed ontological significance. We ought not forget that the ancient Greeks identified man as the *zoon logon echon*, "the animal with reason," or,

---

50. Gen 2:23.
51. John Paul II, "Man's Awareness of Being."
52. The procession of creatures shown to Job also comes to mind.
53. A more rigorist branch of Thomism represented by Edward Feser objects to the idea that animals could participate in the final kingdom of God based on the notion that "the final vision of God must be entirely an experience of the rational intellect, and that animals entirely lack a rational soul" (Hart, "Romans 8:19–22," para. 7). It is sufficient here to point out that this objection would not be applicable to Ulrich's reading of Aquinas for the very reason that creation would only achieve beatitude through the rational soul of the human being.

according to another translation, "the speaking animal."[54] The nominalist claim that words are mere *flatus vocis* could not be further from the truth. It is of little surprise that this wayward philosophy set the stage for materialism, rationalism, and voluntarism with its disdain for the spoken word and its bifurcation of the intellect and the will.[55] Rather, we could argue that—well beyond the observations of J. L. Austin[56]—all speech is in fact performative in a deeply ontological sense that reaches to the core of reality. As D. C. Schindler describes:

> To speak frivolously, to shirk the duty to come to a deep understanding of the real nature of things and give that meaning a genuinely careful articulation, to technologize speech and instrumentalize it altogether for merely practical purposes, to distort the meaning of words through political manipulation and ideology . . . is to bring dis-order into the cosmos.[57]

For this reason, Ulrich also insists that the *form* of the word must never be separated from its *content*. To put it differently, the meaning of words must not be corrupted, and what is spoken must always be *caritas in veritate*. To give a thing a name is to grant it a place in one's own subsistence. A name, a word, represents "the simultaneity of knowledge and love, which is breathed forth, sent on its way, spoken to and with others. Thus a proper word is a word that articulates the essential truth of things [and] shapes this knowing affirmation in a fitting way which makes it accessible to others as what we might call a common good."[58] In this way, we hear the words of Ulrich, who draws our gaze both up to the source of the gift of being in love and out across the rest of creation, which—unable to speak for itself—can only groan and ask us to grant it a loving word and a pathway back to its source through our own "yes" of subsisting love.

---

54. Schindler, "Word as the Center," 74.

55. As Schindler notes, "the problem in Ockham is not his substitute of voluntarism for rationalism, but his simultaneous *separation* of intellect and will, which results in an impoverishment of both, and his collapse of each into the other. This makes Ockham both a rationalist and a voluntarist at the same time—just like John Locke" (Schindler, *Politics of the Real*, 50–51n32).

56. Cf. Austin, *How to Do Things with Words*.

57. Schindler, *Companion*, 87.

58. Schindler, "Word as the Center," 83.

Reflections for Future Contemplation

The concern for the fate of nature in the culture seems ever greater, perhaps as we come to learn the hard way that humanity and the rest of creation are inextricably linked. Today's currents of environmental ethics, caught in a rivalry between anthropocentric and biocentric positions and intrinsic versus instrumental values, could significantly gain from the perspective presented here. This perspective is complementary to that of Wendell Berry, who rejects these dichotomies and the terminology that arises from dualism, such as "ecosystem" and "the environment." Instead of such abstract and sterile notions that displace, disembody, and disconnect us, he reminds us that real names are those of the individual "rivers and valleys; creeks, ridges, and mountains; towns and cities; lakes, woodlands, lanes, roads, creatures, and people."[59] Berry insists that we will only be able to preserve the places where there are communities of people that love them and care for them, for you cannot love what you do not know, and to love something is to call it by its name. Through Ulrich's profound meditation, we see that these names are not mere conveniences, but are true pathways by which that small portion of creation we come to know and love participates in the fullness of our own subsistence.

The question of what it truly *means* to grant a place in our subsistence to the rest of creation remains a mystery. Certainly, its truth is intuited, but a great deal more must be done to unfurl its significance for the way we live our lives. Surely beauty and wonder must play a role. For all that Ulrich discusses truth and goodness, the consideration of beauty is virtually absent from *Homo Abyssus*. This is not surprising, as Aquinas himself makes little mention of it; however, its consideration could be very fruitful, considering beauty's role in the unification of truth and goodness and as the only sensible transcendental quality of being. For those with the proper disposition, beauty induces wonder, the personal experience of being's superabundant intelligibility that gives philosophy its perpetual vitality.

Beauty is a way of appearing specifically *for another* and reveals a certain desire of all creatures to be affirmed as real—as unique, true, good, and beautiful—*by the human person*, but also by other creatures, albeit less fully. The affirmation of the ontological goodness of the other could also

---

59. Berry, *Sex, Economy, Freedom*, 35.

provide a new perspective on the interrelationality within nature. The bee affirms the goodness of the flower and the peahen, the peacock.[60]

Undoubtedly, there is far more upon which to meditate in these reflections.

Conclusion

While we have only scratched the surface of Ulrich's profound meditation on the nature of being, its self-gift, its reception by the human person, and its consequences for all of creation, we have pointed to the value of Ulrich's work on these themes. Not only is he a thinker who receives the full traditions of Western philosophy and Christian thought, but, from them both, he speaks to their most important critics. Thus, he brings these traditions into the present day while, at the same time, reviving their ancient wisdom once again for a culture that has all but forgotten them. Ulrich's vision, though immanently ethical, does not result in a new list of moral obligations or a new formulation of rights to be enshrined in law. Instead, it leads us to an entirely renewed comprehension of what it means to be human, how we can best relate to the world around us and, at the same time, achieve our own fulfillment and that of all creation.

We have seen how God's self-communication takes the form of a total self-gift, purely mediated by being whose meaning is co-determined by the human person in the way he or she receives this gift. In the gift of being, there is a task to be fulfilled and a love to which we must respond. In the words of Stefan Oster, "unless we say 'Yes' to the gift as given and [received], we betray being as love."[61] When *thinking* becomes *thanking*[62] in love and gratitude, this love is communicated forth in speech that is capable of broadening man's subsistence, which is as a doorway through which all of physical creation can return to its source. The human person, as a true shepherd of beings, must call each member by name—not to possess it, but to invite it into a deeper freedom analogous to the relationship between parents and their child. In a separate text, Ulrich describes this relationship in light of the word:

> The mystery of man's becoming himself and receiving himself is most clearly seen in the act of nurturing. In the beginning,

---

60. Does not the cheetah also, in a sense, affirm the goodness of the gazelle?
61. Oster, "Thinking Love," 693.
62. Ulrich, *Homo Abyssus*, 374, 438.

parents communicate to their child, in word and through love, the life-giving power and the unveiling light of the revelatory word. Word and love are the way, the truth, and the light through which the child encounters himself, and undertakes his freedom as gift of the Freedom.[63]

As to whether we will share the eternal glory of heaven with the myriad beautiful non-human creatures with which we have shared the travail of earthly existence, to echo David Bentley Hart, "I would rather defer the question to the end of days, when creation will be restored in the Kingdom, shadows in mirrors will yield to the light of clear knowledge, and (so I am reliably informed) the lion will lie down with the lamb."[64]

Bibliography

Aquinas, Thomas. *Commentary on Aristotle's* Physics. Translated by Pierre H. Conway. https://isidore.co/aquinas/Physics1.htm#8.

———. *Commentary on the Sentences*. Translated by The Aquinas Institute. https://aquinas.cc/la/en/~Sent.I.

———. *De Aeternitate Mundi*. Revised translation by Robert T. Miller. Edited by The Aquinas Institute. https://aquinas.cc/la/en/~DeAeternit.

———. *De Potentia Dei*. Translated by the English Dominican Fathers. Edited and revised by The Aquinas Institute. https://aquinas.cc/la/en/~QDePot.

———. *De Unitate Intellectus contra Averroistas*. https://isidore.co/aquinas/english/DeUnitateIntellectus.htm.

———. *De Veritate*. Translated by Robert W. Mulligan. Chicago: Henry Regnery Company, 1952. https://isidore.co/aquinas/QDdeVer2.htm.

———. *Summa contra Gentiles*. Book II translated by James F. Anderson. Edited by Joseph Kenny. New York: Hanover House, 1955–57. https://isidore.co/aquinas/ContraGentiles2.htm.

———. *Summa Theologica*. Translated by Laurence Shapcote. Edited and revised by The Aquinas Institute. https://aquinas.cc/la/en/~ST.I.

Austin, J. L. *How to Do Things with Words*. 2nd ed. Oxford: Oxford University Press, 1975.

Balthasar, Hans Urs von. *Theo-Logic*. Vol. 1, *Truth of the World*. Translated by Adrian J. Walker. San Francisco: Ignatius, 2000.

Berry, Wendell. *Sex, Economy, Freedom and Community: Eight Essays*. New York: Pantheon, 1994.

Bieler, Martin. "*Analogia Entis* as an Expression of Love according to Ferdinand Ulrich." In *The Analogy of Being: Invention of the Antichrist or the Wisdom of God?*, edited by Thomas J. White, 314–37. Grand Rapids: Eerdmans, 2011.

———. "Introduction." In *Homo Abyssus: The Drama of the Question of Being*, by Ferdinand Ulrich, xv–lv. Washington, DC: Humanum Academic, 2018.

---

63. Ulrich, "Personal Unity," 559.
64. Hart, "Vinculum Magnum Entis," para. 10.

Gonzales, Philip. "A Massive Sea Change in Recent Theology." *Church Life Journal*, Mar. 24, 2021. https://churchlifejournal.nd.edu/articles/a-massive-sea-change-in-recent-theology/.

Goodenough, Ursula, and Terrance W. Deacon. "The Sacred Emergence of Nature." In *The Oxford Handbook of Religion and Science*, edited by Philip Clayton and Zachary Simpson, 853–71. Oxford: Oxford University Press, 2006.

Hart, David Bentley. "Romans 8:19–22." *First Things*, June 2015. www.firstthings.com/article/2015/06/ romans-81922.

———. *A Splendid Wickedness and Other Essays*. Grand Rapids: Eerdmans, 2016.

———. "Vinculum Magnum Entis." *First Things*, Apr. 2015. https://www.firstthings.com/article/2015/04/vinculum-magnum-entis.

Healy, Nicholas J. *The Eschatology of Hans Urs von Balthasar: Being as Communion*. New York: Oxford University Press, 2005.

John Paul II. "Creation as a Fundamental and Original Gift." General Audience, Jan. 2, 1980. https://www.vatican.va/content/john-paul-ii/en/audiences/1980/documents/hf_jp-ii_aud_19800102.html.

———. "Man's Awareness of Being a Person." General Audience, Oct. 24, 1979. https://www.vatican.va/content/john-paul-ii/en/audiences/1979/documents/hf_jp-ii_aud_19791024.html.

Oster, Stefan. "Thinking Love at the Heart of Things: The Metaphysics of Being as Love in the Work of Ferdinand Ulrich." *Communio* 37.4 (2010) 660–700.

Ratzinger, Joseph. *The End of Time*. Mahwah, NJ: Paulist, 2004.

———. *Principles of Catholic Theology: Building Stones for a Fundamental Theology*. San Francisco: Ignatius, 1987.

Schindler, D. C. *A Companion to Ferdinand Ulrich's* Homo Abyssus. Washington, DC: Humanum Academic, 2019.

———. *Plato's Critique of Impure Reason: On Goodness and Truth in the* Republic. Washington, DC: Catholic University of America Press, 2011.

———. *The Politics of the Real: The Church between Liberalism and Integralism*. Steubenville, OH: New Polity, 2021.

———. "What's the Difference? On the Metaphysics of Participation in a Christian Context." *Saint Anselm Journal* 3.1 (2005) 1–27.

———. "The Word as the Center of Man's Onto-Dramatic Task." *Communio* 49.1 (2019) 73–85.

Taylor, Michael Dominic. "A Gift to the World: The Human Person's Place in Creation according to the Thought of Ferdinand Ulrich." *Saint Anselm Journal* 19.1 (2023) 93–107.

Ulrich, Ferdinand. *Homo Abyssus: The Drama of the Question of Being*. Translated by D. C. Schindler. Washington, DC: Humanum Academic, 2018.

———. "The Personal Unity of Glory and Poverty in Freedom as Love." *Communio* 42.3 (2015) 558–63.

Verbeke, Gerard. "Man as a 'Frontier' according to Aquinas." In *Aquinas and Problems of His Time*, edited by Gerard Verbeke and Daniël Verhelst, 195–223. Leuven: Leuven University Press, 1976.

7

The Return of the Angels

The Ecological Turn as a Conversion to the Theology of Creation and to Natural Law

Rocco Buttiglione

In the encyclical *Laudato Si'*, Pope Francis invites us to an ecological conversion.[1] In this short essay, we will try to understand the extent and significance of this ecological conversion. To delve into the meaning of the pope's proposal, we are required to question some of the most entrenched opinions that have been dominating in the field of theology and philosophy in recent decades.

Can the Pope Call for Conversion to Something or Someone Other Than Jesus Christ?

In principle, we cannot deny that there is something scandalous about a pope calling for a conversion to ecology. Isn't it a surrender of the church to the spirit of the times? A kind of idolatry that denies that there is no other name but the name of Jesus Christ that brings us salvation? In order to answer this first and fundamental question, we need to consider the etymology and meaning of the word "ecology." It comes from the Greek and is composed of two parts: *oikos*, which means home, and *logos*, which means law or immanent rule. If we consider the earth as the home of man and all living beings, then ecology is the immanent rule of the life of the earth or, more broadly speaking, of the cosmos. In Platonic philosophy,

---

1. Francis, *Laudato Si'*, §§216–21.

the *logos* is the inner rationality that constitutes the cosmos as such; it differentiates the cosmos from chaos because it introduces within chaos a principle of intelligibility. St. John goes much further than Plato. For St. John, the *Logos* is the Word of God; through the *Logos* all things have been not only ordered but created from nothingness and brought into being.[2] This inner principle of intelligibility is also the Law that regulates the life of the human community and, in particular, the Law of the People of Israel. St. Paul tells us that this Law is written not only in the Tablets of the Law, but also in the heart of every human being.[3] It coincides with the natural law. St. John adds that this inner rationality of nature and human society has become flesh in the person of the man Jesus of Nazareth.[4]

Now we see that the ecological conversion is, in the last instance, a conversion to God, who has created earth and sky; to the natural law that governs both the physical reality surrounding us and the human heart; and to the Savior of man, Jesus Christ, who "is the centre of the universe and of history."[5]

Nothing New under the Sun?

Shall we then say that there is nothing new under the sun and that *Laudato Si'* just repeats a traditional doctrine? Not quite. The pope enters into dialogue with one of the fundamental trends of our society, one so powerful that it has become a force for change in the lives of millions of people, becoming for them a moral obligation. It touches the heart of man at such a profound level that it seems able to either become or generate a new religion. This explains the hesitancy of many Christians with regard to the ecological movement: afraid of the reemergence of pagan religion, they would have preferred that it be condemned outrightly.

The pope made a different decision, choosing another pastoral strategy: the strategy of dialogue and discernment. Discernment means that we ask ourselves: What is the Spirit of God doing in this movement? What is the message it conveys to us? What kind of opportunity does it offer for an encounter between man and the true God, the God of Jesus Christ? Of course, at the same time we must ask ourselves: What are the

---

2. John 1:3.
3. Rom 2:14–15.
4. John 1:14.
5. John Paul II, *Redemptor Hominis*, §1.

dangers implied in this movement? How is the devil trying to distort its positive aspects? Where will it lead us if we do not correct the partiality of some of its formulations? Dialogue and discernment demand of us both human sympathy and a critical approach.

A first striking message is contained precisely in the religious nature of the movement that upends one fundamental trend of our civilization. In modern times, we seem to believe that nature is simply matter in movement, and that man can impose on this matter in movement the form he arbitrarily chooses. This is the myth of Prometheus: man creates a new world, wholly independent from that created by God; this would prove that we don't need to have any God at all. Man, making use of modern science and technology, takes the place of God. This would give us empirical evidence of the fact that God does not exist, and even if he does exist, he makes no inroads into the world of man; thus, we are fully justified in taking no notice of his existence. We live in the world of man, not (or no longer) in the world of God.[6]

The Novelty of the Ecological Approach

This vision is brought into question by two facts. The first is that we have destroyed our natural environment to the extent that the earth might easily become unable in the relatively near future to further support human life. Nature resists humanity's attempt at absolute domination; it has a form of its own that cannot be disregarded or violated without destroying it. The objects of this earth have a form, and in using them man has to respect that form, which is not dependent on man. The second is that man is also an object of this earth. Therefore, claiming that man can manipulate the earth without being restrained by any precept not derived from his arbitrary will would be tantamount to saying that some men (powerful figures of science, economics, communication, and politics) have the right to manipulate others and make them subservient to their arbitrary will. Nature and men are both used to increase the wealth and power of a dominating elite. This wealth and power is measured in money, in exchange values. The earth is used and exploited not to better the lives of human beings (not to maximize use values), but to maximize exchange values—that is, money.

---

6. Marx, *Economic and Philosophic Manuscripts*, 107.

The pope positively evaluates this turn that the ecological movement imposes on our civilization. It invites us to recover an esthetic and religious attitude in the face of reality. It is a religious attitude because the world is not something that we create; it is something that we receive from a power that gives it to us, allowing us to make use of it but also imposing upon us an obligation of respect. There is a certain fundamental and original passive attitude toward reality that needs to be recovered. It is an esthetic attitude because the things of this world have a form. This form ought to be respected, but it also conveys a meaning to us. The world is a world of symbols that must be interpreted, and we have a responsibility to respond to the message contained in those symbols.[7]

One might observe that the religiosity that has been recovered is a natural religiosity, more similar to the pantheistic sense of nature that animates natural religions than to the specific religious form of Christianity. Can the God of Jesus Christ be found along the path of the ecological movement? Is the dialogue Pope Francis has entered into a trap that leads us back to paganism, and not to Christianity?

Are the Old Gods Coming Back?

The ecological movement has rediscovered the concept of form. Animals and trees and grasses and water are not just pure objects, just matter in movement. They have a form; through this form they are related to one another and are constituted as parts of a whole; they cooperate for the good of the other and for the system of which they are a part. This is the concept of the ecosystem, which can be understood in two different ways. A forest or a lake is an ecosystem, but also the whole earth is an ecosystem: an ecosystem of ecosystems. Through this concept, the totality of nature is also related to man: man is part of this Whole. However, man is not a part of this Whole that is exactly equal to all the other parts: he is the part of the Whole in which the Whole becomes conscious of itself and acquires a certain power of decision over itself. Man has the responsibility to preserve the Whole—but he can also refuse the responsibility and actively destroy the ecosystem, placing his particular good against the good of the Whole instead of understanding his own good in light of the good of the Whole.

---

7. Balthasar, *Glory of the Lord* vol. 1.

Up to now, we have learned the truth of the ecological movement in light of the Aristotelian theory of the form.[8] However, this theory is a transposition of an older vision that is proper to all natural religions. To say that the objects of the natural world have a form of their own means to say that they also have a subjectivity of their own. This subjectivity is hypostatized by Greek mythology in the different divinities of the natural world. Every river has its god, and every spring its nymph. The poets have always remained faithful to this perception of reality. Let us make one point clear: the perception of the form does not invalidate the scientific vision of the world as a world of pure objects. St. Thomas (with Aristotle) makes us aware of the fact that the same real object can be the object of different sciences. Each of them considers the object from a particular point of view at the exclusion of all others. To better study and understand one aspect or peculiarity of the object, the scientist puts all others aside. Through this act of putting within brackets all other aspects, the scientist constitutes the formal object of his science; however, in the real world, what is bracketed off is not annihilated or destroyed. The scientist can, now and then, read poetry and see the same object from a completely different point of view, and the philosopher can try to reconstruct in a reflexive and ordered way the totality of real objects.

The ecological movement invites us to see the world as a world of forms, inhabited by magical creatures: elves and naiads and demigods and gods. Is this compatible with a Christian vision of reality?

Is Monotheism Incompatible with the Old Gods?

The pagans had an analogical understanding of the world: in every natural phenomenon, they saw a guiding spirit; in each bush, a faun; in each spring, a naiad. Max Weber has contended that Christian monotheism has desecrated the world of nature, transforming it into raw material deprived of a form and meaning of its own.[9] There is only one God, and he has created all things. Through this belief in one God, Christians unify the ancients' complex and sometimes contradictory worldview and simultaneously (says Weber) oppose God's absolute subjectivity to the absolute objectivity of the things of this world. When belief in God is abandoned, what will be left is only a world of pure objects. This is

---

8. Aristotle, *Metaphysics*, 987b (14–15).
9. Weber, *Economy and Society*, 509.

far from being true (at least for Catholicism): veneration of angels and saints has enhanced within monotheism the perception of the sacred and the sacrality of nature. The Catholic God creates the world according to mathematical concepts, as Galileo reminds us, and really mathematics is—in one sense—the language of God. From a non-monotheistic perspective, it would be difficult to understand the world as a coherent unity, regulated by a system of impersonal mathematical laws. But God does not speak only one language; at once he created a world of forms and of symbols. There is a mathematical *and* a symbolic order of reality. In creating the world of forms, God also created a host of spirits to whom he entrusts the created reality; each of them cooperates in the fulfillment of the destiny of each created thing.[10] Each thing that has a form also has a destiny; it is composed of potentiality and act, and the fulfillment of its proper act is its destiny. In the Catholic vision, the old demigods are transformed into angels and devils. These spirits cooperate with creation in the fulfillment of its purpose, or they oppose its fulfillment and distort its purpose in an act of dis-creation.[11] Some saints also acquire a similar function of protecting particular areas of human activity, and/or some phenomena of nature. Through the *Logos* of God all things were created, in Heaven and on Earth.

The Return of the Angels

The angels are the created beings of Heaven. The disenchantment of the world is not, therefore, a legitimate and necessary consequence of Christianity. The whole symbolic structure of Catholic (and Orthodox) liturgy gives witness to this truth. The liturgy unproblematically makes use of the natural symbols of water and light, bread and wine, and so forth. It is a great merit of Tolkien to have promoted a re-enchantment of the world through fantasies steeped in the wisdom of the Catholic Church.

The question is more complicated for Protestants. On the one hand, the fathers of the Reformation were clearly not against the cult of the angels; this cult is also rooted in Protestant popular devotion. On the other hand, it is equally true that Catholic veneration of angels and saints is a frequent target of Protestant polemists, and it migrates later into the works that issued from the anti-Catholic currents of the Enlightenment.

---

10. Aquinas, *Summa Theologiae*, I, q. 112.
11. Daniélou, *Angels and Their Mission*.

It is considered a form of superstition, a residue of paganism within Christianity. This prejudice has been confirmed and strengthened by a certain trend within contemporary theology that separates faith from religion, even putting them in opposition to each other. The modern man is, according to this vision, a thoroughly secularized being who sees reality only as an object of his own activity, not as being endowed with any kind of subjectivity. To preach the faith to this kind of man is only possible if we divest it from any kind of religiosity, labelled as superstition.[12] In this secularized faith, there is no place for sanctuaries, for angels or saints, for places in which Heaven touches the earth and makes itself more distinctly perceivable; in general, there is no place for the sacred. This is a tremendous problem for traditional Catholic popular piety, which has assumed within Christianity the heritage of natural religiosity, understanding the faith as the accomplishment of religion, not as its negation. This point also seems to be at the center of the controversies surrounding the interpretation of the Second Vatican Council. The so-called progressives see the spirit of the Council in the demythologization of Catholicism; the so-called traditionalists resist and desire to maintain the link between the Christian faith and popular religiosity. The ecological turn brings to evidence the fact that the demand for the sacred, although repressed, was indeed present in the heart of the secularized man.[13] A consequence thereof is the necessity of rethinking the relation of faith and religion in positive terms, and of reevaluating the meaning and value of popular religiosity. It needs, of course, to be purified from spurious and superstitious elements, but it is nonetheless a fundamental element of the Christian faith.

Laudato Si' Demands a Reconsideration of the Law of Nature

Laudato Si' calls for a conversion to Christ as the *Logos* through whom all things were made and who has left in all created beings an imprint of his creative power. To this imprint a specific respect is due: man is allowed to use the world of nature, but he is also called to respect its inner finality and dignity; this dignity of nature constitutes the law of nature.

The idea of the law of nature has been largely set aside in modern philosophy and theology. It contrasts with a certain idea of human

---

12. Cox, *Secular City*.
13. Berger, *Rumor of Angels*.

liberty. The general conviction was (and is) that reality is what man constitutes as such, and the exterior world—the world that precedes human intentionality and which this intentionality finds, in one sense, already made—is indefinitely manipulable, mere prime matter that receives its form only through human intention on the one hand and human technical manipulation on the other. The object is not what it is, but what is constituted by the human subject. The idea of natural law has been seen as a limit to human liberty, a concept forged by social authority in order to restrict the sovereignty of human subjectivity or as a device of the Catholic Church to impose its authority on moral matters. To a certain extent, this is surprising because the concept of natural law was one of the fundamental conceptual tools of the polemics of the Enlightenment against the pretension of the Catholic Church to monopolize the domain of morality. However, modern ecology rediscovers a concept of natural law that is strikingly similar to that of St. Thomas Aquinas.

Each ecosystem has a certain inner balance; this balance must be maintained to preserve the ecosystem's structure as such and the survival of the living organisms that constitute it and are contained in it. These organisms are contained in the structure in the sense that they exist in it, and from it they derive their possibility to survive and reproduce. On the other hand, they constitute the structure in the sense that the structure is not a reality imposed upon them and distinct from them. The structure is nothing but the beings living within it considered in the correct relation among themselves. The structure is the form of their correct relation. This form is the living principle of the structure.

The most beautiful and concise formulation of St. Thomas's conception of the natural law has been given perhaps by Dante: "*Ius est realis et personalis hominis ad hominem proportio, quae servata hominum servat societatem, et corrupta corrumpit.*"[14] It is the idea of the ecosystem applied to human society. The sanction for the transgression of the norms of the natural law does not come from the outside. It is immanent and not transcendent: it is the malfunctioning—and in the end, the destruction—of human society. We can even make a comparison to the Darwinian law of the survival of the fittest.[15] If a species does not behave in accordance

---

14. "Right is a relationship between one individual and another in respect of things and people; when it is respected it preserves human society and when it is violated it destroys it" (Dante, *Monarchia*, II, v, 1).

15. This sentence was of Herbert Spencer, but Darwin made it his own. See Darwin, *Variation of Animals*, 1:6.

with the immanent laws of nature, it will damage its ecosystem and disappear. Of course, ecosystems evolve and so does nature in general. The immanent laws of a social structure can also be modified, but they do not change all at once—evolution takes time. The change obeys structural laws in order to realize a transition from one structure to another; it does not happen arbitrarily. Not all changes are conducive to a new structure. Some (most) of them lead to the decay or disappearance of the ecosystem or social structure entirely. There are some fundamental principles that do not change in time. They determine, in a certain sense, the limits of the changes a structure can undergo without destroying itself.[16] Opposed to this view is the vulgarized evolutionism that has become the dominant social philosophy of our times, which presupposes that random or casual changes always lead to new social structures, or that social structures can be haphazardly constructed or deconstructed.

Man has the responsibility of reasonably conducting processes of social change respecting the immanent laws of social structures and the ecosystem. He cannot govern the ecosystem if he does not first govern the social structure. A social structure entering a path of self destruction must necessarily lead to the destruction of the ecosystem in which it lives, which is, in one sense, entrusted to its care. The natural law governing human society and the natural law governing the ecosystem stay in a necessary relation to one another because man is the shepherd of being. The first causes of the ecosystem's destruction lie in an imbalance within human society.[17] The same *Logos* through whom the word of nature was created has created the nature of man and is the immanent law of the just relation of men among themselves. This is the reason why the ecological turn implies reconsidering the question of natural law.

This is a kind of philosophical revolution. One generation of philosophers has been used to think that, in man, existence precedes essence[18]—that is, that man gives to himself his own essence. But the ecological turn obliges us to recognize that man (like all animals) has an essence that precedes his existential decisions and constitutes the inner measure of these decisions. It remains true that man decides his

---

16. It is interesting to observe the strict parallelism with what St. Thomas says on the natural law, which is immutable in its first principles and can change in the conclusions derived from the principles. See Aquinas, *Summa Theologiae*, I–II, q. 94, art. 4, 5, and 6.

17. Francis *Laudato Si'*, §§101–36.

18. Sartre, *Existentialism Is a Humanism*.

own essence, but this decision does not take place in a vacuum. Man determines himself in the face of the essence offered to him. He can accept this essence—and with it, the responsibility of caring for the created world and leading it to a higher degree of perfection—or he can refuse it, choosing rather to substitute the disorder created by his arbitrary will for the God-given order of things. He destroys creation, or he completes it. God behaves like one of the great artists of the Italian Renaissance in the execution of a great work of art—for instance, a monumental fresco. The masters traced the main lines of the work and then left the details to their collaborators, who completed the piece respecting its main lines; in this way, the assistants became co-creators with the artists.

This also implies a different understanding of the essence of human liberty. Liberty is the freedom to act according to one's own nature, not the right to arbitrarily alter or destroy it. This idea of nature and natural freedom (freedom according to nature) also restores the distinction between the normal and the pathological that the postmodernist trend seeks to eliminate.[19]

Back to the Middle Ages, or forward to a New World Culture?

It seems that the ecological turn brings us back to the Middle Ages, to the rediscovery of the sacrality of nature, the angels, and the old Thomist notion of the natural law. This is certainly true, but it is not however the whole truth. It is not difficult to perceive in *Laudato Si'* the echo of the new anthropological reflection that has been developing in Latin America in recent decades, which has influenced both the Theology of the People and that of the Native Indians.

Rodolfo Kusch and Miguel León-Portilla have offered us a new comprehension of the cosmovisions of the South American peoples. León-Portilla[20] has dealt mainly with the Nahuatl culture and Kush[21] rather with that of the Quechua, but on several points they come to similar conclusions. The natural religions and cultures of Mesoamerica and the Andes see man as immersed in the natural world that surrounds him; he is part of this nature and a brother of all beings that live in the same environment. Man stands at the summit of the pyramid of being, but he

---

19. Foucault, *Madness and Civilization*.
20. León-Portilla, *Aztec Thought and Culture*.
21. Kush, *Indigenous and Popular Thinking*.

is nevertheless still a component part of it, swinging and dancing in the same rhythm of life. It is a rhythm that encompasses life and death, the succession of the seasons and the human labor corresponding to each, respect for the living forms of plants and animals, and the perception of the sacred in the mysteries of nature and life. There are a plurality of gods; they must not however be understood as separate entities. They are rather different manifestations of the Sacred that introduce man into the all-encompassing mystery of Being.[22] Man is profoundly conscious of his contingence. We cannot properly say that he *is*. He rather stands in being[23] in front of the world of nature and as an effect of powers that go beyond his subjective grasp. His being is ephemeral, provisory, and fortuitous. He lives in relation to the human and natural environment he is a part of. We are here exactly at the antipodes of the promethean attitude of the European spirit. This perception of the human *"estár en el mundo"* (to be in the world) has entered into Latin American popular religiosity, where Christian angels and saints have taken the place of the old deities.

Bibliography

Aquinas, Thomas. *Summa Theologiae*. Translated by Fathers of the English Dominican Province. New York: Benziger Bros., 1947. https://aquinas.cc/la/en/~ST.I.
Aristotle. *Metaphysics*. Translated by C. D. C. Reeve. Indianapolis: Hackett, 2016.
Balthasar, Hans Urs von. *The Glory of the Lord*. Vol. 1, *Seeing the Form*. San Francisco: Ignatius, 1982.
Berger, Peter L. *A Rumor of Angels*. New York: Doubleday, 1969.
Buttiglione, Rocco. *Caminos: Hacia una Teología del Pueblo y de la Cultura*. Valparaíso: Ediciones Universitarias de Valparaíso, 2022.
Cox, Harvey. *The Secular City*. Princeton: Princeton University Press, 2013.
Daniélou, Jean. *The Angels and Their Mission*. Manchester, NH: Sophia Institute, 2010.
Dante Alighieri. *Monarchia*. Edited by Pier Giorgio Ricci. Translated by Prue Shaw. Florence: Società Dantesca Italiana, 1965. https://dante.princeton.edu/pdp/monarchia.html.
Darwin, Charles. *The Variation of Animals and Plants under Domestication*. Vol. 1. London: John Murray, 1868.
Foucault, Michel. *Madness and Civilization*. New York: Vintage Books, 1988.

---

22. In these cultures, it is important not to forget that the Sacred is not only the godly or divine; the phenomenon of the Sacred also encompasses the demonic. Plato and then the Christians introduced a clear distinction between the divine and the demonic; natural religions did not. This is the reason why you can have, in the Nahuatl religion, both very high values and horrible human sacrifices. There are *semina Verbi*, but also *semina Diaboli*.

23. We translate with these words the Spanish "está" o "está siendo," in the language of Rodolfo Kush. See Kush, *Indigenous and Popular Thinking*, 158–59.

Francis. *Laudato Si'*. Encyclical, May 24, 2015. https://www.vatican.va/content/francesco/en/encyclicals/documents/papa-francesco_20150524_enciclica-laudato-si.html.

John Paul II. *Redemptor Hominis*. Encyclical Letter, Mar. 4, 1979. https://www.vatican.va/content/john-paul-ii/en/encyclicals/documents/hf_jp-ii_enc_04031979_redemptor-hominis.html.

Kush, Rodolfo. *Indigenous and Popular Thinking in America*. Durham: Duke University Press, 2010.

León-Portilla, Miguel. *Aztec Thought and Culture*. Norman, OK: University of Oklahoma Press, 1967.

Marx, Karl. *Economic and Philosophic Manuscripts*. Moscow: Progress, 1977.

Sartre, Jean Paul. *Existentialism Is a Humanism*. New Haven: Yale University Press, 2007.

Weber, Max. *Economy and Society*. Berkeley: University of California Press, 1978.

8

Differences and Similarities in the Initiatives of the Catholic Church and the European Union to Protect Our Common Home[1]

LÓRÁND UJHÁZI

Along the Road of Dialogue

ON DECEMBER 11, 2019, the European Commission published the European Green Deal,[2] a communication designed to address climate and environmental challenges in a complex way. The European Union (EU) believes that its targets, supported by legal and other considerations, should be achieved according to schedule. The main goal is to reduce greenhouse gas emissions to zero by 2050.[3] The EU intends to enter an extensive dialogue on its policy objectives. In his monograph on environmental protection, Máté Szabó points out that while the EU as a larger unit allows for long-term action against ecological problems, "the traditional values of politics and economy, fragmentation, particular interests and short-term responsiveness" may continue to hamper the EU's activities. This could be reduced by civil cooperation. The monograph remains silent on dialogue with religions.[4] Franziska Petri has devoted several studies to the green diplomacy of the EU. Building on the successes of the

1. This paper is a revised version of a work originally published in *Európai Tükör*: Ujházi, "A Környezetvédelem és a Teremtésvédelem."

2. European Commission, "Communication on the European Green Deal."

3. European Council "European Green Deal"; Krämer, "Planning for Climate and the Environment."

4. Szabó, "Európai Környezetpolitika," 3–4.

EU's environmental diplomacy, it seeks to develop diplomatic relations with all countries and international organizations on green issues. However, Petri says nothing about the churches or the Holy See as a subject of international law.[5]

However, in recent years the Catholic Church has become a prominent advocate for environmental protection. Furthermore, policymakers in the West—including the EU—have lagged far behind the Catholic Church, which has a long-standing theological tradition of honoring creation. However, the emphasis on preserving creation has become more important because of pollution.[6] It should be noted that the Catholic Church and public policy adopted different approaches to environmental protection. The protection of creation is a theological concept that is part of Catholic dogmatic theology. It postulates a personified supernatural being who created the world.[7]

This begs the question of whether it is possible and worthwhile to compare these two assessments of environmental protection and the protection of creation, as they are based on different foundations. While the theology of creation has always been well-established in the tradition of Catholic dogmatic theology, the need to protect the created world (again, because of environmental pollution) did not become significant in the social teachings of the Catholic Church until later. Even still, some conservative tendencies in the Catholic Church consider dialogue with modern international organizations toward that end useless—even harmful—for the integrity of Catholic doctrine.[8] However, the Second Vatican Council broke away from the Catholic Church's state-skeptical and distant attitude toward international organizations.[9] This is summarized in the pastoral constitution *Gaudium et Spes*: "With great respect, therefore, this council regards all the true, good and just elements inherent in the very wide variety of institutions which the human race has established for itself and constantly continues to establish. The council affirms, moreover, that the church is willing to assist and promote all these institutions to the extent that such a service depends on her and can be associated with her mission."[10] In this sense, the public policy approach to environmental

5. Biedenkopf and Petri, "European External Action Service."
6. Zamagni, "Catholic Social Thought."
7. Fergusson, *Creation*; Mitchell, "Catholic Theology of Creation."
8. Alva, "Catholic Church's Perspective." For an example, see Molnar, *Church*.
9. Visioli, "Catholic Church Tested."
10. Paul VI, *Gaudium et Spes*, §42.

protection is an area of common good where the church seeks cooperation, even if environmental protection is not a matter of theology for the State. If we accept the political paradigm that public policy is part of a politics that asserts the common good, then, according to the Catholic Church's approach, public policy is a place of "dialogue and meeting."[11]

Suppose we also accept Guy Peters's claim that the EU is still functioning as a public policy system primarily based on values and an ideological and theoretical orientation.[12] In that case, it is also logical that the church seeks to dialogue with the agents of integration. In his encyclical *Laudato Si'*, Pope Francis calls the "climate . . . a common good."[13] The pope sees facing environmental harm as a shared challenge for mankind, and he seeks opportunities for dialogue with various organizations. As a result, he emphasizes the common denominator, not the differences.

What Connects and What Separates

Social dialogue is a good starting point for comparing the Catholic Church's theology of the protection of creation with the EU's policy. The Catholic faith, based on natural law, has comprehensible areas for natural reason. Such common sense allows for the church to dialogue even with non-believing members of society on several articles of the Christian faith. Why should environmental protection be an exception? Even without accepting the theological principle of creation, it is easy to see that the current economy and equipment used in war cause environmental devastation. Paul VI's *Octogesima Adveniens*, the first encyclical to reflect on environmental pollution, adopted a less theologically motivated approach. The encyclical states, "Man is suddenly becoming aware that by an ill-considered exploitation of nature, he risks destroying it and becoming in his turn the victim of this degradation."[14] John Paul II's encyclicals *Centesimus Annus* and *Sollicitudo Rei Socialis*, which provide a more thorough theological perspective to the protection of creation, sought to formulate common-sense considerations about the degradation of the

---

11. Pontifical Council for Justice and Peace, *Compendium*, §42.
12. Peters, "Policy Transfers."
13. Francis, *Laudato Si'*, §23.
14. Paul VI, *Octogesima Adveniens*, §21.

environment, principles that are accepted even by non-believers based on rational logical argumentation and everyday experiences.[15]

A dialogue based on the common good and reason is not alien to the relationship between the EU and the Catholic Church. The Holy See responds to the EU's public policies. However, those organizations working for a greater political integration within the EU were also willing to incorporate the church's social teaching. Alcide De Gasperi of Italy, Robert Schuman of France, and Konrad Adenauer of Germany were all political leaders with solid Catholic socialization. All three drew heavily from the encyclicals underlying the church's social doctrine, especially Leo XIII's *Rerum Novarum* and Pius XI's *Quadragesimo Anno*. Even though they made it clear that their political initiatives had lay roots, they wished to implement the church's social teaching in European political life and society in many ways.[16]

The protection of creation goes beyond the mere practical issues in the church's approach. In Catholic thinking, the starting point based on a divine mandate[17] has always resulted in respect for the created world. This is also true of the prestigious Catholic authors who never spoke about the protection of creation. Still, their cosmology suggests a deep respect for nature and man's responsibility over it. The works of Augustine, Anthony the Hermit, Ephrem the Syrian, and Evagrius Ponticus already feature the created world as the manifestation of God's love.[18] Even though aspects of the protection of creation were not explicitly laid out, man's responsibility was self-evident due to theological principles.[19] This is true even if authors like Lynn White blame Judeo-Christian culture for environmental pollution because of the biblical expression to "subdue" the created world.[20]

However, Catholic theology has indeed started to emphasize the protection of creation in the modern economic and military contexts.[21] Martin Schlag draws attention to parts of the church's social teaching

---

15. John Paul II, *Sollicitudo Rei Socialis*, §34; John Paul II, *Centesimus Annus*, §37.

16. Prélot, *Storia del Pensiero Politico*.

17. See Gen 2:15.

18. Augustine, *On Genesis*; Christian, "Augustine on the Creation"; O'Meara, "Saint Augustine's Understanding"; Quacquarelli, "Ecologia."

19. Tanzella-Nitti, "Creazione."

20. White, "Historical Roots"; see Gen 1:28.

21. Christiansen, "Church Says 'No'"; Welty, "Theological Landscape"; Woods, "Nature of War and Peace."

that have become more pronounced with changes in social challenges.[22] The EU also gradually developed a wide-ranging green policy,[23] but the environmental issue was not part of the original objectives of European integration.[24] So, the communication between the political bodies promoting European integration and the Catholic Church advanced in other areas of social justice, security, and fundamental rights issues.[25] Fair wages, social benefits, healthcare, and a range of public services are still present in the formulations of the EU and the church. When these Catholic proposals found their way into international organizations' terminology, they abandoned their original theological meanings. The finest example is the principle of subsidiarity. The original theologically based concept was revived in integration organizations and received a peculiar political content.[26] The use of terms that are conceptually different but identical in purpose can provide a basis for dialogue between the church and the secular entity. Of course, the meaning of the original theological concept may change in the new context.

Finding out where the two organizations currently stand in each other's foreign policy is more important. As the Founding Fathers of Europe based the project of a united European continent on specialized and public policies close to the Catholic Church, the popes had also supported integration processes.[27] The individual public policy objectives had a firm Catholic grounding, but after the first years of integration, the communication process came to a halt. Paul VI repeatedly warned of the initial goals of the unification efforts. He emphasized the importance of European values, such as "freedom, justice, the dignity of the human

---

22. Schlag, "Political Life"; Cordes, "Paradigm Shift"; Hehir, "John Paul II."

23. Wilkinson, "Using the European Union's Structural"; Baziadoly, "Major Stages."

24. Jans, *European Environmental Law*; Hertin and Berkhout, "Ecological Modernisation"; Görlach et al., *From Vienna to Helsinki*; Krämer, *Genesis of EC Environmental Principles*.

25. Pasture, "Catholic and Christian Democratic Views"; Lecomte, "Popes and the European Integration"; Kratochvíl and Doležal, *European Union*; Leuștean, *Ecumenical Movement*; Valente, "Santa Sede e l'Europa Unita"; Chelini, "Papal Thought"; Chenaux, "Vatican et l'Europe."

26. Brennan, "Subsidiarity in the Tradition"; Follesdal, "Subsidiarity"; Follesdal, "Competing Conceptions"; Chaplin, "Subsidiarity and Sphere Sovereignty."

27. Pasture, "Catholic and Christian Democratic Views"; Chenaux, "Vatican et l'Europe."

person, solidarity and universal love," which are inseparable from European traditions.[28]

John Paul II and Benedict XVI had a strong vision of Europe, and they generally often provided a specifically European outlook with respect to certain global social issues. As regards the protection of creation, the *Compendium of the Social Doctrine of the Church* devotes considerable space to the protection of the created world. It is not Europe-centered, but it cites a number of international and security documents associated with Europe. The document is interesting in that it places the protection of creation between the political and international community and the support of peace. The *Compendium* was born in the spirit of the Council, relying on the cooperation of the church and the political and international community in respect for great social challenges. Indeed, the *Compendium* regards the environment as a universal common good for humanity.[29] It seems that there are areas where "the traditional defensive measures of States appear to be destined to failure."[30] In these areas, international organizations should introduce "adequate and effective political and juridical instruments"[31] to achieve "an integral development in solidarity."[32] This approach was expressed in many of Benedict XVI's papal declarations specifically for the protection of the created world. The best-known was his 2010 World Day of Peace message, entitled "If You Want to Cultivate Peace, Protect Creation."[33] Also, in his encyclical *Caritas in Veritate*, Benedict XVI touched on the relationship between the protection of creation and international communities.[34] In each case, he explicitly stated that environmental protection presupposes moral, legal, and organizational cooperation.[35]

---

28. Paul VI, "Ad Perpetuam Rei," 965–66.
29. Pontifical Council for Justice and Peace, *Compendium*, §466.
30. Pontifical Council for Justice and Peace, *Compendium*, §370.
31. Pontifical Council for Justice and Peace, *Compendium*, §371.
32. Pontifical Council for Justice and Peace, *Compendium*, §373.
33. Benedict XVI, "Message of His Holiness."
34. Benedict XVI, *Caritas in Veritate*, §§27, 43; Strand, "On Method"; Keating et al., "Benedict XVI as Social Realist," 350.
35. Benedict XVI, "Message of His Holiness," §10.

Pope Francis, or the Completion of Dialogue

Pope Francis undoubtedly created something new by issuing an encyclical that comprehensively discusses the protection of creation. *Laudato Si'* had an impact on ecclesiastical organizations across Europe and even received responses from EU institutions. The Council of the Bishops' Conferences of Europe (CCEE) set up a special committee to promote joint work between the church and the EU in protecting creation and the environment. The committee has made contributions and recommendations on the Green Deal.[36] After his election, the Holy Father explicitly sought public policies that united the two entities instead of separating them. Of these, the issue of the environment is one of the most important. Pope Francis rightly sees that, despite the theological foundation for protecting the created world, success and overall change are unrealistic if we protect creation on purely theoretical grounds. He is aware of the church's possibilities for action: while the Holy See is a subject of international law,[37] it has limited economic, military, or political influence. Therefore, the pope correctly applies the Council's general philosophy of dialogue to the protection of creation. The entire fifth chapter of *Laudato Si'* is about dialogue. This concerns both the local and national levels based on international policy[38] and the principle of subsidiarity.[39] It deals with the relationship between dialogue and transparency,[40] the role of dialogue between politics and the economy,[41] and between religions and science in promoting the protection of creation.[42]

Here the apostolic constitution *Veritatis Gaudium* might also be mentioned, which re-regulates the functioning of ecclesiastical universities; therein, Pope Francis states that classical theological matters should be treated with a transdisciplinary approach.[43] The constitution's appendix suggests several research areas related to the protection of creation.[44]

---

36. COMECE, "Green Deal."

37. Antonini, "Diplomatic Activity"; Graham, *Vatican Diplomacy*; Hanson, *Catholic Church in World Politics*; Arangio-Ruiz, "On the Nature"; Araujo, "International Personality"; Bathon, "Atypical International Status"; Morss, "International Legal Status."

38. Francis, *Laudato Si'*, §§163–75.

39. Francis, *Laudato Si'*, §§176–81.

40. Francis, *Laudato Si'*, §§182–88.

41. Francis, *Laudato Si'*, §§189–98.

42. Francis, *Laudato Si'*, §§199–201.

43. Francis, *Veritatis Gaudium*; Mitchell, "Catholic Theology."

44. Petkovšek, "Theology Facing the Challenges."

Tanzella-Nitti draws attention to the need for theological clarity because, in analytical works,[45] it can be difficult to see differences between political, social, and theological aspects.[46] Scientific deep drilling should not be ignored, as it helps us to understand the identities and differences between international political actors—including the approach of the EU and the church. A number of prestigious Catholic universities are conducting research based on this type of cooperation. As the pontifical universities in Rome have been incorporated into the Erasmus program, the relationship between Catholic universities in member states and pontifical universities is expected to become more profound.

Incidentally, the encyclical *Laudato Si'* is an example of the transdisciplinary method proposed by *Veritatis Gaudium*.[47] It discusses the areas of water, air, and land pollution, waste management, agriculture, industry, and climate change.[48] It devotes a separate subchapter to the loss of biodiversity, the deterioration in the quality of human life, and social decline. It is aware of the complexity of the field and the need for dialogue between the sciences. The pope does not share the opinion of retrograde Catholic groups that there is no point in dialogue with political communities.[49] On the contrary, he takes every opportunity to highlight the protection of creation when making statements before political bodies or international organizations. This was the subject of his speech in the European Parliament, where he also spoke of the importance of protecting the environment. Arguing in theological terms, he claimed that "we are not [nature's] masters. Stewards, but not masters. We need to love and respect nature, but 'instead we are often guided by the pride of dominating, possessing, manipulating, exploiting.'" He linked this to the social sphere: "It is intolerable that millions of people around the world are dying of hunger."[50]

In his message to the European Youth Conference, the pope called for the "care of our common home."[51] In this case, too, the protection of creation appears alongside other social areas. He referred to the

---

45. Tanzella-Nitti, "Come la Religione."

46. Lai and Tortajada, "Holy See"; Ittekkot and Milne, "Encyclical Letter 'Laudato Si'"; Boff, *Creato*; Flecha, *Rispetto del Creato*.

47. Padányi, "Climate Change."

48. Youngs, "Climate Change and EU Security."

49. Molnar, *Church*.

50. Francis, "Address," para. 30; quoting Francis, "General Audience," para. 3.

51. Francis, *Laudato Si'*.

environmental implications of fossil fuels and overconsumption and their social welfare and security aspects.[52] The pope's meetings with prominent EU officials have also raised awareness surrounding environmental protection. For example, it was a topic of discussion with the president of the European Commission,[53] and in meetings with the EU's environment ministers.[54] The defense of our common home is not an ideological matter, but a dialogue between sober-minded parties to find a solution. Moreover, on the latter occasion, the pope highlighted policy areas at the forefront of the EU's attention: resource saving, waste reduction, water management, recycling, etc. The EU's institutions seem open to learning about the church's approach to protecting creation. After the publication of *Laudato Si'*, Laurence Argimon-Pistre, the EU's ambassador to the Holy See, commended the new document. Presenting it before the UN Food and Agriculture Organization, she highlighted the importance of the church's environmental guidelines, the protection of creation, and commitment to the poor.[55] In a private interview, Ursula von der Leyen evaluated the meeting with the pope. She expressed her gratitude and appreciation for *Laudato Si'*. The dialogue between Christianity and European public life has been characterized by *ratio* since the birth of Christianity. Today, protecting creation and the environment is not the only facet of this dialogue, but perhaps it is the most crucial.[56]

Furthermore, European societies are more sensitive to environmental issues. Miranda Schreurs made a comparison between the environmental commitments of the United States, China, and the EU. On the one hand, she believes that European citizens are more dedicated to climate protection. On the other hand, she highlights the EU's energy dependency. As the EU is the biggest importer, it sees the development of alternative energies as particularly important.[57] Schreurs is right about the environmental awareness of EU citizens. However, she only takes account of the external and security aspects of the European environmental landscape. Human or fundamental rights are often palpable in some EU public policies based on Christian values. The right to a healthy environment embodied in fundamental rights documents stems from the

52. San Martín, "Pope to European Youth."
53. Lariver, "Pope Francis Meets."
54. CIDSE, "Press Release."
55. Argimon-Pistre, "Responsibility towards the Environmental Crisis."
56. Lariver, "Pope Francis Meets."
57. Schreurs, "Paris Climate Agreement," 220.

Christian philosophy of creation. The perspective that the EU is more environmentally conscious can be traced not only to the security aspect, but also to the Christian philosophy that still exists in European countries.[58]

Open Questions in Dialogue

Ann Pettifor's study on the EU's green policy shows that achieving results *a priori* depends on realizing a complex social change in mentality.[59] No success is likely if the program does not entail this comprehensive social change. In their 2017 study, Tilman Altenburg and Dani Rodrik add that the EU can only achieve its ambitious objectives by completely replacing outdated technology with new resources.[60] Old tech is based on a different philosophy and was not developed with due regard for environmental awareness. Unfortunately, even today the EU's economy, industry, and agriculture are largely based on these technologies. Pope Francis also talks about the complexity of environmental issues. In his view, the protection of creation necessarily affects the economy, the financial world, the eradication of poverty, social issues, the arms trade, and the issue of war.[61]

Another matter is how economic and short-term political interests will limit genuine cooperation. Pope Francis often describes international agreements as ineffective.[62] This is even more pronounced in the apostolic exhortation *Laudate Deum*.[63] Some analyses of EU public policy have come to the same conclusion.[64] Alicja Sikora points out that environmental protection has become commonplace, unlike many other European public policies. However, she warns that no ambitious plans can be implemented without a new lifestyle.[65] Robert Pollin pointed to

---

58. Raith, "'Global Pact.'"
59. Pettifor, *Case for the Green New Deal.*
60. Altenburg and Rodrik, "Green Industrial Policy."
61. Francis, *Laudato Si'*, §§66, 104, 198, 200, 225.
62. For instance, a comment on the Rio Agreement: "Although the summit was a real step forward, and prophetic for its time, its accords have been poorly implemented, due to the lack of suitable mechanisms for oversight, periodic review and penalties in cases of non-compliance" (Francis, *Laudato Si'*, §167). Elsewhere: "The Conference of the United Nations on Sustainable Development, 'Rio+20' (Rio de Janeiro 2012), issued a wide-ranging but ineffectual outcome document" (Francis, *Laudato Si'*, §169).
63. Francis, *Laudate Deum.*
64. Krämer, "Planning for Climate."
65. Sikora, "European Green Deal."

the weaknesses of the EU's Green Deal even before its final adoption.[66] He believes the biggest stumbling block to climate neutrality or environmental protection is the reluctance of (Europe's) welfare societies to give up growth.[67] Pope Francis points out the same: profitability cannot be the only criterion of the economy.[68] The forms of economic crisis management are wrong and only strengthen the rule of money. Measures and actions based on the criteria of profitability, however lengthy and costly they are, do not lead to a real cure but rather result in a new crisis.[69] The most outstanding merit of the pope is that he has raised to a high level of communication the idea that the only solution is to change our lifestyle. Although the EU's public policies sometimes imply the need for far-reaching social transformations, they dare not call it by its name. In essence, the pope is saying that a green policy can only be achieved by dismantling the consumer society on which Western economic policy is based and which is, above all, responsible for environmental damage.[70] This makes it possible to care for others and the environment. The Holy Father aims to develop "attitudes" that consider "the impact of our every action and personal decision on the world around us."[71] However, this is opposed to the consumer mentality that sustains the current economic conditions on which the Western and European economies are based.

Conclusion

Due to environmental damage in the second half of the twentieth century, the protection of creation became increasingly pronounced in Catholic social teaching.[72] The Second Vatican Council had the merit of seeing the church leave behind a refusal to cooperate with international organizations. The common good emerged as a connecting factor that the church should promote in cooperation with the political community.

66. Pollin, "Global Green Growth."
67. Chomsky and Pollin, *Climate Crisis*.
68. Francis, *Laudato Si'*, §185.
69. Francis, *Laudato Si'*, §189.
70. Francis, *Laudato Si'*, §209.
Francis, *Laudato Si'*, §208.
71. Francis, *Laudato Si'*, §208.
72. This is not to claim that the church did not have a theological concept about the created world beforehand.

The social aspects of European integration, which began in the 1950s, overlapped with Catholic social teaching in many areas. Given the shared values, this allowed for communication. Later, several lines of fracture emerged in the values of the EU and the Catholic Church. However, Pope Francis emphasizes common points rather than opposing positions to promote specific areas of the common good. Since he explicitly places the protection of the created world among public goods, cooperation in this area is beyond dispute. "The gravity of the ecological crisis demands that we all look to the common good." All this urges the church to "embark[] on a path of dialogue."[73] Pope Francis was the first to issue an encyclical specifically on protecting creation. His predecessors referred to the importance of the subject in many cases, but they linked the protection of creation to individual areas of Catholic social teaching. The encyclical *Laudato Si'* does the opposite: its starting point is the created world, to which other societal challenges are connected.

The EU sees itself as an alliance of values that treats environmental protection at a high public policy level. Its criteria sometimes overlap with Catholic social teaching. The EU could be a good partner for the Holy See, especially since the Holy See expects that, in a globalized world, individual states need more strength to achieve ambitious goals.

Pope Francis envisages that the EU should play a role beyond Europe in environmental matters.[74] However, it should be remembered that in the case of the EU there are economic and budgetary constraints that limit the achievement of its lofty goals. In this context, Drew Christiansen and Walter Grazer highlight that the EU's public policy logic and the protection of creation are bound to diverge on one level.[75] The latter is based on theological teachings, with which essentially secular-oriented public policy cannot engage. The defense of creation can only be understood from a theological point of view. A modern market economy based on growth cannot comprehend what these relevant theological aspects—such as a modest life rather than growth—signify. This approach is alien to doctrines insistent on the supremacy of growth and the EU's environmental policy.

Several analyses today point out that the EU's current green policy does not provide the basis for ending the misuse of wealth. Its strategies cannot address systemic injustices. While the EU has committed to

73. Francis, *Laudato Si'*, §201.
74. Zengarini, "Pope Francis."
75. Christiansen and Grazer, *"And God Saw."*

becoming climate-neutral by 2050, achieving this goal would require a substantial economic and social transformation throughout Europe. However, the biggest problem is the lack of will or sincerity currently found only in the teaching of the Catholic Church at the universal level. We should admit that only by living more modestly and making consumption more restrained can we achieve results in the protection of creation. Cooperation between the EU and the Catholic Church at the level of communication, operation, or diplomacy is essential and necessary, but it will always remain haphazard as long as no one faces up to this fact.

Bibliography

Altenburg, Tilman, and Dani Rodrik. "Green Industrial Policy: Accelerating Structural Change towards Wealthy Green Economies." In *Green Industrial Policy: Concept, Policies, Country Experiences*, edited by Tilman Altenburg and Claudia Assmann, 1–21. Geneva, Bonn: UN Environment; German Development Institute/Deutsches Institut für Entwicklungspolitk, 2017. https://drodrik.scholar.harvard.edu/files/dani-rodrik/files/altenburg_rodrik_green_industrial_policy_webversion.pdf.

Alva, Reginald. "The Catholic Church's Perspective of Human Dignity as the Basis of Dialogue with the Secular World." *Stellenbosch Theological Journal* 2 (2017) 64–75.

Antonini, Orlando. "The Diplomatic Activity of the Holy See." *Communication* 12 (2015) 5–15.

Arangio-Ruiz, Gaetano. "On the Nature of the International Personality of the Holy See." *Revue Belge de Droit International* 29 (1996) 354–69.

Araujo, Robert J. "The International Personality and Sovereignty of the Holy See." *Catholic University Law Review* 50 (2001) 291–336.

Argimon-Pistre, Laurence. "Responsibility towards the Environmental Crisis, the Poor and the Future Generations." In *Laudato Si': On Care for Our Common Home: Compilation of Speeches of the Last Encyclical Letter at FAO*, 16–27. Rome: Food and Agriculture Organization, 2016. https://www.fao.org/3/i5461b/I5461B.pdf.

Augustine. *On Genesis*. Washington, DC: The Catholic University of America Press, 1991.

Bathon, Matthew. "The Atypical International Status of the Holy See." *Vanderbilt Journal of Transitional Law* 34 (2001) 597–632.

Baziadoly, Sophie. "The Major Stages in the Construction of European Environmental Law." In *The Environment and the European Public Sphere*, edited by Christian Wenkel, 244–62. Winwick: White Horse, 2020.

Benedict XVI. *Caritas in Veritate*. Encyclical Letter, June 29, 2009. https://www.vatican.va/content/benedict-xvi/en/encyclicals/documents/hf_ben-xvi_enc_20090629_caritas-in-veritate.html.

———. "Message of His Holiness Pope Benedict XVI for the Celebration of the World Day of Peace." Jan. 1, 2010. https://www.vatican.va/content/benedict-xvi/en/messages/peace/documents/hf_ben-xvi_mes_20091208_xliii-world-day-peace.html.

Biedenkopf, Katja, and Franziska Petri. "The European External Action Service and EU Climate Diplomacy: Coordinator and Supporter in Brussels and Beyond." *European Foreign Affairs Review* 26 (2021) 71–86.

Boff, Leonardo. *Il Creato in Una Carezza*. Assisi: Cittadella, 2000.

Brennan, Patrick McKinley. "Subsidiarity in the Tradition of Catholic Social Doctrine." Working Paper Series, Villanova University Charles Widger School of Law, 2012. https://digitalcommons.law.villanova.edu/cgi/viewcontent.cgi?article=1182&context=wps.

Chaplin, Jonathan. "Subsidiarity and Sphere Sovereignty: Catholic and Reformed Conceptions of the Role of the State." In *Things Old and New: Catholic Social Teaching Revisited*, edited by Francis McHugh and Samuel Natale, 175–202. Washington: University Press of America, 1993.

Chelini-Pont, Blandine. "Papal Thought on Europe and the European Union in the Twentieth Century." *Religion and Society* 37 (2009) 131–46.

Chenaux, Philippe. "Le Vatican et l'Europe (1947–1957)." *Storia delle Relazioni Internazionali* 1 (1988) 48–83.

Chomsky, Noam, and Robert Pollin. *Climate Crisis and the Global Green New Deal*. London: Verso, 2020.

Christiansen, Drew. "The Church Says 'No' to Nuclear Weapons: Pastoral and Moral Implications." *Civiltà Cattolica* (2017) 1–14.

Christiansen, Drew, and Walter Grazer. *"And God Saw That It Was Good": Catholic Theology and the Environment*. Washington: United States Catholic Conference, 1996.

Christian, William A. "Augustine on the Creation of the World." *Harvard Theological Review* 46 (1953) 1–25.

Commission of the Bishops' Conferences of the European Union. "Green Deal: Final Report of the Interfaith Youth Convention Is Now Online." Mar. 14, 2022. https://www.comece.eu/final-report-of-the-interfaith-youth-convention-is-now-online/.

Cordes, Paul Josef. "Paradigm Shift in the Social Doctrine of the Church." In *Free Markets and the Culture of Common Good*, edited by Martin Schlag and Juan Andrés Mercado, 83–92. Berlin: Springer, 2012.

European Commission. "Communication on the European Green Deal." Dec. 11, 2019. https://eur-lex.europa.eu/resource.html?uri=cellar:b828d165-1c22-11ea-8c1f-01aa75ed71a1.0002.02/DOC_1&format=PDF.

European Council. "European Green Deal." 2020. https://www.consilium.europa.eu/en/policies/green-deal/#:~:text=The%20European%20Green%20Deal%20is%20a%20package%20of%20policy%20initiatives,a%20modern%20and%20competitive%20economy.

Fergusson, David. *Creation*. Grand Rapids: Eerdmans, 2014.

Flecha, José-Roman. *Il Rispetto del Creato*. Milan: Jaca, 2001.

Follesdal, Andreas. "Competing Conceptions of Subsidiarity." In *Federalism and Subsidiarity*, edited by E. James Fleming and Jacob T. Levy, 214–30. New York: NYU Press, 2014.

———. "Subsidiarity." *Journal of Political Philosophy* 6 (1998) 190–218.

Francis. "Address of Pope Francis to the European Parliament." Nov. 25, 2014. https://www.vatican.va/content/francesco/en/speeches/2014/november/documents/papa-francesco_20141125_strasburgo-parlamento-europeo.html.

———. "General Audience." June 5, 2013. https://www.vatican.va/content/francesco/en/audiences/2013/documents/papa-francesco_20130605_udienza-generale.html.

———. *Laudate Deum.* Apostolic Exhortation, Oct. 4, 2023. https://www.vatican.va/content/francesco/en/apost_exhortations/documents/20231004-laudate-deum.html.

———. *Laudato Si'.* Encyclical, May 24, 2015. https://www.vatican.va/content/francesco/en/encyclicals/documents/papa-francesco_20150524_enciclica-laudato-si.html.

———. *Veritatis Gaudium.* Apostolic Constitution, Jan. 29, 2018. https://press.vatican.va/content/salastampa/en/bollettino/pubblico/2018/01/29/180129c.html.

Görlach, Benjamin, et al. *From Vienna to Helsinki.* Wuppertal: Institut für Klima, 1999.

Graham, Robert. *Vatican Diplomacy.* New York: Princeton University Press, 1959.

Hanson, Eric. *The Catholic Church in World Politics.* New York: Princeton University Press, 1987.

Hehir, Bryan. "John Paul II, Continuity and Change in the Social Teaching of the Church." In *Readings in Moral Theology*, edited by Charles E. Curran and Richard McCormick, 247–63. New York: Paulist, 1986.

Hertin, Julia, and Frans Berkhout. "Ecological Modernisation and EU Environmental Policy Integration." *Journal of Environmental Policy and Planning* 5 (2003) 39–56.

International Family of Catholic Social Justice Organizations. "Press Release: EU Environment Ministers Pressed to Meet Papal Challenge on Climate Change." Sept. 15, 2015. https://www.cidse.org/2015/09/15/eu-environment-ministers-pressed-to-meet-papal-challenge-on-climate-change/.

Ittekkot, Venugopalan, and Eleanor Milne. "Encyclical Letter 'Laudato Si': A Gentle but Firm Nudge from Pope Francis." *Environmental Development* 17 (2016) 1–3.

Jans, Jan H. *European Environmental Law.* Groningen: Kluwer Law International, 2000.

John Paul II. *Centesimus Annus.* Encyclical Letter, May 1, 1991. https://www.vatican.va/content/john-paul-ii/en/encyclicals/documents/hf_jp-ii_enc_01051991_centesimus-annus.html.

———. *Sollicitudo Rei Socialis.* Encyclical Letter, Dec. 30, 1987. https://www.vatican.va/content/john-paul-ii/en/encyclicals/documents/hf_jp-ii_enc_30121987_sollicitudo-rei-socialis.html.

Keating, Maryann, et al. "Benedict XVI as Social Realist in *Caritas in Veritate*." *Journal of Markets and Morality* 14 (2011) 345–58.

Krämer, Ludwig. *The Genesis of EC Environmental Principles.* Bruges: Collège d'Europe, 2003.

———. "Planning for Climate and the Environment: The EU Green Deal." *Journal for European Environmental and Planning Law* 17 (2020) 267–306.

Kratochvíl, Petr, and Tomáš Doležal. *The European Union and the Catholic Church.* Hampshire: Macmillan, 2015.

Lai, Theodore, and Cecilia Tortajada. "The Holy See and the Global Environmental Movements." *Frontiers in Communication* 6 (2021) 1–13.

Larivera, Luciano. "Pope Francis Meets European Commission President at the Vatican." Jesuit European Social Centre, June 10, 2021. https://jesc.eu/pope-francis-meets-european-commission-president-at-the-vatican/.

Lecomte, Bernard. "The Popes and the European Integration." In *The Popes and Sixty Years of European Integration*, edited by the Delegation of the European Union to the Holy See, 9–14. Vatican City: L'Osservatore Romano, 2017. https://www.eeas.europa.eu/sites/default/files/the_popes_and_sixty_years_of_european_integration.pdf.

Leuștean, Lucian. *The Ecumenical Movement and the Making of the European Community*. Oxford: Oxford University Press, 2014.

Mitchell, Donald W. "Catholic Theology of Creation: Nature's Value and Relation to Humankind." *Claritas: Journal of Dialogue and Culture* 4 (2015) 69–74.

Molnar, Thomas. *The Church, Pilgrim of Centuries*. Grand Rapids: Eerdmans, 1990.

Morss, John R. "The International Legal Status of the Vatican." *European Journal of International Law* 26 (2015) 927–46.

O'Meara, John. "Saint Augustine's Understanding of the Creation and Fall." *Maynooth Review* 10 (1984) 56–62.

Padányi, József. "Climate Change, Migration and Christian Communities." In *Budapest Report on Christian Persecution 2021*, edited by Lóránd Ujházi et al., 271–80. Vác: Mondat, 2021.

Pasture, Patrick. "Catholic and Christian Democratic Views on Europe before and after World War II." In *Christian Democracy across the Iron Curtain: Europe Redefined*, edited by Piotr H. Kosicki and Sławomir Łukasiewicz, 25–57. London: Palgrave, 2018.

Paul VI. "Ad Perpetuam Rei." *Acta Apostolicae Sedis* 56 (1964) 965–67.

———. *Gaudium et Spes*. Pastoral Constitution, Dec. 7, 1965. https://www.vatican.va/archive/hist_councils/ii_vatican_council/documents/vat-ii_const_19651207_gaudium-et-spes_en.html.

———. *Octogesima Adveniens*. Apostolic Letter, May 14, 1971. https://www.vatican.va/content/paul-vi/en/apost_letters/documents/hf_p-vi_apl_19710514_octogesima-adveniens.html.

Peters, B. Guy. "Policy Transfers between Governments: The Case of Administrative Reforms." *West European Politics* 20 (1997) 71–88.

Petkovšek, Robert. "Theology Facing the Challenges of the Modern Anthropological Crisis." *Bogoslovni Vestnik* 79 (2019) 17–31.

Pettifor, Ann. *The Case for the Green New Deal*. New York: Verso, 2019.

Prélot, Marcel. *Storia del Pensiero Politico*. Milan: Mondadori, 1975.

Pollin, Robert. "Global Green Growth for Human Development." 2016 UNDP Human Development Report Think Piece. New York: United Nations Development Programme, 2016.

Pontifical Council for Justice and Peace. *Compendium of the Social Doctrine of the Church*. May 26, 2006. https://www.vatican.va/roman_curia/pontifical_councils/justpeace/documents/rc_pc_justpeace_doc_20060526_compendio-dott-soc_en.html.

Quacquarelli, Antonio. "L'ecologia nei Riflessi del Linguaggio Simbolico dei Padri della Chiesa." *Vetera Christianorum* 28 (1991) 5–24.

Raith, Jasmin. "The 'Global Pact for the Environment'—A New Instrument to Protect the Planet?" *Journal for European Environmental and Planning Law* 15 (2018) 3–23.

San Martín, Inés. "Pope to European Youth: Make Less War, Eat Less Meat." *Crux*, July 12, 2022. https://cruxnow.com/vatican/2022/07/pope-to-european-youth-make-less-war-eat-less-meat.

Schlag, Martin. "Political Life: Peace, Freedom, and Justice in Society." In *Handbook of Catholic Social Teaching: A Guide for Christians in the World Today*, edited by Martin Schlag, 97–101. Washington, DC: Catholic University of America Press, 2017.

Schreurs, Miranda A. "The Paris Climate Agreement and the Three Largest Emitters: China, the United States, and the European Union." *Politics and Governance* 4 (2016) 219–23.

Sikora, Alicja. "European Green Deal—Legal and Financial Challenges of the Climate Change." *ERA Forum* 21 (2021) 681–97.

Strand, Vincent. "On Method, Nature and Grace in *Caritas in Veritate*." *Nova et Vetera* 15.3 (2017) 835–52.

Szabó, Máté. "Európai Környezetpolitika, Európai Civil Társadalom." European Booklets 63. Budapest: Government Strategic Analysis Centre, 2004. https://mek.oszk.hu/18600/18697/18697.pdf.

Tanzella-Nitti, Giuseppe. "Come la Religione Interpreta la Vita Biologica: La Visione del Cristianesimo su Vita Biologica e Immortalità." *Philosophical News* 11 (2015) 141–52.

———. "Creazione." In *Dizionario Interdisciplinare di Scienza e Fede*, edited by Giuseppe Tanzella-Nitti and Alberto Strumia, 300–316. Rome: Città Nuova, 2002.

Ujházi, Lóránd. "A Környezetvédelem és a Teremtésvédelem mint Találkozási pont a Katolikus Egyház és az Európai Unió Kapcsolatában. Protection of Environment and Creation as a Meeting Point between the Catholic Church and the European Union." *Európai Tükör* 25.1–2 (2022) 71–90.

Valente, Massimiliano. "La Santa Sede e l'Europa Unita, dalla Conferenza dell'Aja al Trattato di Maastricht (1948–1992)." In *Fede e Diplomazia: Le Relazioni Internazionali della Santa Sede nell'Età Contemporanea*, edited by Massimo de Leonardis, 381–407. Milan: EDUCatt, 2014.

Visioli, Matteo. "The Catholic Church Tested for Confessionalism: The Vatican II Doctrinal Principles." *Journal of Law and Religion* 33 (2018) 155–71.

Welty, Emily. "The Theological Landscape of the Nuclear Nonproliferation Treaty: The Catholic Church, the World Council of Churches and the Bomb." *Global Policy* 7 (2016) 396–404.

White, Lynn. "The Historical Roots of Our Ecologic Crisis." *Science* 155.3767 (1967) 1203–7.

Wilkinson, David. "Using the European Union's Structural and Cohesion Funds for the Protection of the Environment." *Review of European Community and International Environmental Law* 3 (1994) 119–26.

Woods, Mark. "The Nature of War and Peace: Just War Thinking, Environmental Ethics, and Environmental Justice." In *Rethinking the Just War Tradition*, edited by Michael W. Brough et al., 17–35. New York: University of New York Press, 2007.

Youngs, Richard. "Climate Change and EU Security Policy: An Unmet Challenge." Carnegie Endowment for International Peace, May 2014. http://www.jstor.com/stable/resrep12774.

Zamagni, Stefano. "Catholic Social Thought, Civil Economy and the Spirit of Capitalism." In *The True Wealth of Nations: Catholic Social Thought and Economic Life*, edited by Daniel Finn, 63–94. Oxford: Oxford University Press, 2010.

Zengarini, Lisa. "Pope Francis: A Healthy Environment Is Right of Every Human Being." Vatican News, Sept. 29, 2021. www.vaticannews.va/en/pope/news/2021-09/francis-healthy-environment-human-right.html.

9

Being, Creation, and Education

The Gift of Distinguishing What Is Real from What Is Not

ALEJANDRO SERANI MERLO

The Animal's Subjective Experience

FROM A PHENOMENOLOGICAL POINT of view, the living human being can be characterized as an "awakened animal." This metaphorical and insightful description points out the radical behavioral difference between human beings and other animals. The living human being lives "in reality" and perceives sensorial aspects of reality, but more radically, the human being apprehends "reality as reality."[1]

Jakob von Uexküll (1864–1944), the pioneer of contemporary ethological studies, was the first to emphasize that each non-human animal species in nature is able to respond to specific and fixed cues in its surrounding ambiance (*Umwelt*). In that sense, each animal is "isolated" in its own environment.[2] In keeping with the proposals of Konrad Lorenz (1903–89), each animal species reacts to a limited number of "innate trigger stimuli," which elicit specific phylogenetically acquired behaviors.[3]

However, animals are not mere automata. Their rich and plastic behavior results from the interaction of many factors: the affective and organic states of the animal, the inherited patterns of action already

---

1. Zubiri, *Inteligencia Sentiente*, 54–67.

2. Uexküll, *Ideas para una Concepción*, 37–79; Uexküll, *Mondes Animaux*, 28–37, 91–173.

3. Lorenz and Leyhausen, *Biología del Comportamiento*, 7–53.

mentioned, and other acquired behavioral responses—either through classical conditioning[4] or operant conditioned behaviors.[5]

Despite the enormous variability of complex animal behaviors, each animal is confined to its own environment—an environment to which it is phylogenetically adapted. Stimuli that do not pertain to a species' specific pattern of innately triggered responses are simply ignored by the animals' sensorial perceptual apparatus, and consequently fall out of the scope of their behavior. This is why animals are so vulnerable to any environmental change that could inadvertently interfere with the innate functional behavioral circuit of their species. In fact, minimal—even inadvertent—human interventions in some ecosystems can eventually produce massive ecological disasters.

Although animals affect their environment through their behavior, they are ignorant concerning what really goes on. We could thus compare their conscious status to sleepwalking. In fact, they seem to perceive other animals exclusively as objects, and only as much as those objects represent a benefit or risk to their well-being or survival. Results from ethological research suggest that animals do not have the self-awareness to know that they are subjects in the real world; neither do they perceive other animals as such. To them, what is referred to as "the environment" is nothing but a part of their subjective sensory experience.

From Uexküll's briefly summarized views, we can draw the conclusion that animals do not have intersubjective experiences and applying this term to the experience of animals would be a mere anthropomorphic projection. Even in groups, each animal really lives alone; this renders meaningless, for instance, the human term "loneliness" when extended to animals. These results must however be complemented with common sense observations in higher animals. Our remarks do not intend in any way to deny the rich variety of sensorial objects and affective experiences of animals. They only intend to show the difficulties that arise when we try to objectively conceive the "purely" animal consciousness as a model for understanding human perceptual experience.

---

4. Pavlov, *Fisiología y Psicología*, 21–50, 70–90.

5. Skinner, *Beyond Dignity and Freedom*; Catania, "Operant Behaviorism of B. F. Skinner."

The Living Human as an Awakened Animal

From a philosophical point of view, it is quite surprising that the characterization of inner animal experience and behavior, which emerges from contemporary ethological studies, resembles what some modern philosophers—such as Locke, Berkeley, Hume, and Kant—conceive as human sensory perception. It seems therefore that, in the paradigm of modern philosophy, the cognitive capacities of human beings were interpreted in terms of animal experience.

Modern philosophers then, depriving animal and human sensory perception of any real capacity for knowledge, as they usually do, tend to reduce human perception to a sheer subjective experience—moreover, to a subjective experience without subject. As the German philosopher Hans Jonas has well pointed out, the consequences of this misleading characterization of human perception have been the division of modern philosophers into two branches: the empiricists, leading to materialist scientism, or the idealists, leading to subjective rationalism.[6] Both of these modern tendencies have a common point: the devaluation of the cognitive capacity of sensory perception in human beings when it works in synergy with higher capacities.

In accordance with common sense, and supported by a long philosophical tradition, we can affirm that human beings, unlike non-human animals, are able to apprehend reality "as reality." For human beings, things do not just happen—they challenge us about the meaning of *what* is happening. Each of us has experienced how uncomfortable it is for humans when we don't understand what is going on.

The human sensory apparatus does not only apprehend what is harmful or safe in our surrounding perceptual space. For humans—beyond being harmful or safe, painful or pleasant, useless or useful—things simply *are* in themselves. That's why children universally ask their parents, "What is this?" As human animals, we live not merely in an environment, but in a world of things that constitutes itself as the *real* world.

Contemporary studies of human developmental psychology have provided us with interesting insights on these crucial topics, which need to be further elucidated through philosophical reflection. Unfortunately, some of the theoretical interpretations of this experimental data are usually contaminated with untenable philosophical presuppositions. I

---

6. Jonas, *Phenomenon of Life*, 127–34; Serani Merlo and Lailhacar, "Conducta Animal"; Serani Merlo, "Crítica de Hans Jonas."

consider the theory of the Swiss biologist, psychologist, and philosopher Jean Piaget as a paradigmatic example in this respect. Through methodical observations, Piaget has provided invaluable insights on children's cognitive development: for example, how they react differently to the same question at different early stages of their development.[7] When asked at an early age about the location of the name of the sun, they usually respond "in the sun." Later in their development, they affirm that the name of the sun is "in the air." Still later, they answer that the name is "in the tongue," and finally that it is "in the brain or in the mind." A realist philosopher can see in these observations an illustration of the infant's continuous growth in intellectual maturation. They start from a crude but firm affirmation of the existence of real things in the world (names are in things), then they progress to the consciousness that things are apprehended by an immaterial act (names are in the air), afterward that the fruit of the intellectual act is a concept expressed by a word (names are in the tongue), and finally that there is an intelligent subject that apprehends reality (names are in the mind).[8]

Surprisingly, from his remarkable observations, Piaget's conclusion is the opposite of what appears to be common sense or of what a reasonable psychologist or realist philosopher would affirm. In fact, in what appears to be a continuous process of maturation, Piaget sees a discontinuous development containing disconnected stages. One stage follows the other, but the previous stages are not integrated into the subsequent ones. Piaget seems to be applying a Darwinian theoretical framework to developmental psychology in which species arise one from another by mutation and chance. Piaget thinks that the first stage—which he calls naïve realism—is followed by others as equally false as the first. Eventually, the child would arrive to a mature awareness that reality consists in ideas created by the mind. A child's progression in knowledge would thus be a discontinuous transit from ingenious realism to "mature" Piagetian constructivism.

Piaget and other contemporary constructivists do not seem puzzled in any way by the inconsistencies in their theory. In fact, how can a theory of knowledge, which is supposed to describe a natural and progressive process of development, pretend that the starting point of knowledge is the generation of a delusion of the existence of a real world outside their

---

7. Piaget, *Representación del Mundo*, 61–83.
8. Piaget, *Representación Del Mundo*, 61–83.

heads? The culmination of the process would be the recognition that reality does not exist.

Of the many points that can be drawn from this kind of explanation, let us limit ourselves to presenting the two most curious ones. First, one must suppose that those theorists were well-intentioned in telling us what *really* occurs in cognitive development. How else could they pretend to affirm true notions about something, without also supposing the existence of such thing? Second, how do they explain that children are, according to them, constructing reality in their minds while also maintaining the delusion that there is a world that exists outside their heads? It is in fact surprising that children everywhere continue to believe that the world exists, even if Piaget thinks that they are not able to affirm it.

Let us then seriously evaluate these constructivist theories by examining their conclusion. According to Piaget's theory, children proceed in their cognitive development from a starting point in which they naïvely affirm the existence of a world outside their heads. The culminating point in this process is a moment in which they would become conscious of the fact that there is not a real world outside their heads, while however continuing to intuitively affirm that the outside world does exist. One wonders which is worse: to be deceived without the ability to know you are deceived, or to still be deceived, but consciously. The first situation would be like what we have described concerning animals; the second would be a sort of situation in which an animal had the possibility of being human but insisted on continuing to be an animal. The latter could be described as a kind of voluntary somnambulism.

One could compare the situation of the supposedly naïve child described by Piaget with the case of the metaphysical transcendental illusion in the sense of Kant.[9] Human beings are curious animals that consistently affirm the existence of real things outside their heads, even if they don't have any means to sustain what they affirm. Why would they insist on a delusion, even if they could have the means to be aware of it? It is as if each one of us, instead of being given a guardian angel, was given a Cartesian evil genius that constantly made us believe in a real world—even if a real world didn't *really* exist. We could continue *ad nauseam* developing the innumerable inconsistencies that derive from the philosophical, psychological, and pedagogical constructivist doctrines.

---

9. Kant, *Crítica de la Razón Pura*, 297–307.

After what we have seen, we can pose some crucial questions: What if—contrary to the constructivist theory—children are right to assume that there is a real world outside their minds, and that they are real beings in the world? What happens if, despite the obvious difficulties that we encounter to know things, we have the possibility of knowing the real world, at least in its most general and fundamental traits? What if, instead of denying the intrinsic capacity of our faculties to attain firm knowledge, we recognized their intrinsic and factual limitations?

If that is in fact the case, we must then ask ourselves how we arrived at this point—at a point where the absurd stands for the truth and the truth for absurdity. There are certainly many answers to this question to be addressed on different epistemological levels; I will focus however on only one aspect.

Sinning against the Intelligence

I suggest that we moderns have sinned against intelligence, which is perhaps one of the worst of all possible sins. Intelligence is the capacity for apprehending the real world, and human will is the capacity and power to love real things, inspiring real intelligent actions that are motivated by genuine love. To deprive intelligence from its very nature of attaining the real, and to deny against all evidence any capacity to know by our sensory perceptual faculties, equates to transforming the experience of reality into delirium. It is literally the world upside-down. I am firmly convinced that the sole remedy for this absurdity is to abandon all these psychological, pedagogical, and philosophical ideas and humbly try to follow the way of little children.

I sustain that one of the first, greatest, and most transcendental acquisitions of children in their development is the ability to make the distinction between what is real and what is not. The language of children distinguishes quite early on what is real from what is fake, what is true from what is false, what is genuine from what is deceptive. But the fact that human language acquires this distinction very early on, does not imply that every child at any time can always distinguish what is real from what is not. If children can do it sometimes—and they learn that it is not always easy—then it is because they are endowed by nature with the capacity of doing it. We call that capacity "intelligence." Intelligence—etymologically: "to read in the interior of things"—is thus the capacity to read what things are. It is thus a genuine and surprising human capacity that opens the living human being to the world of real things. But although in principle intelligence does recognize reality as such, that is not, in concrete instances, always the case.

In addition to affirming that the main acquisition in early childhood is the awakening of intelligence, I am also convinced that human education of every kind can in fact be characterized as "supporting child realism." Child education—and human education in general—is nothing but promoting, developing, sustaining, enforcing, and enriching intelligence in order to pursue a truly human life in the real world. This includes all of the activities that immediately derive from these goals.

Intelligent cognitive performance is not a spontaneous acquisition; it takes time and effort. In fact, the acquisition of this capacity takes a lifetime, and even an entire life is not enough. This is exactly what intelligence is for: it has the hard task of teaching us what is real from what is not; what kind of reality this is, in contrast to others; how much reality is contained in nature; how much reality is contained in practical things; how much reality is contained in ethics, politics, poetry, architecture, and religion. Intelligence must enlighten our life by indicating what nature really is, what people really are, and who God really is—including all the real, practical consequences therefrom.

What Piaget sees very early in the lives of children, and what he calls "naïve realism," is in fact the very first awakening of humanity. It is certainly an incipient, immature, imperfect realism, but not at all *naïf*. The spontaneous impulse of the child to affirm the connatural affinity of reality and thought is not the fruit of animistic beliefs or blind causal evolutionary processes. Instead, the strong and early realistic instinct of children is the first announcement of the most impressive cognitive capacity that a human being can have: plain natural intelligence.

Intelligence and the Gift of Creation

The gift of creation is fundamentally and radically the gift of being, and the reception of being with gratitude supposes the apprehension of being as good. Aquinas sustained the profound metaphysical identity and convertibility of being, goodness, truth, alterity, and unity.[10] All these transcendental notions of being are the different "faces," "blossoms," or

---

10. Aquinas, *Quaestiones Disputatae de Veritate*, q. 1, a. 1.

"fruits" of being, in our mind. This identity and convertibility are difficult to understand for our modern minds. However, it seems as if modernity has discovered the immensity of evil, falsehood, ugliness, and disunity—at least, this seems to be the predominant meaning of the word "reality" in contemporary literature, art, cinema, ethics, and politics.

If, as it seems, we have been rescued from the ingenuity of realism, we have also been rescued from the ingenuity of affirming the reality of goodness, being, truth, beauty, and unity. Human beings have been disenchanted, and disenchantment has dissolved our candid ingenuity. The disappearance of ingenuity in turn has led to permanent suspicion.[11] It is as if one could say, "Modern realism created the modern world, and modernity saw that all was evil." But evil, as St. Augustine saw, has no positive being in itself.[12] We could not then be confident of truth because what really exists is falsehood; we could not praise beauty because what really exists is ugliness; we could not desire unity because what exists is disunity. Paradoxically, modern cultural tendencies are the confirmation by contrast of the metaphysical validity of the convertibility of being. In fact, it seems that the fall of the angel of being has also dragged down in its descent the angels of goodness, truth, beauty, and unity.

The gift of creation is then principally the gift of being, but thereby also the gift of goodness, the gift of truth, the gift of beauty, and the gift of unity. If we are incapable of receiving in our minds and hearts the gift of reality, we will necessarily be deprived of the other transcendental gifts. If reality is nothing but a naïve belief, a delusion, or a collective delirium, what can we expect from the rest of the transcendentals of being?

And reality for us creatures—as we are familiar with from Aquinas—is contingent. Creatural reality is received, and it is received as a gift. We can refer to "given reality" in a very strict sense. What we admire, what we receive, what we use, what we pray for, is given reality proceeding from a real giver. Given reality is the participation of real being in the source of being.

Even if the Western philosophical tradition acknowledges Greek philosophers for their metaphysical discovery of being, God was never explicitly invoked in ancient Greece as the source of the gift of being. According to the Judeo-Christian scriptures, Moses asked God:

---

11. See Ricoeur, *Freud and Philosophy*, 33, 35.
12. Augustine, *De Natura Boni*, §4.

> "If I come to the people of Israel and say to them, 'The God of your fathers has sent me to you,' and they ask me, 'What is his name?' what shall I say to them?" God said to Moses, "I AM WHO I AM." And he said, "Say this to the people of Israel, 'I AM has sent me to you.'"[13]

Theologically and metaphysically understood, this means that Being in itself (*Ipsum Esse Subsistens*) does not receive from another what he himself gives. "God is subsisting being itself."[14] God does not receive his being, he *is* Being by itself. In fact, the primary gift endowed by the Creator is "being itself."

We exist through a participation in being that comes from God. This participation in being is freely given in an act of pure love—not by necessity, as some Gnostic or pantheist doctrines claim.

Conclusion

Biological and animal life are for us living humans the most basic gifts in the realm of creation; however, intelligence and free will are the most precious ones. Moreover, in absolute terms, the highest gifts received by humanity are supernatural grace, theological virtues, and the spiritual gifts that give us the unbelievable possibility of sharing in the intimate trinitarian life of God.

Intelligence allows us to contemplate the immensity of the cosmos and to praise the Great Giver for it. Each time we acquire true knowledge—even concerning the tiniest issue—it expands in us the universe we are given and that we receive through our intelligence. Moreover, since the reality of things has been created and given by love for us, the reception of this gift opens new possibilities for a grateful and loving dialogue with God.

Both natural and supernatural gifts induce wonder over the fact that there is "something rather than nothing." Based on this, the realm of formal education should be radically reformulated by strictly following the entire range of possibilities opened up by each of the gifts of nature and spirit. Formal educational processes for children should closely align with the birth and development of each of their senses, feelings, and movements: sensation, imagination, memory, perceptual experience, love and

13. Exod 3:13–14.
14. Aquinas, *Summa Theologiae*, I, q. 4, a. 2.

hate, pleasure and pain, joy and sadness, anger and calmness, hope and discouragement, walking, running, dancing, coordination, equilibrium, and so on. Intellectual education should follow the reinforcement of the natural operations of intuition, judgment, and reasoning, and afterward, the progressive culture of the intellectual and moral virtues. Scientific and artistic virtues in the realm of theoretical and practical intelligence, and the moral virtues of temperance, fortitude, prudence, and justice, must be the guiding criteria by which formal education should be reorganized. In doing so, we could avoid rigidity and monotony, and above all, we must respect the individual nature of each child.

I am really convinced that, in times of confusion and painful deception, we must leave aside the rationalistic, pragmatic, and technocratic models of formal education predominantly installed in the Western world. The critical situation of modern Western civilization offers an outstanding opportunity for generating educational programs that could be consistent with the confirmation and development of the natural and supernatural gifts of creation.

Bibliography

Augustine. *De Natura Boni contra Manichaeos Liber Unus.* https://www.augustinus.it/latino/natura_bene/index.htm.
Aquinas, Thomas. *Quaestiones Disputatae de Veritate.* Leonine Edition text, edited by The Aquinas Institute. https://aquinas.cc/la/en/~QDeVer.Q1.A1.
———. *Summa Theologiae.* Leonine Edition text, transcribed and revised by The Aquinas Institute. https://aquinas.cc/la/en/~ST.I.Q4.A2.
Catania, A. Charles. "The Operant Behaviorism of B. F. Skinner." In *The Behavioral and Brain Sciences* 7.4 (1984) 473–75.
Jonas, Hans. *The Phenomenon of Life: Toward a Biological Philosophy.* Chicago: The University of Chicago Press, 1966.
Kant, Immanuel. *Crítica de la Razón Pura.* Mexico: Taurus, 2010.
Lorenz, Konrad, and Paul Leyhausen. *Biología del Comportamiento: Raíces Instintivas de la Agresión, el Miedo y la Libertad.* Mexico: Siglo XXI, 1971.
Pavlov, Ivan. *Fisiología y Psicología.* Madrid: Alianza, 1968.
Piaget, Jean. *La Representación del Mundo en el Niño.* Madrid: Ediciones Morata, 1997.
Ricoeur, Paul. *Freud and Philosophy: An Essay on Interpretation.* Translated by Denis Savage. New Haven: Yale University Press, 2008.
Serani Merlo, Alejandro. "La Crítica de Hans Jonas al Monismo Materialista." In *Filosofía de la Mente y Psicología: Enfoques Interdisciplinarios,* edited by Pablo López-Silva and Francisco Osorio, 87–98. Santiago de Chile: UAH/Ediciones, 2020.
Serani Merlo, Alejandro, and Yvan Lailhacar. "La Conducta Animal y lo Transanimal en el Hombre en la Biología Filosófica de Hans Jonas." *Intus Legere Filosofía* 8.2 (2014) 9–22.

Skinner, Burrhus Frederic. *Beyond Dignity and Freedom*. Indianapolis: Hackett, 2002.
Uexküll, Jakob von. *Ideas para una Concepción Biológica del Mundo*. Madrid: Calpe, 1922.
———. *Mondes Animaux et Monde Humain*. Paris: Éditions Denoël, 1965.
Zubiri, Xavier. *Inteligencia Sentiente*. Madrid: Alianza y Sociedad de Estudios y Publicaciones, 1980.

10

A Field Hospital for Catholic Bioethics

The Conciliar Methodology of *Laudato Si'* and *Fratelli Tutti*

M. THERESE LYSAUGHT

"'*LAUDATO SI', MI SIGNORE*'—'PRAISE *be to you, my Lord!*'"[1] So opens Pope Francis's resplendent encyclical on the gift of creation and the care for our common home, *Laudato Si'*. And so likewise it ends: "Praise be to you! Amen!"[2]

Some might write off these phrases as rhetorical flourishes. I would suggest that they are two of the most important sentences in the document. With elegant simplicity, they provide a luminous hermeneutical frame crucial for interpreting the content that lies between them. As importantly, as these words resound—"'*Laudato si', mi signore*'—'*Praise be to you, my Lord!*'"—they ripple through the disciplines of Catholic theology, inviting us to return to the heart of the Christian life (which is, ineluctably, worship) and, in so doing, to begin to hear in a new way the harmonics of a deeply conciliar methodology.

In this chapter, I have been asked to reflect on *Laudato Si'* and the gift of creation as it is manifested in Catholic bioethics. When I embarked on this task, I presumed that I would review and expand on the scholarly literature on *Laudato Si'* and bioethics. To my surprise, seven years after its promulgation, little has been written on this topic, even though environmental issues lay at the very founding of the field of bioethics.[3] Less

---

1. Francis, *Laudato Si'*, §1, emphasis in original.
2. Francis, *Laudato Si'*, §246.
3. My literature search surfaced three essays on *Laudato Si'* and Catholic bioethics: Hamel, "Call to Conversion"; Austriaco, "Bioethics in *Laudato Si'*"; and Labrecque,

surprising is Nicanor Austriaco's reflection, "Bioethics in *Laudato Si'*: The Ecological Law as a Moral Principle." Here Austriaco suggests that, in the encyclical, "Francis proposes that the natural moral law can be reimagined as an ecological *moral law*."[4] This is an odd claim insofar as reference to law in *Laudato Si'* is minimal.[5] He also focuses almost exclusively on the encyclical's implications for the standard, limited focus of Catholic bioethical issues: abortion, contraception, and genetically modified organisms.[6] This is also (at best) odd, given Pope Francis's specific critiques of Catholic moral theology, as we will see further below.[7]

Faced with this lacuna, one must ask: Why have Catholic bioethicists not turned to *Laudato Si'* as a source for informing the field as they have with other papal encyclicals on bioethical issues? Pope Francis specifically states that *Laudato Si'* is a work of moral theology, intentionally "added to the body of the Church's social teaching."[8] The encyclical explicitly focuses on key themes in Catholic bioethics—science, religion, and ethics; technology and the technocratic paradigm; nature; health and illness; the human person, human dignity, and human flourishing; virtues; abortion; genetics; the elderly; children; and more. And, as noted earlier, ecology and environmental questions have long been understood as foundational to the field of bioethics.

"Catholic Bioethics." Hamel notes that Van Renesselaer Potter—who is considered to be the founding figure of bioethics—"intended 'bioethics' to refer to 'the questions about humankind's relationship with its environment, and the survival of the human species in the face of environmental threats, such as pollution, overpopulation, and nuclear war'" (Hamel, "Call to Conversion," 236–37, citing Brody, *Future of Bioethics*, 178). See also Labrecque, "Catholic Bioethics," 669.

4. Austriaco, "Bioethics in *Laudato Si'*," 657, emphasis added.

5. Of the twenty references to law in *Laudato Si'*, only four refer to the natural or moral law (§§68–69, 155). The remaining citations refer to the laws of the Sabbath or Jubilee as economic alternatives, or to civil law.

6. While genetics is mentioned frequently in *Laudato Si'*, abortion is mentioned only once and contraception not at all. Thus, this is a very odd—and therefore telling—reading of the encyclical.

7. *Evangelium Vitae* forwards the same narrow focus. Even though it reprises *Gaudium et Spes* §26 and its long list of actions opposed to life in paragraph 3, in the end, *Evangelium Vitae* only focuses on the standard, narrow set of issues: abortion, which it mentions seventy-eight times (§§8, 11, 13, 14, 16, 17, 18, 19, 27, 54, 57, 58–62, 68–74, 81, 89, 91); euthanasia, with thirty-eight references (§§8, 11, 15, 18, 19, 20, 27, 57, 63–67, 68–74, 81, 89); contraception (§§13, 16, 17, 23, 91), with nods to infanticide, the death penalty, war, genocide, and artificial reproduction. Shifting the discourse from moral to legal evaluations, abortion and euthanasia are labeled as "crimes against life" (§§11, 18).

8. Francis, *Laudato Si'*, §15.

Undoubtedly, the lacuna is rooted in large part in the firewall that is adamantly maintained between much of Catholic bioethics and what is considered to be a separate theological field: Catholic social doctrine.[9] Thus, *Laudato Si'*, with its focus on putatively "social" issues such as ecology, economics, and social policy, holds little interest for traditional Catholic bioethicists. But I would also suggest that it has another, more powerful root: the tenacious grip of a manualist moral framework. Over the past sixty years, the neo-Scholasticism underlying the manualist tradition has largely been critiqued by philosophically and theologically robust methodologies across the Catholic theological disciplines. But Catholic bioethics has largely resisted the call of *Optatam Totius* for the renewal of moral theology.[10] Adherence to this framework accounts, at least in part, for Austriaco's idiosyncratic reading of the encyclical.

What if we were to read *Laudato Si'* as an encyclical on bioethics? To do so, as Austriaco notes, finds Pope Francis squarely in continuity with his predecessors on key issues. But we also find something more profound: instead of manualist Scholasticism, we find a powerful conciliar *theological* vision that has transformative implications for moral theology and Catholic bioethics.[11] To make this argument, in the following, I read *Laudato Si'* (along with *Fratelli Tutti*) alongside two encyclicals considered central for Catholic bioethics: *Humanae Vitae* and *Evangelium Vitae*. In doing so, one sees a gradual evolution: from an understandably manualist moral framework in *Humanae Vitae*, that continues in *Evangelium Vitae*, though now mixed with conciliar insights; the latter of which come into fuller expression and proper balance in *Laudato Si'/Fratelli Tutti*.[12]

---

9. For an analysis of this issue, see Lysaught and McCarthy, "Social Praxis"; Lysaught and McCarthy, *Catholic Bioethics and Social Justice*.

10. Paul VI, *Optatam Totius*, §16.

11. Since 2013, it has been commonplace for Pope Francis's detractors to characterize his work as "pastoral," with the not-always-subtle claim (sometimes implicit, sometimes explicit) that, unlike his predecessor popes, he is neither an intellectual nor a theologian. Debunking this myth is the aim of Massimo Borghesi's important book *The Mind of Pope Francis*. For a catalog of Francis's detractors, see Borghesi, *Mind of Pope Francis*, xv–xxx. Borghesi drills down into the genesis of these critiques in his equally important *Catholic Discordance*. This putative critique further supports the argument offered in this chapter, given the nominalist genesis of the problematic split between "theology" and "pastoral application," as detailed in Pinckaers, *Sources of Christian Ethics*, 257.

12. In this chapter, I consider *Laudato Si'* and *Fratelli Tutti* together. The roots of *Fratelli Tutti* are evident in *Laudato Si'*. While the phrase "social friendship" does not appear in *Laudato Si'*, the concept is integrated throughout, from frequent use of the term "fraternity" (§§11, 70, 82, 92, 201, 221), related concepts such as civic friendship

As a thorough-going analysis of these three documents is beyond the scope of this chapter, to make this comparison I focus on two theological questions: Who is God in each document? And who, correspondingly, is the human person? The answers to these questions reveal that *Humanae Vitae* and *Evangelium Vitae* continue to be shaped by a neo-Scholastic understanding of God, so aptly described by Servais Pinckaers, with correlative accounts of anthropology, agency, and ethics. In contrast, at the heart of *Laudato Si'* stands a conciliar vision of God—the ceaselessly self-giving transcendent God who, in love and mercy, endlessly comes astonishingly near to us in creation and Christ. This shift in the operative theology of God—from the lawgiver who judges and condemns to the Samaritan who perpetually reaches out to us in love, who continually draws near to us in our woundedness, who always seeks to encounter us in redemptive mercy—entails powerful and intertwined implications for moral agency and what it means to *imago Dei*. These implications are captured in the central figures of *Evangelium Vitae* and *Laudato Si'/Fratelli Tutti*: Cain and St. Francis of Assisi.[13] I close by identifying five implications of *Laudato Si'* for Catholic bioethics.

---

and social love (e.g., §§142 and 228–31), and the frequent reference to creation as our "Sister" and those in our communities as "brothers and sisters." Further, in advancing the notion of integral *ecology*, Pope Francis repeatedly points to the connection between the demise of the environment and of human fraternity, e.g.: "The human environment and the natural environment deteriorate together; we cannot adequately combat environmental degradation unless we attend to causes related to human and social degradation" (Francis, *Laudato Si'*, §48; cf. §§6, 49, 51, 61, 93, 119, 122, 137, 139, 141, 142, 145, 148, 156). These documents also have a parallel structure. In *Laudato Si'*, the one left battered by the side of the road is creation (§§17–61 and §§75–96); in *Fratelli Tutti*, it is humanity, both poor and rich (§§9–53). But this brokenness is not just a spiritual condition. *Fratelli Tutti* makes clear that large swathes of humanity have been materially robbed, abused, abandoned, and discarded. In *Fratelli Tutti*, it is the fraternal love of the Good Samaritan that can begin to remedy this brokenness through the practice of social friendship (*à la* St. Francis). Likewise, *Laudato Si'* details how God's grace through human action can begin to remedy these ills and create a new future through a practice of social friendship with creation, as witnessed by St. Francis.

13. As I will argue in this chapter, St. Francis serves as an icon for Pope Francis's theology and anthropology, but equally for his larger theological project. In addition to his witness regarding creation and social friendship, St. Francis also provides an icon for Pope Francis's emphases on dialogue, peace, interfaith engagement, economic critique, and rebuilding the church itself. Pope Francis notes, importantly, that St. Francis is a person "much loved [even by] non-Christians" (Francis, *Laudato Si'*, §10), thereby providing a different and more deeply theological starting point than natural law for finding common ground with people of good will.

The Tentacles of Nominalist Moral Theology

Since the opening of his papacy, Pope Francis has had stark words for the field of Catholic moral theology. Key concerns were laid out in his September 2013 interview with Fr. Anthony Spadaro. Here, he lamented an undue focus on "small-minded rules," an excessively narrow and decontextualized focus on "issues related to abortion, gay marriage, and the use of contraceptive methods"—issues at the heart of Catholic bioethics.[14] He calls out a legalist, restorationist "obsess[ion] with the transmission of a disjointed multitude of doctrines to be imposed insistently," an inability to prioritize the essential truths of the Christian *kerygma*, a search for "disciplinarian solutions [and an] exaggerated doctrinal 'security'" rooted in "a past that no longer exists."[15] He expressed concern that under such a regime, "faith becomes an ideology among other ideologies."[16]

Pulling no punches, Pope Francis identifies the theological problem at the heart of our current struggles—the perennial plague combatted since Augustine and Aquinas: a subtle, shape-shifting Gnosticism:

> This worldliness can be fuelled in two deeply interrelated ways. One is the attraction of gnosticism, a purely subjective faith whose only interest is a certain experience or a set of ideas and bits of information which are meant to console and enlighten, but which ultimately keep one imprisoned in his or her own thoughts and feelings. The other is the self-absorbed promethean neopelagianism of those who ultimately trust only in their own powers and feel superior to others because they observe certain rules or remain intransigently faithful to a particular Catholic style from the past. A supposed soundness of doctrine or discipline leads instead to a narcissistic and authoritarian elitism, whereby instead of evangelizing, one analyzes and classifies others, and instead of opening the door to grace, one exhausts his or her energies in inspecting and verifying. In neither case

---

14. Spadaro, "Interview with Pope Francis."

15. Spadaro, "Interview with Pope Francis." Pope Francis continues these critiques in *Evangelii Gaudium*, §§35, 45, 49, and 83, and *Gaudete et Exsultate* (2018).

16. Spadaro, "Interview with Pope Francis." Elsewhere he expands on these points: "With the holy intent of communicating the truth about God and humanity, we sometimes give them a false god or a human ideal which is not really Christian. In this way, we hold fast to a formulation while failing to convey its substance. This is the greatest danger. Let us never forget that 'the expression of truth can take different forms. The renewal of these forms of expression becomes necessary for the sake of transmitting to the people of today the Gospel message in its unchanging meaning'" (Francis, *Evangelii Gaudium*, §41).

is one really concerned about Jesus Christ or others. These are manifestations of an anthropocentric immanentism. It is impossible to think that a genuine evangelizing thrust could emerge from these adulterated forms of Christianity.[17]

While these deformations of moral theology certainly reflect the influence of Gnosticism and new forms of modernism, they also echo Servais Pinckaers's critique of the distortions introduced into theology—and therefore, moral theology—by nominalism.[18] As Pinckaers notes, William of Ockham's fourteenth-century interventions shattered and atomized the multifaceted set of unities that shaped the Thomistic worldview, what we might call a polyhedric theological synthesis.[19] Most significantly, Ockham's foundational move—the reconceptualization of freedom—introduced a profound mutation into the understanding of God. As Pinckaers states:

> [Ockham's] thought was dominated by the idea of divine omnipotence, which enabled him to carry his idea of freedom to an absolute degree. For him, the divine will was totally free; it governed moral law itself and all the laws of creation. What God willed was necessarily just and good precisely because he willed it. Law, and all moral value or qualification, flowed from this will.[20]

Thus, at the heart of Ockham's conception of God was power—God's power to Will, to command, to establish the Law, even capriciously.

As defining attributes of God, these could not help but redefine the *imago Dei* as well. But they did so in a contorted manner—the essence of the human person was now, likewise, will and power but only as an extrinsic reflection; the intrinsic, participative connection between God and humanity now, like all other realities, had been severed:

---

17. Francis, *Evangelii Gaudium*, §94.

18. Nominalism is a philosophical theory forwarded most notably by William of Ockham that, at its root, denied the existence of metaphysical universals, holding that only particular, concrete individuals exist. This, effectively, severed necessary connections and relations between entities—God, people, creation. This had significant implications for epistemology, science, theology, ethics, political theory, and more. See Spade and Panaccio, "William of Ockham."

19. According to Pinckaers, "With Ockham, freedom, by means of the claim to radical autonomy that defines it, was separated from all that was foreign to it: reason, sensibility, natural inclinations, and all external factors. Further separations followed: freedom was separated from nature, law, and grace; moral doctrine from mysticism; reason from faith; the individual from society" (Pinckaers, *Sources of Christian Ethics*, 242).

20. Pinckaers, *Sources of Christian Ethics*, 246.

> Thus, divine and human freedom were conceived as two absolutes, but with this difference: God was omnipotent in regard to his creatures and could, consequently, impose his will upon us. Having removed from both divine and human wills all dependence upon their respective natures, Ockham could no longer find any links between man and God as with other freedoms, except those issuing from the divine will, acting with the force of obligation.[21]

Moral agency, as a result, became completely reshaped; no longer a framework of happiness and virtues recursively generated by and ordered to charity, it shifted almost entirely to a framework of law and obligation, of obedience and judgment. For Pinckaers:

> Law and obligation thus held the central position in Ockham's moral theory; they became its inmost core. Obligation was for [Ockham] the very essence of morality.... Moral obligation was determined and refined by law. Law therefore confronted human freedom in the form of obligations issuing from the divine will and, to some extent, assumed the role of this will. First came the divine law, communicated to us through revelation in the Bible, particularly the Decalogue and the evangelical precepts.... Natural law was no longer based, for [Ockham], on human nature and its inclinations, which reason could reveal. It consisted rather in the authority of right reason presenting directly to the human will the orders and obligations that emanated from the divine will, without there being any need whatsoever to justify them, since the justification of the law could be found only in the divine will itself.[22]

Pinckaers goes on to persuasively describe how thoroughly Ockham's vision became the overriding framework for the manualist tradition that emerged in the seventeenth century and that continued to shape moral theology up until the Council. It is with the remnants of this nominalist methodology that Pope Francis rightly takes issue. And one area where such remnants doggedly persist is in the field of Catholic bioethics.

---

21. Pinckaers, *Sources of Christian Ethics*, 248.
22. Pinckaers, *Sources of Christian Ethics*, 248–49.

Lawgiver or Good Samaritan?

Humanae Vitae is, admittedly, a short document. Promulgated shortly after the close of the Council in 1968, it is not surprising that it reflects a strongly manualist theology of God. Here God is the God described by Pinckaers—the largely voluntarist God of the post-Scholastic period. God is repeatedly affirmed as Creator;[23] except for one reference to God as love,[24] *every other mention* of God refers to God's will or to God as the one who established the law by designing, planning, and ordering nature.[25] Thus, we hear that "the natural law, too, declares the will of God,"[26] that "the objective moral order . . . was established by God,"[27] that in his "loving design,"[28] "God has wisely ordered laws of nature,"[29] that "the teaching of the Church regarding the proper regulation of birth is a promulgation of the law of God Himself."[30]

God here is a distant lawgiver—one that could be mistaken for the Deist god, but for the possibility of the help of grace through the sacraments, as we will see below. Apart from the ongoing involvement in the creation of new human lives, God's work seems largely confined to the past. Notably absent is a robust account of Christ, who here appears almost exclusively to affirm the magisterium's doctrinal authority[31] and as a model for marriage per Ephesians.[32]

In *Evangelium Vitae*, three decades later, God inches closer. Here we begin to move past a strictly manualist theology to a conciliar vision of a God whose intrinsic, participatory relation to humanity is affirmed. God is affirmed as the One whose life we are called to share, who has loved us in Christ.[33] Humanity, we hear, is a "manifestation of God in the world," "the glory of God," "a reflection of God himself," "the summit

---

23. Paul VI, *Humanae Vitae*, §§1, 8, 10, 13, 16, and 25.
24. Paul VI, *Humanae Vitae*, §8.
25. Paul VI, *Humanae Vitae*, §§8, 11, 13, 19, 30.
26. Paul VI, *Humanae Vitae*, §4.
27. Paul VI, *Humanae Vitae*, §10.
28. Paul VI, *Humanae Vitae*, §§8, 14.
29. Paul VI, *Humanae Vitae*, §11.
30. Paul VI, *Humanae Vitae*, §20.
31. Paul VI, *Humanae Vitae*, §§4, 6.
32. Paul VI, *Humanae Vitae*, §§8, 25.
33. John Paul II, *Evangelium Vitae*, §§1, 34 and 2–3, 28, 31.

of God's creative activity."[34] Each person is "precious" in God's eyes; all who are threatened or diminished learn of God's concern for them.[35] Yet the primary point, it seems, where God and humanity meet in "loving and fatherly providence" is in procreation,[36] insofar as unborn children are singled out as "the personal objects of God's loving and fatherly providence."[37]

Evangelium Vitae also offers a richer Christology. The encyclical lifts up Jesus's outreach to the poor, sick, and suffering[38] and his kenotic offering in his Incarnation and the cross.[39] But subtly, Christ's mission—and in fact the Gospel itself—becomes narrowed to a focus on life. The document steadily thrums a litany of links between Jesus and life. Summing these up, it notes:

> To proclaim Jesus is itself to proclaim life. For Jesus is "the word of life" (1 Jn 1:1). In him "life was made manifest" (1 Jn 1:2); he himself is "the eternal life which was with the Father and was made manifest to us" (1 Jn 1:2). By the gift of the Spirit, this same life has been bestowed on us. It is in being destined to life in its fullness, to "eternal life," that every person's earthly life acquires its full meaning.[40]

While concretely, the document focuses on protecting human life temporally, the christological focus is largely on eternal life.[41]

Yet despite these affirmations, many sections of *Evangelium Vitae* continue to convey a profound sense of humanity's distance from God.[42] The controlling image of God's engagement with humanity is Cain, who surfaces repeatedly throughout the document. Again, God here is the voluntarist God of neo-Scholasticism, God whose Will is inscrutable and, perhaps, capricious.[43] God comes close to Cain, but in this proximity, he

---

34. John Paul II, *Evangelium Vitae*, §§34, 35.
35. John Paul II, *Evangelium Vitae*, §32.
36. John Paul II, *Evangelium Vitae*, §§43, 44, 92.
37. John Paul II, *Evangelium Vitae*, §61.
38. John Paul II, *Evangelium Vitae*, §§32, 33, 47.
39. John Paul II, *Evangelium Vitae*, §§33, 47, 50–51.
40. John Paul II, *Evangelium Vitae*, §80; see also §29.
41. John Paul II, *Evangelium Vitae*, §§1, 37–38.
42. John Paul II, *Evangelium Vitae*, §37.
43. John Paul II, *Evangelium Vitae*, §8. As the encyclical notes, the text of Genesis does not give a reason why God preferred Abel's sacrifice to that of Cain.

almost exclusively admonishes, avenges, curses, punishes, and judges.[44] We hear that because of sin, creation has become "a place of scarcity, loneliness and separation from God";[45] we live in a moment when "the sense of God [has been] lost," "eclipse[d]," a time where "the systematic violation of the moral law [has produced] a kind of progressive darkening of the capacity to discern God's living and saving presence."[46] Thus, God remains a God of law and commandment,[47] of will,[48] who has designed and planned,[49] and who "is always merciful even when he punishes."[50] Significantly, one of the most extensive and recurring christological foci in the document pertains to the commandments, particularly the commandment "You shall not kill."[51]

With *Laudato Si'* and *Fratelli Tutti*, this manualist theology is finally left behind. Here, one theme rings clear: the ever-transcendent God is startlingly close to us. No longer is creation bereft of God; *Laudato Si'* sings creation as a locus of God's presence.[52] Not only does "the universe unfold[] in God, who fills it completely,"[53] but in creation, God actively and intentionally *encounters us*. Indeed, "'the divine and the human meet in the slightest detail in the seamless garment of God's creation,'" no longer simply in procreation but in every moment and every space, including "'in *the last speck of dust* of our planet.'"[54] But even more, via "the Spirit of life [that] dwells in every living creature [God] calls us to enter into relationship with him."[55] By contemplating creation, we can "discover in each thing a teaching which God wishes to hand on to us since, 'for the believer, to contemplate creation is to hear a message, to listen to a paradoxical and silent voice.'"[56] Even further, in creation God

---

44. John Paul II, *Evangelium Vitae*, §§8–9, 21, 53, 74.

45. John Paul II, *Evangelium Vitae*, §9.

46. John Paul II, *Evangelium Vitae*, §§21–24.

47. John Paul II, *Evangelium Vitae*, §§13, 28, 38, 41, 48, 49, 52, 54, 55, 57, 61, 62, 65, 72, 74, 75.

48. John Paul II, *Evangelium Vitae*, §25.

49. John Paul II, *Evangelium Vitae*, §§22, 25, 36, 44, 52, 56, 67.

50. John Paul II, *Evangelium Vitae*, §9.

51. Exod 20:13. See John Paul II, *Evangelium Vitae*, §§22, 25, 36, 44, 52, 56, 67.

52. Francis, *Laudato Si'*, §88.

53. Francis, *Laudato Si'*, §233.

54. Francis, *Laudato Si'*, §9, emphasis added.

55. Francis, *Laudato Si'*, §88.

56. Francis, *Laudato Si'*, §85; see also §§11, 233: "Hence, there is a mystical meaning to be found in a leaf, in a mountain trail, in a dewdrop, in a poor person's face" (Francis,

comes *so* close so as to love us *tangibly*: "The entire material universe," we hear, "speaks of God's love, his *boundless* affection for us. Soil, water, mountains: everything is, as it were, a caress of God."[57] Indeed, every creature "is the object of the Father's tenderness ... Even the fleeting life of the least of beings is the object of his love, and in its *few seconds* of existence, God enfolds it with affection."[58]

Thus, in *Laudato Si'*, God's heart, open to us and all of creation, constantly reaches out, calls us, ceaselessly offers the gift of the divine self, the divine word, and divine love.[59] Yet, Pope Francis rightly notes, "this call to love could be misunderstood" if not inextricably tied to the person and work of Jesus Christ.[60] Thus, where *Laudato Si'* details the ways that God reaches out to us via creation, in *Fratelli Tutti* we find this same gratuitous, open, merciful God reaching out to us in the figure of the Good Samaritan. The Samaritan, of course, for both Luke and *Fratelli Tutti* is Jesus himself, who as God's Word incarnate "had an open heart,"[61] but was nonetheless "despised and rejected by men."[62] In the christoform Samaritan, God comes close and encounters us again, this time not simply in our createdness, but in our woundedness. As in creation, in the Samaritan God compassionately reaches out to us, gratuitously and tenderly, with extraordinary affection, to touch, caress, and heal our wounded selves.

There is sin in this parable—the personal and structural sin of the robbers who left the man wounded. And there is law—the laws the

---

Laudato Si', §233). And in §221, where Pope Francis speaks of "the awareness that each creature reflects something of God and has a message to convey to us, and the security that Christ has taken unto himself this material world and now, risen, is intimately present to each being, surrounding it with his affection and penetrating it with his light" (Francis, *Laudato Si'*, §221).

57. Francis, *Laudato Si'*, §84.

58. Francis, *Laudato Si'*, §77. To be clear, Pope Francis is not advancing a version of pantheism or panentheism. Rather, the vision here is a sacramental one, where the materiality of each particular aspect of creation can mediate God's encounter: "God is intimately present to each being, without impinging on the autonomy of his creature" (Francis, *Laudato Si'*, §80). This presence can be perceived through eyes shaped by faith per *Lumen Fidei*.

59. As he notes, creation—itself an order of love (Francis, *Laudato Si'*, §77)—"can only be understood as a gift from the outstretched hand of the Father of all, and as a reality illuminated by the love which calls us together into universal communion" (Francis, *Laudato Si'*, §76).

60. Francis, *Fratelli Tutti*, §62.

61. Francis, *Fratelli Tutti*, §84.

62. Isa 53:3.

Samaritan (God) violates in order to come close to the wounded man (us).[63] But we are far afield from the nominalist God of the manualist tradition. Rather than obligation and imperative, in *Laudato Si'* and *Fratelli Tutti* God extends an invitation: to "Go and do likewise";[64] namely, to love the neighbor—the neighbor who is, first, this *God* with a heart open to the world who comes near to *each* of us in compassionate mercy.

Cain or St. Francis?

Turning to the theology of the human person and human agency, *Humanae Vitae* opens on a promising note. In its very first line, it affirms that in the profound work of the transmission of human life, married couples "collaborate freely and responsibly with God the Creator."[65] Indeed, marriage almost glimmers with the inner dynamism of the Trinity insofar as

> husband and wife, through that mutual gift of themselves, which is specific and exclusive to them alone, develop that union of two persons in which they perfect one another, cooperating with God in the generation and rearing of new lives. The marriage of those who have been baptized is, in addition, invested with the dignity of a sacramental sign of grace, for it represents the union of Christ and His Church.[66]

---

63. As noted earlier, the natural or moral laws are not absent from *Laudato Si'* but are in fact mentioned four times (Francis, *Laudato Si'*, §§68–69 and 155). Law appears more frequently in *Fratelli Tutti*, but here the bulk of the references are to the great commandment and the law of love or charity (Francis, *Fratelli Tutti*, §§39, 56, 60, 61, 66, 88, 181) as well as to the moral law (§§207, 208, 210, 265). They are, rather, properly ordered to a larger theological framework. For comparison, the word *law* appears fifty-three times in *Humanae Vitae*—a *much* shorter document—and most of those citations refer to natural, moral, or biological laws; only one refers to civil law. The term *law* appears 103 times in *Evangelium Vitae*, with about 38 references to the moral/divine/natural/canonical/God's law and 65 to civil law. The latter figure is important, as we see in *Evangelium Vitae* a shift in Catholic bioethics to legal activism—which I would suggest is a deformation of Christian discipleship. *Fratelli Tutti* likewise attends seriously to civil law but primarily to affirm its proper political function and the importance of government over against growing threats to the rule of law (Francis, *Fratelli Tutti*, §§159, 164, 173, 174, 177, 196, 206, 231, 257, 264, 266, 267).

64. Luke 10:37.

65. Paul VI, *Humanae Vitae*, §1.

66. Paul VI, *Humanae Vitae*, §8; see also §9.

But as quickly as the next sentence, this collaboration shifts from a free and creative action to a "duty" to be fulfilled.[67] From here forward, human agency consists almost exclusively in "faithful observance" of God's will, known via the objective moral order of the natural law.[68] Parenthood is cast as an "obligation[]" grounded in "biological processes" that dictate "proper functions."[69] "Reason and will must exert control" over our "innate drives and emotions"[70]; "self-denial" and "self-discipline" are prescribed.[71] In fact:

> From this it follows that [married persons] *are not free* to act as they choose in the service of transmitting life, as if it were wholly up to them to decide what is the right course to follow. On the contrary, *they are bound* to ensure that what they do corresponds to the will of God the Creator.[72]

For "one is not the master of the sources of life but rather the minister of the design established by the Creator."[73] Humans are to obediently and dutifully observe these laws under penalty of judgment and condemnation,[74] but in fact such obedience is only possible if God *chooses* to "come[] to [our] help with the grace by which the goodwill of men is sustained and strengthened."[75] Thus, as God is the distant law-maker whose essence is his Will, human agency is primarily conceptualized in *Humanae Vitae* as the dutiful following of laws that stand between us and the divine.

---

67. Paul VI, *Humanae Vitae*, §1; see also §10.
68. Paul VI, *Humanae Vitae*, §§4, 10, 12, 13, 19, 23, 26.
69. Paul VI, *Humanae Vitae*, §10.
70. Paul VI, *Humanae Vitae*, §10; see also §21.
71. Paul VI, *Humanae Vitae*, §21.
72. Paul VI, *Humanae Vitae*, §10, emphasis added.
73. Paul VI, *Humanae Vitae*, §13. Continuing: "Just as man does not have unlimited dominion over his body in general, so also, and with more particular reason, he has no such dominion over his specifically sexual faculties" (Paul VI, *Humanae Vitae*, §13; see also §17). Furthermore, the greatest challenge is that humanity seeks to exercise "domination and rational organization [over] the forces of nature," "extend[ing] this control over every aspect of his own life" (Paul VI, *Humanae Vitae*, §2). This latter point is echoed in *Evangelium Vitae*: "On a more general level, there exists in contemporary culture a certain Promethean attitude which leads people to think that they can control life and death by taking the decisions about them into their own hands" (John Paul II, *Evangelium Vitae*, §15).
74. Paul VI, *Humanae Vitae*, §§14, 16.
75. Paul VI, *Humanae Vitae*, §§20, 35.

Like *Humanae Vitae*, *Evangelium Vitae* begins on a positive note, affirming that the human vocation is "supernatural," "sharing the very life of God";[76] because of God's "boundless love" via the Incarnation, every human being is "united . . . in some fashion" with Christ,[77] who has poured out his blood for all of us in the Passion.[78]

Yet despite these occasional theological affirmations, human agency throughout *Evangelium Vitae* is, again, almost entirely defined with regard to the law. Every person can "by the light of reason and the hidden action of grace, come to recognize [the sacred value of human life] in the natural law written in the heart."[79] The "individual conscience . . . stands before God in its singleness and uniqueness,"[80] but this encounter is largely an encounter of judgment—the "definitive meeting with God" coming after our death.[81] As mentioned earlier, the character who dominates this document—who stands before God in conscience—is Cain. The world bequeathed to us by Adam's fall and Cain's murder of Abel is wracked by "a veritable structure of sin . . . a veritable 'culture of death.'"[82] Seated on his throne,[83] God is the master, the owner, who holds the power of life and death in his hands.[84] We are obliged to obey God's will via God's commands, to meet his demands, sometimes in fear.[85]

Thus, the image of human agency and the human person that emerges from *Evangelium Vitae* is ambiguous.[86] We share in God's lordship, should God so choose, but with limits: "Man's life comes from God; it is his gift, his image and imprint, a sharing in his breath of life. God therefore is the sole Lord of this life: man cannot do with it as he wills."[87] This sharing in God's life and work is elusive since "only those who recognize that their life is marked by the evil of sin can discover in an

---

76. John Paul II, *Evangelium Vitae*, §2; see also §22.
77. John Paul II, *Evangelium Vitae*, §2.
78. John Paul II, *Evangelium Vitae*, §25.
79. John Paul II, *Evangelium Vitae*, §2.
80. John Paul II, *Evangelium Vitae*, §§24, 90.
81. John Paul II, *Evangelium Vitae*, §65.
82. John Paul II, *Evangelium Vitae*, §12; see also §24.
83. John Paul II, *Evangelium Vitae*, §25.
84. John Paul II, *Evangelium Vitae*, §§39, 46, 55, 66.
85. John Paul II, *Evangelium Vitae*, §§48, 49, 52, 68, 73.
86. Oddly, *Evangelium Vitae* says little about human agency. Given its concern with the "culture of death," its focus is more vaguely directed at "society."
87. John Paul II, *Evangelium Vitae*, §39.

encounter with Jesus the Saviour the truth and the authenticity of their own existence."[88] God remains distant to us, only coming near in judgment or capriciously.

In the end, our primary—perhaps, sole—task as human persons and disciples is "to defend and promote life, to show reverence and love for it."[89] Not surprisingly, our main mode of cooperating with God is in procreation.[90] Echoing *Humanae Vitae*, the "specific responsibility [that we are] given for human life as such . . . reaches its highest point in the giving of life through procreation by man and woman in marriage."[91] Even here, positive acts like "respect, love, and promot[ing] the life of every brother and sister" are cast again in terms of the law: "an absolute imperative," a "requirement[]," made clear by the "Spirit [who] becomes the new law."[92]

In *Laudato Si'* and *Fratelli Tutti*, a very different account of human and Christian agency emerges. Where Cain dominates *Evangelium Vitae*, *Laudato Si'* and *Fratelli Tutti* open with meditations on St. Francis. In St. Francis, "concern[] for God's creation and for the poor and outcast" meet.[93] Not accidentally, the same words used to describe God throughout these documents are those used to describe St. Francis: openhearted, self-giving, encounter, love, awe, wonder, praise, joy, care, "intimately united" to every creature "by bonds of affection."[94]

In these documents, the human person is not simply a rational being of a subsistent nature, nor one obliged to hew to commandments of the natural law, nor (as elsewhere) one defined by some unitary capacity

---

88. John Paul II, *Evangelium Vitae*, §32. John Paul II cites Gregory of Nyssa in a claim that undercuts his arguments elsewhere about the intrinsic theological value of all human life: "'Man, as a being, is of no account; he is dust, grass, vanity. But once he is adopted by the God of the universe as a son, he becomes part of the family of that Being, whose excellence and greatness no one can see, hear, or understand . . . Man surpasses his nature: mortal, he becomes immortal; perishable, he becomes imperishable; fleeting, he becomes eternal; human, he becomes divine'" (John Paul II, *Evangelium Vitae*, §80).

89. John Paul II, *Evangelium Vitae*, §42.
90. John Paul II, *Evangelium Vitae*, §43.
91. John Paul II, *Evangelium Vitae*, §43.
92. John Paul II, *Evangelium Vitae*, §§76–77; see also §79.
93. Francis, *Laudato Si'*, §10. He continues that St. Francis "shows us just how inseparable the bond is between concern for nature, justice for the poor, commitment to society, and interior peace" (Francis, *Laudato Si'*, §10).
94. Francis, *Laudato Si'*, §11; see also Francis, *Fratelli Tutti*, §§1–5; and *Laudato Si'*, §§1, 10–12.

such as autonomy or freedom or even relationality.[95] Rather, here theological anthropology—what it means to be a human person created in God's image—catches fire. We see (via Bonaventure) "that *each creature bears in itself a specifically Trinitarian structure, so real that it could be readily contemplated if only the human gaze were not so partial, dark and fragile.*"[96] Imbued with this trinitarian structure, humans—and all creatures—originally tended toward God and each other in a constant, dynamic—dare we say, perichoretic?—harmonious relationship; everything was interconnected.[97] Sin ruptured this harmony, fragmenting reality. We are, as in the parable, wounded.

Yet this trinitarian structure remains our nature and call. To be in God's image and likeness now means not to simply follow external laws but to embody God's trinitarian presence in the world. It means to work to heal these ruptures—first in ourselves, then in creation and the world. St. Francis witnesses that this is possible. As Pope Francis notes, "It is significant that the harmony which Saint Francis of Assisi experienced with all creatures was seen as a healing of that rupture. Saint Bonaventure held that, through universal reconciliation with every creature, Saint Francis in some way returned to the state of original innocence."[98]

As such, St. Francis provides an icon of what it means to be human. Almost every description of the human person in these documents resonates with the depiction of St. Francis and of the Good Samaritan. "Our openness to others, each of whom is a 'thou' capable of knowing, loving and entering into dialogue," Pope Francis proclaims, "remains the source

---

95. Importantly, *Laudato Si'* and *Fratelli Tutti* offer a thoroughly *theological* anthropology—grounded in scripture, doctrine, sacraments, and saints. Not only is it a theocentric anthropology, it is also christoform. Thus, rather than starting with science, philosophy, psychology, ethnography, or secular reason, and from these positing a "natural" understanding of the human person to which theology and revelation must be added (often resulting in a supererogatory vision of the human person posited only for people of faith), these encyclicals invert the method, positing a theological vision of the human person which—intriguingly—can be confirmed by the best of science, ethnography, psychology, and maybe even philosophy.

96. Francis, *Laudato Si'*, §239, emphasis in original; see also Francis, *Fratelli Tutti*, §85. He continues: "Saint Bonaventure went so far as to say that human beings, before sin, were able to see how each creature 'testifies that God is three.' The reflection of the Trinity was there to be recognized in nature 'when that book was open to man and our eyes had not yet become darkened'" (Francis, *Laudato Si'*, §239). These comments echo Pope Francis's beautiful account of faith as a way of seeing detailed in *Lumen Fidei*.

97. Francis, *Laudato Si'*, §240; see also §66.

98. Francis, *Laudato Si'*, §66.

of our nobility as human persons."⁹⁹ As a receptivity, this openness is an "attitude of the heart, one which approaches life with serene attentiveness, which is capable of being fully present to someone without thinking of what comes next, which accepts each moment as a gift from God to be lived to the full."¹⁰⁰ At the same time, this openness enables what he calls the "law of *ekstasis*," a dynamic love that "draws [us] out of [ourselves] and towards others," moving us beyond ourselves "'in the sincere gift of self to others.'"¹⁰¹ Without this movement toward others, we "cannot live, develop [or] find fulfilment."¹⁰² In fact, it is only by "go[ing] outside'" of ourselves and encountering others that we can fully *know* ourselves.¹⁰³ And as we do, we "'find a *fuller* existence *in* [the other].'"¹⁰⁴ In fact, "we come to experience others as our 'own flesh.'"¹⁰⁵

Thus, the anthropology of *Laudato Si'* and *Fratelli Tutti* is one of trinitarian dynamism.¹⁰⁶ As *Laudato Si'* notes:

99. Francis, *Laudato Si'*, §119. The term "open" occurs twenty-nine times in *Laudato Si'* and seventy-six times in *Fratelli Tutti*. Further, "when our hearts are authentically open to universal communion, this sense of fraternity excludes nothing and no one" (Francis, *Laudato Si'*, §92). Turning to Aquinas, Pope Francis notes, "Yet if the acts of the various moral virtues are to be rightly directed, one needs to take into account the extent to which they foster openness and union with others. That is made possible by the charity that God infuses. Without charity, we may perhaps possess only apparent virtues, incapable of sustaining life in common" (Francis, *Fratelli Tutti*, §91).

100. Francis, *Laudato Si'*, §226. Furthering the christological connections, Pope Francis continues that Jesus embodied and modeled this attitude for us (Francis, *Laudato Si'*, §226).

101. Francis, *Fratelli Tutti*, §§87–88. Importantly, Pope Francis points out that, theologically grounded, this self-gift is not transactional but is rather completely gratuitous: "Fraternal love can only be gratuitous; it can never be a means of repaying others for what they have done or will do for us. That is why it is possible to love our enemies. This same gratuitousness inspires us to love and accept the wind, the sun, and the clouds, even though we cannot control them. In this sense, we can speak of a 'universal fraternity'" (Francis, *Laudato Si'*, §228; see also Francis, *Fratelli Tutti*, §250). Elsewhere, this divine love "is the fundamental moving force in all created things" (Francis, *Laudato Si'*, §77). That we are to imitate God's gratuity, see Francis, *Laudato Si'*, §220. Pope Francis also emphasizes gratuity in *Fratelli Tutti*, §§139–41.

102. Francis, *Fratelli Tutti*, §87.

103. Francis, *Fratelli Tutti*, §88. Continuing: "'I communicate effectively with myself only insofar as I communicate with others'" (Francis, *Fratelli Tutti*, §87).

104. Francis, *Fratelli Tutti*, §88, emphasis added.

105. Francis, *Fratelli Tutti*, §84. "Saint Thomas Aquinas," he notes, "sought to describe the love made possible by God's grace as a movement outwards towards another, whereby we consider 'the beloved as somehow united to ourselves'" (Francis, *Fratelli Tutti*, §93).

106. I would suggest that this theological anthropology has its counterpart in the

> The human person grows more, matures more, and is sanctified more to the extent that he or she enters into relationships, going out from themselves to live in communion with God, with others and with all creatures. In this way, they make their own that trinitarian dynamism which God imprinted in them when they were created.[107]

But *Fratelli Tutti* adds one more piece. For we participate in this trinitarian dynamism not simply by mandate or imitation. Rather, Jesus's words "compel us" not only to recognize Christ in the Samaritan, but "to recognize Christ himself in each of our abandoned or excluded brothers and sisters."[108] God, in other words, is encountered in both the Samaritan and in the one left at the side of the road. In the parable, God not only comes close—God recursively encounters God. As such, the parable is an icon of the work of the Trinity active in our midst. Thus, as we respond in love to the one who shows us mercy (God), we are drawn into the ec-static openness of the Trinity, simultaneously enabled to embody God's grace to those we encounter—particularly creation and those at the peripheries—while encountering God there anew.[109]

---

ecclesiology of *Evangelii Gaudium* and the reflections of *Lumen Fidei*. In bringing these four documents into conversation, we would find, I believe, that the trinitarian dynamism outlined here equally animates Pope Francis's vision for the conversion and healing of each of us (*Lumen Fidei*), of the church (*Evangelii Gaudium*), of creation (*Laudato Si'*), and of the world (*Fratelli Tutti*).

107. Francis, *Laudato Si'*, §240. He continues: "In this way, [Bonaventure] points out to us the challenge of trying to read reality in a Trinitarian key" (Francis, *Laudato Si'*, §239; see also Francis, *Fratelli Tutti*, §85). "Everything is interconnected, and this invites us to develop a spirituality of that global solidarity which flows from the mystery of the Trinity" (Francis, *Laudato Si'*, §240).

108. Francis, *Fratelli Tutti*, §85. The full paragraph reads:

> For Christians, the words of Jesus have an even deeper meaning. They compel us to recognize Christ himself in each of our abandoned or excluded brothers and sisters (cf. Mt 25:40.45). Faith has untold power to inspire and sustain our respect for others, for believers come to know that God loves every man and woman with infinite love and "thereby confers infinite dignity" upon all humanity. We likewise believe that Christ shed his blood for each of us and that no one is beyond the scope of his universal love. If we go to the ultimate source of that love which is the very life of the triune God, we encounter in the community of the three divine Persons the origin and perfect model of all life in society. Theology continues to be enriched by its reflection on this great truth. (Francis, *Fratelli Tutti*, §85)

109. As noted earlier, the notion of social friendship developed in *Fratelli Tutti* is the correlate between persons of the social friendship advocated in *Laudato Si'* between persons and the environment. As Pope Francis notes, "A correct relationship with the created world demands that we not weaken this social dimension of openness to others,

"Praise be to you, my Lord!"

What a stunning prospect: that when we live as we are truly created and called to be, we can—by grace—live ever more deeply into the inherently trinitarian structure of human nature, becoming creatures in whom God recursively meets God amid the world's material realities. Through us, by grace, God's trinitarian presence can infuse even the most mundane moments in the most obscure or quotidian places. It is as if Aquinas's *exitus/reditus* scheme has been transposed from the cosmic arc of salvation history into our daily lives.

In *Laudato Si'* and *Fratelli Tutti*, Pope Francis is calling us to a vibrant and powerful anthropology, grounded in a robustly theological vision of the Trinity, that is lived not as adherence to commandments, norms, and precepts, but as the constant embodiment of the divine character revealed in Christ via scripture, the Good Samaritan, and the *alter Christus*, St. Francis: openness, hospitality, joy, dialogue, vulnerability, love, care, and interconnectedness.

But our account of the theological anthropology of *Laudato Si'* still needs one more piece. For what happens when we are encountered by God, or when God encounters God? Again, St. Francis points the way—"*Laudato si', mi signore!*" What other response can there be but praise, awe, wonder, joy! As Pope Francis notes, "When we can see God reflected in all that exists, our hearts are moved to praise the Lord for all his creatures and to worship him in union with them."[110] This is the response called forth from the center of one's being to encountering the extraordinary gift of God's merciful love.

It is not an accident that the word *praise* occurs thirty times in *Laudato Si'*, including, as noted earlier, in both the opening and closing sentences. Indeed, the encyclical again echoes the inner life of the Trinity—the endless delight, love, joy, and praise among the three Persons.[111]

---

much less the transcendent dimension of our openness to the 'Thou' of God. Our relationship with the environment can never be isolated from our relationship with others and with God" (Francis, *Laudato Si'*, §119).

110. Francis, *Laudato Si'*, §87. Or elsewhere: "'When we contemplate with wonder the universe in all its grandeur and beauty, we must praise the whole Trinity'" (Francis, *Laudato Si'*, §238, quoting John Paul II, "General Audience," §4). Thus, the world—and all its people—are not problems to be solved but "a joyful mystery to be contemplated with gladness and praise" (Francis, *Laudato Si'*, §12).

111. Notably, this theme of praise connects to Pope Francis's first apostolic exhortation's emphasis on joy; see *Evangelii Gaudium* (2013). I thank Guy Valponi for this and other insights incorporated into this chapter.

If such is the life of the Trinity, then "the heart of what it is to be human"[112] becomes clear—it is worship. This is signaled not only in the icon of St. Francis, but equally in Pope Francis's withering critiques of the "distorted" modern anthropologies and the "reductive anthropological visions"[113] that lie at the heart of both our ecological crisis[114] and the fragmentation of the human community.[115] For what lies at the heart of these distorted anthropologies is idolatry, the worship of "a deified market."[116] We become what we worship because worship lies at the heart of who we are.

As noted earlier, in *Laudato Si'* the same Person who gazes with tangible love upon each of our wounded selves is the same One who gazes upon all of creation with tenderness via creation; but this same Person further unites creation and our brokenness in a third locus of encounter: the Eucharist. "It is in the Eucharist," Pope Francis notes, "that all that has been created finds its greatest exaltation."[117] Here God comes the closest of all, "reach[ing] our intimate depths through a fragment of matter."[118] Here we find "the living centre of the universe, the overflowing core of love and of inexhaustible life."[119] Here we recursively encounter anew the One who via the double-movement of *kenosis* encountered us in our own bodily reality and then suffered the wounding of that body unto death and who was raised by the God who reaches out across the farthest of distances.

To put it differently, to perform this trinitarian identity fully and authentically—to become who we are created and called to be as human persons—calls us to recursively navigate between the loci of creation, Eucharist, and the poor as St. Francis did, encountering in each place God's

---

112. Francis, *Laudato Si'*, §11.
113. Francis, *Fratelli Tutti*, §22; see also Francis, *Laudato Si'*, §69.
114. Francis, *Laudato Si'*, §§115–36.
115. Francis, *Fratelli Tutti*, §22.
116. Francis, *Laudato Si'*, §56. Elsewhere: "'In today's world, many forms of injustice persist, fed by reductive anthropological visions and by a profit-based economic model that does not hesitate to exploit, discard and even kill human beings. While one part of humanity lives in opulence, another part sees its own dignity denied, scorned or trampled upon, and its fundamental rights discarded or violated'" (Francis, *Fratelli Tutti*, §22). The violence we wreak on creation and others comes from "our hearts, wounded by sin," creating sickness everywhere (Francis, *Laudato Si'*, §2). Another way to display the anthropology of *Laudato Si'* and *Fratelli Tutti* would be to outline the negative anthropology contained in these critiques. That would be an interesting and useful analysis.
117. Francis, *Laudato Si'*, §236.
118. Francis, *Laudato Si'*, §236.
119. Francis, *Laudato Si'*, §236.

merciful, joyful love again and again, being drawn into and participating in God's trinitarian life again and again, and being transformed more fully into our deepest identities again and again. To ignore any of the three leads to a misshapen theology and practice.

Thus, in *Laudato Si'* a truly conciliar moral theology begins to come into full bloom. Not only is nominalist theology and method left behind. We find here a moral theology deeply informed by the structure of the Council, opening as it does with *Sacrosanctum Concilium* and closing with *Gaudium et Spes*. Built into this structure lies a hermeneutic—a framework rooted in the sacramental encounter with the triune God, that shapes and empowers not only the agency of individuals but primarily the agency of the Body of Christ as missionary disciple(s), that moves beyond itself to bring God's love to the pain of the world. *Laudato Si'* hears this vision, centering worship as the hermeneutical key—the font and summit—of both a theological anthropology and moral theology. This is the vision of Vatican II: a moral theology of missionary discipleship/social friendship whereby the church (as moral agent) moves from worship to the world, where we again encounter Christ—this time in the sacramental locus of the peripheries. In so doing, the church is recursively converted as we return to its liturgical gathering.[120]

How might *this* conciliar vision reshape Catholic bioethics?

A Field Hospital for Catholic Bioethics

The foregoing account is not meant to draw a sharp distinction—or rupture, as some do—between the papacy of Pope Francis and his predecessors. For certainly, as Pope Francis notes, "All revealed truths derive from the same divine source and are to be believed with the same faith."[121] And certainly, in the broader works of Paul VI, John Paul II, and Benedict XVI we see a growing attention to the sacramental center of a conciliar theological (and, therefore, moral) method. Paul VI, for example, in his homily opening the 1968 CELAM session in Bogotá, noted the church's long tradition of recognizing "in the poor the sacrament of Christ . . . in perfect analogical and mystical correspondence with" the reality of the

---

120. For further development of this argument, see Lysaught, "War or Peace?"; Lysaught, "Peripheries and the Eucharist." Hamel, "Call to Conversion," also notes how Pope Francis's account of creation itself in *Laudato Si'* is deeply sacramental.

121. Francis, *Evangelii Gaudium*, §36.

Eucharist.¹²² Prayer and sacrament pervade the corpus of John Paul II.¹²³ And with Benedict XVI's *Deus Caritas Est*, we see a major shift toward the foundational nature of worship for moral methodology.¹²⁴ But such integration, puzzlingly, seems to stop at the doors of Catholic bioethics.¹²⁵

What might it mean to reimagine Catholic bioethics through the lens of *il Poverello* instead of Cain, for it to shed the last remnants of nominalism—especially its habit of reading "St. Thomas and the Fathers . . . through 'nominalist lenses'"¹²⁶—and turn to the Council's sacramental-ecclesial vision for its renewed methodology? *Laudato Si'* provides at least four important starting points for next steps.

First, *Laudato Si'* presses us to examine the *theology* presumed in Catholic bioethics. Insofar as moral theology is often deemed little more than "applied theology," scant attention is paid to the powerfully operative but often implicit theological presuppositions that shape its methodology. Who is the God that stands behind Catholic bioethics? What Christology is operative—on the rare occasions Jesus is mentioned at all? What ecclesiology or sacramental theology? In what, beyond simple assertions of "human dignity," does our theological anthropology consist? And what is our operative account of moral agency?

---

122. Paul VI, "Santa Misa," cited in Luciani, *Pope Francis*, 901.

123. Lysaught, "Roman Catholic Teaching."

124. See Lysaught, "Roman Catholic Teaching"; Lysaught, "Love and Liturgy." Insofar as Benedict XVI did not issue an encyclical on "bioethics" strictly speaking, he is not included in this analysis. Further elucidation of the argument in this chapter would trace the many points of contact between *Laudato Si'*, *Deus Caritas Est*, and *Caritas in Veritate*. Francis himself connects his sacramental theology of encounter to Benedict XVI: "I never tire of repeating those words of Benedict XVI which take us to the very heart of the gospel: 'Being a Christian is not the result of an ethical choice or a lofty idea, but the encounter with an event, a person, which gives life a new horizon and a decisive direction'" (Francis, *Evangelii Gaudium*, §7, quoting Benedict XVI, *Deus Caritas Est*, §1).

125. In *Humanae Vitae* and *Evangelium Vitae*, the sacraments receive scant or peculiar mention. In *Humanae Vitae*, the sacraments are described solely as means to bolster married couples in their weaknesses, burdens, duties, and failings that make it difficult to adhere to the law (Paul VI, *Humanae Vitae*, §§25, 29, 35). The closest discussion of sacramentality in *Evangelium Vitae* occurs primarily in chapter 1, "The Voice of Your Brother's Blood Cries Out to Me from the Ground." In perhaps an attempt to parallel the spilling of Abel's blood by Cain, *Evangelium Vitae* focuses almost exclusively on the blood of Christ. But insofar as it frames this discussion with the letter to the Hebrews, sacramentality is almost entirely framed by concepts of the law (John Paul II, *Evangelium Vitae*, §§25–29). Oddly, the *body* of Christ is not substantively mentioned in the document.

126. Pinckaers, *Sources of Christian Ethics*, 253.

Second, *Laudato Si'* challenges us to reevaluate the *methodology* that shapes Catholic bioethics. Pinckaers and others have made clear that manualist moral theology relied on a methodology that was deeply theologically flawed. Sprouted from the same nominalist root, it is the mirror image of the methodology of the secular bioethics that Catholic bioethics endlessly critiques—a method based on a radical, atomizing understanding of freedom that plays itself out in principles and law. As the culture wars have made painfully clear, the nominalist emphasis on law in the realm of morality has spilled over into an excessive focus by many in Catholic bioethics on the mechanisms of civil law as the almost exclusive way to address what have been labelled as "preeminent" moral issues.[127] This has deeply distorted and damaged the church's practice of the Gospel and witness in the public sphere. As such, both branches of this nominalist root (secular and Catholic bioethics) are simply modalities of power, played out as either internalized or overt forms of biopolitics.

Third, *Laudato Si'* demonstrates how a conciliar methodology will illuminate a new array of *critically important questions*. Such a methodology will ask: What, really, do we worship? What idols shape our practice of medicine, our culture—even our church—and thereby misshape our understanding of ourselves and our practice of medicine? *Laudato Si'* and Pope Francis's corpus as a whole relentlessly center the idol to which most of us are enthralled: economics.[128] It will privilege questions of the poor and the earth—universal health care, clean water, food security, gross disparities in infant or maternal mortality rates for babies and women of color—over what Paul Farmer has referred to as "the quandaries of the fortunate"—questions regarding technologies only available to the wealthy (e.g., preimplantation genetic diagnosis).[129] And—further received through *Laudato Si'*—a conciliar bioethics will foreground questions of integral ecology, an expansion of Paul VI's notion of integral human development that not only encompasses the environmental

---

127. John Paul II, *Evangelium Vitae*, §§68–75. See n7 above.

128. While John Paul II called out the idolatries of "money, ideology, class, [and] technology" (John Paul II, *Sollicitudo Rei Socialis*, §37).

129. A bioethics informed by the Council and *Laudato Si'* "must integrate questions of justice in debates on the environment, so as to hear *both the cry of the earth and the cry of the poor*" (Francis, *Laudato Si'*, §49, emphasis in original). See also Farmer, *Pathologies of Power*, 175. Farmer might note that both *Donum Vitae* and *Dignitatis Personae* focus neither on the earth or the poor, but on the quandaries of the fortunate.

responsibilities of Catholics and Catholic institutions, but also equally gives attention to environmental racism, poverty, and health.[130]

Finally, *Laudato Si'* restores a more theologically authentic *vision of the Christian life*. No longer is moral theology a neo-Pelagian or Kantian practice of self-righteousness managed by dutiful obedience to externally imposed rules aimed simply at access to the Eucharist as a pseudo-magical means of grace. Rather, it is a joyful practice of missionary discipleship by those who, together as part of Christ's living presence in the world, body forth God's trinitarian love for all those encountered.[131] It is a practice of growth, not only in virtue, but toward the trinitarian structure inherent in our very selves as we heal the ruptures in our selves, our lives, creation, and the world.

In these ways, *Laudato Si'*—and Pope Francis's corpus more broadly—provide what we might call a field hospital for Catholic bioethics. It provides a starting point for healing the wounds inflicted on our discipline by nominalist manualism that desiccated our theology and prevented us from seeing the vast landscape of issues crying out for theological analysis and ministerial accompaniment. Certainly, such a transformed bioethics might be difficult to translate into guidelines or practices for a clinical setting deeply shaped by neoliberal economics—another insight from *Laudato Si'* requiring further exploration. But perhaps that is no longer the most important locus for Catholic bioethics.[132] Perhaps instead of trying

---

130. Hamel highlights a raft of ecological issues crucial for Catholic bioethics: the ways that environmental degradation harms both the eco-sphere and human health; the ways that climate change is already having the most significant and devastating impacts on poor and vulnerable communities across the globe; the ways that practices like energy conservation, waste management, food sourcing, chemical usage, and architecture are all deeply consonant with—and called for by—the Catholic tradition; see Hamel, "Call to Conversion." Labrecque echoes the above, adding issues such as compulsive consumerism and the throwaway culture, human trafficking, etc.; see Labrecque, "Catholic Bioethics."

131. As Pope Francis notes in his interview with Spadaro, "I have a dogmatic certainty: God is in every person's life. God is in everyone's life. Even if the life of a person has been a disaster, even if it is destroyed by vices, drugs or anything else—God is in this person's life. You can, you must try to seek God in every human life. Although the life of a person is a land full of thorns and weeds, there is always a space in which the good seed can grow. You have to trust God" (Spadaro, "Interview with Pope Francis").

132. As Pope Francis writes in *Evangelii Gaudium*,
> In her ongoing discernment, the Church can also come to see that certain customs not directly connected to the heart of the Gospel, even some which have deep historical roots, are no longer properly understood and appreciated. Some of these customs may be beautiful, but they no longer serve as means of communicating the Gospel. We should not be afraid to re-examine

to carve out influence in the clinical setting or civil legislatures, it is time to reimagine Catholic bioethics as a practice of the church as a field hospital. In his now-classic articulation of this image, Pope Francis states:

> I see clearly . . . that the thing the church needs most today is the ability to heal wounds and to warm the hearts of the faithful; it needs nearness, proximity. I see the church as a field hospital after battle. It is useless to ask a seriously injured person if he has high cholesterol and about the level of his blood sugars! You have to heal his wounds. Then we can talk about everything else. Heal the wounds, heal the wounds . . . . And you have to start from the ground up . . . .
>
> How are we treating the people of God? . . . . The church's ministers must be merciful, take responsibility for the people and accompany them like the good Samaritan, who washes, cleans and raises up his neighbor. This is pure Gospel. God is greater than sin. . . . The first reform must be the attitude. The ministers of the Gospel must be people who can warm the hearts of the people, who walk through the dark night with them, who know how to dialogue and to descend themselves into their people's night, into the darkness, but without getting lost. The people of God want pastors, not clergy acting like bureaucrats or government officials. The bishops, particularly, must be able to support the movements of God among their people with patience, so that no one is left behind. But they must also be able to accompany the flock that has a flair for finding new paths.
>
> Instead of being just a church that welcomes and receives by keeping the doors open, let us try also to be a church that finds new roads, that is able to step outside itself and go to those who do not attend.[133]

How transformative would it be to practice a Catholic bioethics that goes out beyond the walls of hospitals and academies to heal the wounds of

---

them. At the same time, the Church has rules or precepts which may have been quite effective in their time, but no longer have the same usefulness for directing and shaping people's lives. Saint Thomas Aquinas pointed out that the precepts which Christ and the apostles gave to the people of God "are very few." Citing Saint Augustine, he noted that the precepts subsequently enjoined by the Church should be insisted upon with moderation "so as not to burden the lives of the faithful" and make our religion a form of servitude, whereas "God's mercy has willed that we should be free." This warning, issued many centuries ago, is most timely today. It ought to be one of the criteria to be taken into account in considering a reform of the Church and her preaching which would enable it to reach everyone. (Francis, *Evangelii Gaudium*, §43)

133. Spadaro, "Interview with Pope Francis."

people and society in the streets?[134] Might it echo the practice of the early church that went out to the poor and the sick; that pioneered the practices and institutions that have become what we know as modern healthcare?[135]

Laudato Si' pushes us to ask: How might Catholic bioethics look different refracted through the lens of the Good Samaritan and *il Poverello*? Standing as an exemplar of the christoform-trinitarian anthropology at the heart of Pope Francis's moral-theological vision, St. Francis points Catholic bioethics toward a theological anthropology that resembles not the abstract human agent of the natural law or philosophical phenomenology, but toward the *alter Christus*—one who via prayer, sacrament, and loving immersion among creation and the poor becomes simultaneously poor and ever more and more like the God who encountered him there. He points us toward a methodology that resembles not nominalism but the fullness of the Gospel: a searing critique of economics, relentless accompaniment of the poor, a prioritizing of creation, and more. So converted, Catholic bioethics might become a true agent of evangelization—a discipline truly ministering to the wounded of the world via Samaritan-like social friendship, thereby helping to both heal society and rebuild the church.

Bibliography

Austriaco, Nicanor. "Bioethics in Laudato Si': The Ecological Law as a Moral Principle." *National Catholic Bioethics Quarterly* 15.4 (Winter 2015) 657–63.

Benedict XVI. *Caritas in Veritate*. Encyclical Letter, June 29, 2009. https://www.vatican.va/content/benedict-xvi/en/encyclicals/documents/hf_ben-xvi_enc_20090629_caritas-in-veritate.html.

———. *Deus Caritas Est*. Encyclical Letter, Dec. 25, 2005. https://www.vatican.va/content/benedict-xvi/en/encyclicals/documents/hf_ben-xvi_enc_20051225_deus-caritas-est.html.

Borghesi, Massimo. *Catholic Discordance: Neoconservatism vs. the Field Hospital Church of Pope Francis*. Collegeville, MN: Liturgical Press, 2021.

———. *The Mind of Pope Francis: Jorge Mario Bergoglio's Intellectual Journey*. Collegeville, MN: Liturgical Press, 2017.

Brody, Howard. *The Future of Bioethics*. New York: Oxford University Press, 2009.

Congregation for the Doctrine of the Faith. *Dignitatis Personae*. Sept. 8, 2008. https://www.vatican.va/roman_curia/congregations/cfaith/documents/rc_con_cfaith_doc_20081208_dignitas-personae_en.html.

———. *Donum Vitae: Instruction on Respect for Human Life in Its Origin and on the Dignity of Procreation*. Feb. 22, 1987. https://www.vatican.va/roman_curia/congregations/cfaith/documents/rc_con_cfaith_doc_19870222_respect-for-human-life_en.html.

---

134. Lysaught, "Peripheries."
135. Risse, *Mending Bodies, Saving Souls*; Stark, *Rise of Christianity*.

Farmer, Paul. *Pathologies of Power*. Los Angeles: University of California Press, 2003.

Francis. *Evangelii Gaudium*. Apostolic Exhortation, Nov. 24, 2013. https://www.vatican.va/content/francesco/en/apost_exhortations/documents/papa-francesco_esortazione-ap_20131124_evangelii-gaudium.html.

———. *Fratelli Tutti*. Encyclical Letter, Oct. 3, 2020. https://www.vatican.va/content/francesco/en/encyclicals/documents/papa-francesco_20201003_enciclica-fratelli-tutti.html.

———. *Gaudete et Exsultate*. Apostolic Exhortation, Mar. 19, 2018. https://www.vatican.va/content/francesco/en/apost_exhortations/documents/papa-francesco_esortazione-ap_20180319_gaudete-et-exsultate.html.

———. *Laudato Si'*. Encyclical, May 24, 2015. https://www.vatican.va/content/francesco/en/encyclicals/documents/papa-francesco_20150524_enciclica-laudato-si.html.

———. *Lumen Fidei*. Encyclical Letter, June 29, 2013. https://www.vatican.va/content/francesco/en/encyclicals/documents/papa-francesco_20130629_enciclica-lumen-fidei.html.

Hamel, Ronald P. "A Call to Conversion: Toward a Catholic Environmental Bioethics and Environmentally Responsible Health Care." In *Catholic Bioethics and Social Justice: The Praxis of US Healthcare in a Globalized World*, edited by M. Therese Lysaught and Michael McCarthy, 235–52. Collegeville, MN: Liturgical Press, 2019.

John Paul II. *Evangelium Vitae*. Encyclical Letter, Mar. 25, 1995. https://www.vatican.va/content/john-paul-ii/en/encyclicals/documents/hf_jp-ii_enc_25031995_evangelium-vitae.html.

———. "General Audience." Aug. 2, 2000. https://www.vatican.va/content/john-paul-ii/en/audiences/2000/documents/hf_jp-ii_aud_20000802.html.

———. *Sollicitudo Rei Socialis*. Encyclical Letter, Dec. 30, 1987. https://www.vatican.va/content/john-paul-ii/en/encyclicals/documents/hf_jp-ii_enc_30121987_sollicitudo-rei-socialis.html.

Labrecque, Cory Andrew. "Catholic Bioethics in the Anthropocene: Integrating Ecology, Religion, and Human Health." *National Catholic Bioethics Quarterly* 15.4 (Winter 2015) 665–71.

Luciani, Rafael. *Pope Francis and the Theology of the People*. Maryknoll, NY: Orbis, 2017. Kindle.

Lysaught, M. Therese. "Love and Liturgy." In *Gathered for the Journey: Moral Theology in Catholic Perspectives*, edited by David Matzko McCarthy and M. Therese Lysaught, 24–42. Grand Rapids: Eerdmans, 2007.

———. "The Peripheries and the Eucharist: Pope Francis, the *Teología del Pueblo*, and the Conversion of Catholic Bioethics." *Perspectiva Teológica* 51.3 (2019) 421–42. https://faje.edu.br/periodicos/index.php/perspectiva/article/view/4221/4388.

———. "Roman Catholic Teaching on International Debt." *Journal of Moral Theology* 4.2 (2015) 1–27.

———. "War or Peace? Toward a Better Kind of Biopolitics." Presentation at "Pope Francis, Vatican II, and the Way Forward," Loyola University Chicago's Hank Center, Mar. 25–26, 2022. https://www.luc.edu/media/lucedu/ccih/formsdocumentsandpdfs/Lysaught%20Remarks.pdf.

Lysaught, M. Therese, and Michael McCarthy, eds. *Catholic Bioethics and Social Justice: The Praxis of US Healthcare in a Globalized World*. Collegeville, MN: Liturgical Press, 2019.

———. "A Social Praxis for US Health Care: Revisioning Catholic Bioethics via Catholic Social Thought." *Journal of the Society of Christian Ethics* 38.2 (Fall/Winter 2018) 111–30.

Paul VI. *Gaudium et Spes*. Pastoral Constitution, Dec. 7, 1965. https://www.vatican.va/archive/hist_councils/ii_vatican_council/documents/vat-ii_const_19651207_gaudium-et-spes_en.html.

———. *Humanae Vitae*. Encyclical Letter, July 25, 1968. https://www.vatican.va/content/paul-vi/en/encyclicals/documents/hf_p-vi_enc_25071968_humanae-vitae.html.

———. *Optatam Totius*. Decree, Oct. 28, 1965. https://www.vatican.va/archive/hist_councils/ii_vatican_council/documents/vat-ii_decree_19651028_optatam-totius_en.html.

———. "Santa Misa para los Campesinos Colombianos." Homily, Aug. 23, 1968. https://www.vatican.va/content/paul-vi/es/homilies/1968/documents/hf_p-vi_hom_19680823.html.

Pinckaers, Servais. *Sources of Christian Ethics*. 3rd ed. Translated by Mary Thomas Noble. Washington, DC: Catholic University of America Press, 1995.

Risse, Gunter. *Mending Bodies, Saving Souls: A History of the Hospital*. London: Oxford University Press, 1999.

Spadaro, Anthony. "Interview with Pope Francis." 2013. https://www.vatican.va/content/francesco/en/speeches/2013/september/documents/papa-francesco_20130921_intervista-spadaro.html.

Spade, Paul Vincent, and Claude Panaccio. "William of Ockham." In *The Stanford Encyclopedia of Philosophy*, edited by Edward N. Zalta. Spring 2019 edition. https://plato.stanford.edu/archives/spr2019/entries/ockham/.

Stark, Rodney. *The Rise of Christianity: How the Obscure Jesus Movement Became the Dominant Religious Force in the Western World in a Few Centuries*. San Francisco: HarperSanFrancisco, 1997.

11

The Opposite of Anthropocentrism

Commodity Fetishism, Ecological Crisis, and
a Sacramental View of the World

WILLIAM CAVANAUGH

THE ROOT OF THE ecological crisis is commonly said to be anthropocentrism, the glorification of the human person to a position of mastery over nature. As Pope Francis puts it near the beginning of *Laudato Si'*, "We have come to see ourselves as [the earth's] lords and masters, entitled to plunder her at will."[1] Rather than seeing humans as part of nature, anthropocentrism elevates humans to a uniquely privileged position while simultaneously reducing the natural world to mere raw material to be used for our benefit. The natural world is instrumentalized and disenchanted, reduced to inert matter. Anthropocentrism thereby leads to the exploitation of nature and the breakdown of natural systems, what Francis calls the "tyrannical and irresponsible domination of human beings over other creatures."[2] Lynn White's famous article "The Historical Roots of Our Ecologic Crisis" similarly lays the blame on Western anthropocentrism. He declares, "Especially in its Western form, Christianity is the most anthropocentric religion the world has seen . . . Christianity . . . not only established a dualism of man and nature but also insisted that it is God's will that man exploit nature for his proper ends."[3] Where Francis and White differ is on the biblical roots of the crisis. White traces anthropocentrism to the biblical creation story that directs humans to

1. Francis, *Laudato Si'*, §2.
2. Francis, *Laudato Si'*, §83.
3. White, "Historical Roots," 1205.

subdue the earth, giving them dominion over the fish of the sea and the birds of the air: "God planned all of this explicitly for man's benefit and rule: no item in the physical creation had any purpose save to serve man's purposes."[4] Francis, on the other hand, blames a misreading of the Bible and sees the creation story as God-centered, not human-centered. Francis reminds us that "'The earth is the Lord's' (*Ps* 24:1)" and that "We are not God."[5] He declares, "Clearly, the Bible has no place for a tyrannical anthropocentrism unconcerned for other creatures."[6]

The critique of anthropocentrism is not without merit: humanity in the aggregate has certainly assumed a position of domination and exploitation of the world's resources, with devastating consequences for the other living things on the planet, both animals and plants. I will suggest nevertheless that there is something important missing in this critique. In the first place, the critique of anthropocentrism treats humanity or "man" in the aggregate and does not distinguish among:

1. The captains of industry whose constant search for shareholder value drives ecological degradation;
2. The relatively affluent consumers whose lifestyle demands the continued exploitation of natural resources;
3. The billions whose levels of consumption barely rise above subsistence; and
4. The workers whose labor constitutes another resource to be exploited.

The critique of anthropocentrism, in other words, tends to avoid class analysis, and is therefore too blunt an instrument.[7] In the second place, even people in affluent consumer cultures often experience the contemporary economy not as domination but as powerlessness; we feel like cogs, not masters. As Ivan Illich pointed out several decades ago, we have moved from an age of instrumentalization—subjects using tools to achieve ends—to an age of all-encompassing systems, in which the

---

4. White, "Historical Roots," 1205.
5. Francis, *Laudato Si'*, §67.
6. Francis, *Laudato Si'*, §68.
7. This is not to say that those who critique anthropocentrism *always* avoid consideration of class inequality. Francis, for example, notes that "twenty percent of the world's population consumes resources at a rate that robs the poor nations and future generations of what they need to survive" (Francis, *Laudato Si'*, §95).

subject stands inside the system and adjusts to its dictates. We seem to be subject to powers that might be of human creation but are far beyond human control.[8]

These two challenges to the critique of anthropocentrism—class analysis and the sense of powerlessness over human creations—come together in Karl Marx's critique of commodity fetishism. The consumerism that drives ecological destruction puts commodities, not humans, at the center and, far from disenchanting and instrumentalizing the material world, makes fetishes of commodities. The dynamics of commodity fetishism reveal almost the precise opposite of anthropocentrism: commodities become the center of concern and take on life, while human beings are hidden, and life is drained away from them. In this brief chapter, I will suggest how we become subjected to—rather than dominant over—created things, and then I will explore a Christian response that restores the proper relationships among people, things, and God.

The Power of Commodities and the Subjugation of Humans

For Marx, the instrumentalization of material things typifies the spirit of pre-capitalist societies, not capitalism. People have long made tables for use, and their value is easily understood in terms of their social function and the labor that went into them. In capitalism, however, the use value of commodities is eclipsed by their exchange value, that is, what they can be exchanged for in the market. What matters now is not the table as useful for writing on, but the table as exchangeable for other commodities through the medium of money. Value becomes located not in the satisfaction of human needs or the labor that went into the production of the commodity, but rather in the commodity itself.[9] The commodity transcends the merely material realm and, as Marx says, abounds in "metaphysical subtleties and theological niceties."[10] The commodity enters the market to be exchanged for other commodities, and human need and human labor are hidden from view. Relations among humans are replaced by relations among things. Marx calls this "fetishism" because it

---

8. See David Cayley's summary of Illich's views on the shift from instrumentalization to systems in Cayley, *Ivan Illich*, 244–54. Cayley notes that Illich wrote little about this shift; most of his ideas came across in interviews with Cayley.

9. Marx, *Capital*, 128, 163–64.

10. Marx, *Capital*, 163.

is the attribution of power to an inanimate object, a type of enchantment. Marx writes:

> It is nothing but the definite social relation between men themselves which assumes here, for them, the fantastic form of a relation between things. In order, therefore, to find an analogy we must take flight into the misty realm of religion. There the products of the human brain appear as autonomous figures endowed with a life of their own, which enter into relations both with each other and with the human race. So it is in the world of commodities with the products of men's hands.[11]

Far from being reduced to inert matter, the table begins dancing of its own free will and enters into relationship with other commodities.

At the same time, the surplus value of the labor that produces the commodities is appropriated as profit by the ownership class. Marx explains that producers come into social contact with each other only in the act of exchange, and so social relations "do not appear as direct social relations between persons in their work, but rather as material [*dinglich*, or "thingly"] relations between persons and social relations between things."[12] In other words, in capitalism "persons exist for one another merely as representatives and hence owners, of commodities"—not as persons.[13] For workers, the result of this inversion of persons and things is that commodities buy people, and not vice-versa. "The objective conditions essential to the realization of labour are *alienated* from the worker and become manifest in *fetishes* endowed with a will and soul of their own. *Commodities*, in short, appear as the purchasers of *persons* . . . . It is not the worker who buys the means of production and subsistence, but the means of production that buy the worker to incorporate him into the means of production."[14]

As Marx points out, however, in a capitalist market control of the system also eludes the owners of capital. Exchange-value—one ton of iron for two ounces of gold, for example—is beyond the will and actions of the exchangers. "Their own movement within society has for them the form of a movement made by things, and these things, far from being

---

11. Marx, *Capital*, 165.
12. Marx, *Capital*, 166.
13. Marx, *Capital*, 178–79.
14. Marx, *Capital*, 1003–4.

under their control, in fact control them."[15] This arrangement is, furthermore, thought to be subject to certain iron-clad economic "laws" that must be obeyed as if they were simply natural laws, like that of gravity. Fetishism comes with a certain kind of fatalism; we believe we are fated to obey forces beyond our control, and we cannot change them.

According to Marx, there was no commodity fetishism in medieval Christendom because social relations, though unequal and exploitative, were not hidden under the guise of relations among things. Services were in kind and payments were in kind; every serf knew how much of his labor was in the service of his lord. "The social relations between individuals in the performance of their labor appear at all events as their own personal relations, and are not disguised as social relations between things."[16] By contrast, the worker under capitalism sells his labor for wages, and he sees owners of capital as job providers rather than as appropriators of the surplus value of his work. The consumer, meanwhile, sees only products, and the conditions of production are hidden from view. This is especially true today of online shopping. The consumer encounters nothing but images of products; with a few clicks, the product can be made magically to materialize on the doorstep, with no human interaction involved at all. Marx was concerned with the invisibility of the treatment of workers, but we must add the invisibility of the treatment of the earth. The consumer simply does not see the strip mining of metals, the pollution of groundwater, the expenditure of energy, and the acceleration of global warming; nor do we see the young Thai girls making fifty cents an hour working in a factory surrounded by barbed wire, the people working in the Amazon warehouse whose every movement is monitored, with "time off task" recorded to the second. The tremendously destructive consequences for the earth and for the people who produce our stuff are all hidden behind the shiny images of the products we buy.[17]

What we have in many ways is the opposite of anthropocentrism and the instrumentalization of material goods. Rather than anthropocentrism, the human beings who labor to make and deliver commodities are marginalized, exploited, and hidden from view; we are under the control of the things we make, not vice-versa. And rather than instrumentalization, material goods are enchanted, endowed with life and invested with dreams that transcend the merely material. In advertisements, Amazon

15. Marx, *Capital*, 167–68.
16. Marx, *Capital*, 170.
17. Kantor et al., "Amazon That Customers Don't See."

boxes adorned with a smile dance and sing, while the Amazon workers—who complain of being treated like robots—are invisible to us. In his work on "advertising as religion," Sut Jhally argues that advertising in fact substitutes for the social relations that are hidden in the current economy. We now have relationships with products, not people. Advertising gives inanimate objects personalities.[18]

As Mary Douglas has made clear, people in all societies communicate through material goods: "Goods in their assemblage present a set of meanings.... They are read by those who know the code and scan them for information."[19] In older, non-market societies, however, the relationship between people and the material world was more transparent; most of the things people possessed were made by themselves or by people they knew. Material things were rooted in a closer, more direct relationship with nature and with the producers of our goods. Such relationships were embedded in goods as part of their meaning. In the modern economy, by contrast, relationships with both the natural environment and with the people who produce our goods are hidden; as Jhally writes, "The world of goods in industrial society offers no meaning, its meaning having been 'emptied' out of them. The function of advertising is to refill the emptied commodity with meaning."[20] In fact, Jhally argues, the power of advertising depends on this emptying; the magic of advertising is freed to work on a blank slate.

Jackson Lears's history of consumer culture similarly argues that advertising both accelerates and compensates for the collapse of Christian structures of meaning in the twentieth century. In the United States, consumer culture eroded a Protestant sensibility of self-denial and work. Capitalism's "creative destruction" of ethnicity, family, religion, and community left a void to be filled by the investment of meaning in commodities. The growing distance between manufacturers and buyers was overcome by personalizing the impersonal commodity.[21] Both the need for an ever-expanding consumption of goods to meet the challenge of overproduction and the need for meaning in a world of disrupted social relations were met by consumerism as a new type of religion. The exploitation of both the natural environment and workers is hidden by the investment of ultimate meanings in commodities.

18. Jhally, "Advertising as Religion."
19. Douglas and Isherwood, *World of Goods*, ix.
20. Jhally, "Advertising as Religion."
21. Lears, *Fables of Abundance*, 380.

There are innumerable studies of consumerism as a new religion. One recent empirical study by researchers from the United States and Israel entitled "Brands: The Opiate of the Nonreligious Masses?" found that brand loyalty is inversely related to traditional religious practice: the less people practice a traditional religion like Christianity, the more intense their loyalty to certain brands.[22] For this reason, Jhally borrows religious language to label the dominant stages through which advertising passes.[23] The first stage, the 1890s to the 1920s, he calls "idolatry"; the dominant focus in advertising was the power of the product to transform our world. Vague forms of sacred symbolism were used to show the enhancement, awe, and rapture that products could bring. As an ad in *Printers' Ink Monthly* noted in 1926, advertisements were "beginning to occupy the place in inspiration that religion did several hundred years ago."[24] The next stage, the 1920s to the 1940s, Jhally calls "iconology"; for Jhally, an icon is a symbol that means something. Now ads are focused less on what products can do and more on connecting them to transcendent aspirations for status, freedom, sex, happiness, and so on. The next few decades complete the shift from the product to the person; this is the stage labeled "narcissism," wherein ads show the fantasized completion of the self, as people undergo magical transformations by using a product. Using the right body spray makes one irresistibly attractive. Jhally calls the final stage "totemism," in which products or brands are badges of group membership and therefore "religion," in Durkheim's terms.

What we have seen so far is that the ravenous consumption of the earth and destruction of the environment is inadequately characterized by anthropocentrism and the instrumentalization and disenchantment of the material world; rather, it is marked by the hiding of people behind products and the elevation of goods to the realm of the transcendent. The modern economy is commodity-centric, not anthropocentric; anthropocentrism is more a fantasy than a reality. It is important to note that Marx's proposed cure was not less but more anthropocentrism and instrumentalization, doing away with the mystifications of God and

---

22. Shachar et al., "Brands," 92–110.

23. Jhally, *Codes of Advertising*, 201–2. Jhally later co-wrote a textbook entitled *Social Communication in Advertising* that adds a fifth stage, *mise-en-scène*, to describe more recent advertising, in which commodities in advertisements are props arranged in a theatrical production directed by the consumer. See Leiss et al., *Social Communication*, 566–80.

24. Quoted in Marchand, *Advertising the American Dream*, 265.

fetishized commodities, and returning alienated "man" to a place of control over and use of material goods. A Christian cure would be quite different, returning God to the center, thereby healing human relationships both with other human beings and with the material creation.

Theocentric Creation

To explore a Christian approach, it would help to examine theologically some of the terms that Jhally uses loosely, beginning with idolatry. Idolatry in the Bible is, in broadest terms, the worship of a created thing instead of the Creator. Old Testament critiques of idolatry anticipate Marx's analysis of commodity fetishism in some intriguing ways. The exchange in Marx whereby inanimate objects are endowed with life while life is drained away from their human makers is found already in the Bible, as is the theme of humans being controlled by their own creations. There is a persistent biblical theme in which the worship of idols of metal and stone turns the worshiper into a similarly lifeless object. This mirroring effect is explicitly stated in Ps 115:

> Their idols are silver and gold,
> the work of men's hands.
> They have mouths, but do not speak;
> eyes, but do not see . . . .
> Those who make them are like them;
> so are all who trust in them.[25]

The God of life is contrasted with the lifeless gods made by human hands out of metal. Those who make such idols or trust in them will become as lifeless as they are.

This theme is elaborated throughout the Bible. The lifelessness of idolaters in the Bible is most commonly expressed in terms of human body parts that do not function as they would in a living person. This theme is common in Isaiah's critique of idolatry:

> They shall be turned back and utterly put to shame,
> who trust in graven images,
> who say to molten images,
> "You are our gods."[26]

---

25. Ps 115:4–8. This language is repeated almost identically in Ps 135:15–18.
26. Isa 42:17.

Idolaters are regarded as deaf and blind.[27] The idolater

> sees many things, but does not observe them;
> his ears are open, but he does not hear.[28]

In the following chapter, Isaiah again associates

> the people who are blind, yet have eyes,
> who are deaf, yet have ears![29]

with those who form "no god."[30] In the next chapter, Isaiah mocks the man who uses half a piece of wood to cook dinner and the other half to make an idol to worship. The man becomes as lifeless, blind, and stupid as the block of wood. "All who make idols are nothing, and the things they delight in do not profit; their witnesses neither see nor know.... They know not, nor do they discern; for he has shut their eyes, so that they cannot see, and their minds, so that they cannot understand."[31]

The exchange of human life for the lifelessness of idols is expressed in other ways in the Bible as well. Second Kings 17:15 says of the Israelites, "They went after false idols, and became false."[32] Jeremiah proclaims:

> Thus says the LORD:
>
> > "What wrong did your fathers find in me
> >   that they went far from me,
> > and went after worthlessness, and became worthless? ...
> > Has a nation changed its gods,
> >   even though they are no gods?
> > But my people have changed their glory
> >   for that which does not profit."[33]

Hosea reports:

> But they came to Ba'al-pe'or,
>   and consecrated themselves to Ba'al,
>   and became detestable like the thing they loved.[34]

---

27. Isa 42:18–19.
28. Isa 42:20.
29. Isa 43:8.
30. Isa 43:10.
31. Isa 44:9–18; cf. Isa 6:9–10.
32. 2 Kgs 17:15.
33. Jer 2:5–11.
34. Hos 9:10.

I could multiply examples, but the point should be clear: the exchange of life and lifelessness between alienated workers and animated commodities is found in the Bible, long before it was identified by Marx.

More generally in the biblical view, the false gods that people create come to dominate over them. In 1 Sam 8, the rejection of God as king, equated with serving other gods, leads to dire consequences: the king-god will take your sons and daughters, your land and harvest, your slaves and flocks, and "you shall be his slaves."[35] In Jer 5, the Israelites' worship of foreign gods leads to their subjection to foreign masters: "As you have forsaken me and served foreign gods in your land, so you shall serve strangers in a land that is not yours."[36] If the people want to serve other masters, let them serve other masters. The sin and the punishment are the same thing: the people have made for themselves false gods, gods of death instead of the Lord of life. The people put their trust in their own creations and bowed down to serve them. And so, they shall; they shall be servants of their own creations, and their own creations will make them pay.

Jesus's saying about serving Mammon echoes this theme.[37] As he makes clear, idolatry in the Bible is not exclusively about the explicit worship of other named gods. Paul similarly labels greed idolatry.[38] Jhally's identification of idolatry in advertising is, in other words, quite traditional; the Abrahamic traditions have long recognized the idolatry of material objects. For Jhally, however, theological terms are useful to indicate mystification; both idol and icon describe two different stages in advertising strategy. For Catholic phenomenologist Jean-Luc Marion, by way of contrast, they are two fundamentally different stances toward the created world. The idol—and its opposite, the icon—is not a particular thing or class of things. Rather, "the icon and the idol determine two manners of being for beings, not two classes of beings."[39] Idolatry is in the subject's gaze, not in the object itself; there is nothing inherently idolatrous about material things. For Marion, there is something of a genuine experience of the divine in the idolatrous gaze; he is sympathetic with the need to find meaning in the material world. The problem with idolatry is the reduction of the divine to a human measure; idolatry "is characterized solely by the subjection of the divine to the human

---

35. 1 Sam 8:17.
36. Jer 5:19.
37. Matt 6:24.
38. Col 3:5.
39. Marion, *God without Being*, 8.

conditions for experience of the divine, concerning which nothing proves that it is not authentic."[40]

According to Marion, the first intention of the gaze is to aim at the divine. The gaze searches visible things, "transpiercing" them, seeing through them, as it were, seeing nothing, restlessly looking for the divine and not finding it. The gaze finally stops on an idol, something that presents itself as visible, splendid, and luminous enough to fill the gaze. The gaze finds itself dazzled by the idol. When the gaze stops, its aim settles, and the not-aimed-at disappears. All else drops from view, and the gaze stands ravished. Marion makes clear that when the gaze stops, it does not, "at least at first, arise from an ethical choice: it reveals a sort of essential fatigue."[41] The journey is long and belief in an invisible divinity is hard for a carnal being to sustain over the long haul. We long to see the divine, to feast on what our heart longs for. Our gaze invests the idol with all these longings. We are not so much fooled as overwhelmed by both weariness and longing.

The fact that we invest the idol with our longings and seek satisfaction in it indicates the essential mirroring function of the idol. Marion describes the gaze as a kind of radar signal that bounces off the idol and returns to the self, indicating its position relative to the idol. Because the idol subjects the divine to the conditions set by a human experience of the divine, the divine is cut to the measure of the human, and mirrors back to the human its own experience: "the idol always culminates in a 'self-idolatry.'"[42] Idolatry is marked by a kind of self-worship, a narcissism that can only find its own desires and aspirations reflected back to it in its acts of veneration. Nevertheless, Marion does not simply deny the presence of the divine in this experience. The idol, according to Marion, "presents a certain low-water mark of the divine."[43] The idol is less God, more human experience of the divine—but perhaps not entirely devoid of some inchoate participation in the divine life.

Though the idols Marion has in view are primarily objects of art and metaphysical concepts, I would like to relate his analysis of idolatry to the fetishism of commodities. For Jhally, idolatry and narcissism are two different stages of advertising strategy. For Marion, they are intertwined dynamics in the way that humans encounter the material world. As a

40. Marion, *Idol and Distance*, 6.
41. Marion, *God without Being*, 13.
42. Marion, *God without Being*, 28.
43. Marion, *God without Being*, 14.

Christian, Marion assumes that we have a natural tendency, a "first intention," to seek the divine. The restless gaze seeks God, but because we are creatures we seek God in the creation, in the material world. Most commodities are not the "saturated phenomena," the great works of art that Marion has in mind in his analysis of idolatry. But in a world of fetishized commodities, where the commodity, in Jhally's words, "performs magical feats of transformation and bewitchment, brings instant happiness and gratification, captures the forces of nature, and holds within itself the essence of important social relationships,"[44] it is not hard to see how we are dazzled by commodities, investing in them longings for self-transcendence while all else drops from view. The result is a narcissism in which the commodity serves as a mirror, and the social conditions of production—the people who make and deliver the products and the earth whose resources are consumed in their making—disappear from view. There *is* a kind of anthropocentrism in idolatry; what appears to be the worship of something else is really self-worship. But this narcissism is less dominance over creation than an idolatrous subjection of humanity to artifacts of our own making. Our experience is not simply of being "lords and masters," in Pope Francis's words; for the workers who produce and bring us commodities, the experience is often one of exploitation, and even for those on the consuming end of the exchange, the experience is more being dazzled and enthralled by commodities, while serving the inscrutable and pitiless will of the market.

For Jhally, the goal is to disenchant commodities and return humanity to the center. For Marion, the goal is to return both material things and humans to iconic status, both pointing to God, who is at the center. The restoration of a right relationship between humans and creation for material things must avoid both the exaltation of things to divine status and their hollowing out into mere reflections of human desire. For humans, it must also avoid both the self-worship of idolatry and the degradation and disappearance of the human laborer. The restoration of right relationship on these terms can only take place by the restoration of God to the center; a theocentric, not anthropocentric or commodity-centric world.

Marion's contrast of the idol with the icon is helpful here. For Jhally, iconology describes the way that advertising uses commodities as symbols for deeper strands of human meaning related to happiness, belonging, transcendence, and so on. Ads imply, usually subconsciously,

---

44. Jhally, "Advertising as Religion."

that a certain kind of car, for example, is the key to freedom and self-transcendence. For Marion, similarly, an icon is a kind of window to the divine, but the encounter with the living God is of a very different kind than the way that Jhally's commodity-icon promises an encounter with transcendence. For Marion, an object is rendered an icon by a certain kind of gaze, but the human person is not in control of that gaze. "The icon does not result from a vision but provokes one. The icon is not seen, but appears."[45] Rather than the mirroring effect of the idol, where divinity is cut to the measure of the human, the icon is a kind of window to the divine, but it is a window opened by God, not by us. The icon furthermore does not simply render God visible. Rather than saturating and dazzling the gaze with visibility, the invisible always remains invisible, even as presented by the icon. As Marion writes, the icon

> attempts to render visible the invisible as such, hence to allow that the visible not cease to refer to an other than itself, without, however, that other ever being reproduced in the visible . . . . The icon summons the gaze to surpass itself by never freezing on a visible, since the visible only presents itself here in view of the invisible. The gaze can never rest or settle if it looks at an icon; it always must rebound upon the visible, in order to go back in it up the infinite stream of the invisible.[46]

The icon, then, never delivers the divine to the human grasp. The divine in the icon is not grasped but received as a gift. God is never reducible to the human search for self-transcendence; the human aspiration for self-transcendence within the visible world renders little more than a mirror of ourselves. Authentic contact with the divine can only take place on God's terms, when God is received as a gift through the gift of God's creation. The icon inverts the gaze of idolatry. The gaze belongs not to the human person but to the icon. The icon sees us, regards us; "the icon opens in a face that gazes at our gazes in order to summon them to its depth."[47] The icon is not to be seen but to be venerated. In this sense, Marion implies, there is an ethical component to the icon's gaze. We must ask, "What does the icon want?" The icon is not simply a window for our contemplation, but a door through which we are summoned to walk. The icon puts in motion not just an aesthetics, but an ethics.

---

45. Marion, *God without Being*, 17.
46. Marion, *God without Being*, 18.
47. Marion, *God without Being*, 19.

Although Marion has proper Christian icons painted on wood in view in his analysis, his contrast of idols and icons as two ways of seeing can be useful for a more general account of a Christian relationship to creation. As Junius Johnson's recent theology of beauty points out, "Like the icon, the creature, properly understood, is totally given to the signification of God because it exists only for this purpose."[48] The purpose of creation is to point to God. As the book of Wisdom declares:

> For from the greatness and beauty of created things
> comes a corresponding perception of their Creator.[49]

Like the icon, each creature in its own way opens a door to another world, to heaven. "Ever since the creation of the world his invisible nature, namely, his eternal power and deity, has been clearly perceived in the things that have been made."[50] The being of creatures is ecstatic; the center of all creatures is in God. And yet, this theocentric vision is not a turning away from this world to another world, a turning away from created things and toward God. Because the center of all creatures is in God, one finds creatures by turning toward God. It is in God that creatures are shown to be what they really are. The purpose of creatures is the purpose of the icon. As John Chryssavgis writes in his book *Creation as Sacrament*, "The icon aspires to the inner vision of all, the world as created and intended by God."[51] We only see the creation rightly when we see it in God.

As Marion points out, even icons do not render God visible, and most creatures are even more imperfect, participating in God in a way that both reveals and conceals. The language of Chryssavgis and *Laudato Si'* on creation as sacrament[52] perhaps captures this dynamic best, because a sacrament always both provides access to an invisible grace while cloaking that grace in material signs. Creatures image God but are not God. Sacraments present in ordinary material form what those material elements are not. There is a necessary negation in a sacramental worldview, both presence and absence. The unlikeness between God and creatures, however, is the condition of the intimacy between God and creatures. This is precisely because God is not a being but the very ground of Being;

---

48. Johnson, *Father of Lights*, 185.
49. Wis 13:5.
50. Rom 1:20.
51. Chryssavgis, *Creation as Sacrament*, 114.
52. Francis, *Laudato Si'*, §§9, 235.

God is present in each thing, as Aquinas says, "innermostly."[53] So the complete otherness of God does not diminish the beauty of the creation. On the contrary, as Johnson writes, "the greatness of the difference is what guarantees that there will be no competition, and so God is free to pour Godself richly into creatures without fear that they will be in danger of no longer being creatures or of being seen as more than creatures."[54] A sacramental view of creation thus avoids both the instrumentalization and the idolization of the material world. Creation is neither reduced to raw material for the satisfaction of human wants, nor is it fetishized, exalted to the status of the divine. A proper relationship to creation sees it as God's gift, both saturated with the presence of God and yet for that reason eccentric, pointing to a center outside itself in God. In a sacramental view, creation comes alive precisely in its witnessing to the gift that grounds its being.

The Incarnation makes the relationship between Creator and creation personal; that relationship is not merely one of cause and effect, but the uniting of Creator and creation in the person of Christ. Humanity and divinity are united in Christ, but in a way that avoids both the instrumentalization and the idolatry of human being. The Incarnation is a more complete way for humanity to image God. In Christ, humanity expresses both what it is and what it is not: true God. In Christ, humanity mediates divine presence, even though divine presence is not circumscribed by Christ's humanity. Humanity in all its flaws is in one way negated in Christ in order to reveal God, but—at the same time—Christ reveals what it is to be truly human; for, as Natalie Carnes puts it, "what could be more human than to reveal God?"[55] The first creation story in Genesis makes clear that humanity was created for that purpose.

As the story in Genesis continues, however, it becomes clear that material creation has been disfigured by human sin, but our distorted relationships to the material world have disfigured our human relationships in equal measure. Christ as sacrament comes to effect a cosmic restoration, and we are invited to participate in his sacramental Body. The twinned narcissisms of consumerism and the degradation of human labor stem from the loss of the human person's fundamental role as liturgical celebrant of the sacramental reality of the world.[56] The liturgy of the

53. Aquinas, *Summa Theologiae*, I, q. 8, a. 1.
54. Johnson, *Father of Lights*, 81–82.
55. Carnes, *Image and Presence*, 13.
56. Chryssavgis, *Creation as Sacrament*, 4.

Eucharist restores bread and wine to what they are intended to be: signs that draw us back to the Creator. The Eucharist has an eschatological orientation, realizing in history a foretaste of the final reconciliation and restoration of all things. The eschatological dimension of the Eucharist is not an escape from the world, but a sign of what—despite our sin—the created world is now: a reflection of the glory of God. Our role as celebrants is to uncover this glory in a fallen world. More than simply signs that remind us of God, however, the presence of Christ in the Eucharist incorporates us into a Body in which we not only see but feel the presence of our fellow creatures: "If one member suffers, all suffer together; if one member is honored, all rejoice together."[57]

There is, of course, nothing automatic about the effects of the sacraments in the world. Our receiving of the Eucharist is often terribly compromised by our sin. The sacrament of Reconciliation is in some ways the key to all the sacraments, for we must live penitentially in order to see the world and our role in it rightly. But more than just an act of seeing, a sacramental view of the world must be practiced. It must be an ethic, and not simply an aesthetic. It is easy for those who occupy positions of relative privilege to romanticize the created world and enjoy its fruits while turning a blind eye to the human labor that makes such privilege possible. For this reason, *Laudato Si'* demands that all ecology must be an integral ecology, one that weaves together concern for the created environment with concern for human well-being. As Pope Francis writes, "When we speak of the 'environment', what we really mean is a relationship existing between nature and the society which lives in it."[58] Nature is not something separate from human being. More than an aesthetic, then, an integral ecology must also be a political economy. An integral ecology cares for the vulnerable earth and the vulnerable human persons who live on it; there is no sharp distinction between humans and nature. As Pope Francis writes, "Any approach to an integral ecology, which by definition does not exclude human beings, needs to take account of the value of labour."[59] The critique of commodity fetishism is not merely a critique of the way we see commodities, but of the way we fail—by design—to see the conditions of production and the consumption of both laborers and natural resources that is hidden from our view. A true aesthetics is only made possible by the economic, social, and political conditions in

---

57. 1 Cor 12:26.
58. Francis, *Laudato Si'*, §139.
59. Francis, *Laudato Si'*, §124.

which we can *see* both the human persons who labor to produce our stuff and the condition of the earth where such production takes place. Chryssavgis may be right that ecological correction should put contemplation before action—we must, he says, stop what we are doing and *see* the creation differently[60]—but seeing is difficult in an economy that is designed to hide the consumption of the earth and workers from our sight.

What we need are economies that restore the conditions of production to visibility. In *Caritas in Veritate*, Pope Benedict writes of the importance of *"forms of economic activity marked by quotas of gratuitousness and communion."*[61] The chapter on economic development begins with a reflection on charity or love as gift, the principle of gratuitousness that must form the basis of a truly human economy. As both Benedict and Francis recognize, scale is important; one can only love another person or another creature if one can see them. The healing of material creation and human relations depends on economies that restore the visibility of both, not merely in their empirical form, but in what they most truly are: sacraments, bearers of the beauty of God.

Conclusion

The idea that anthropocentrism causes the consumption of the earth's resources and the degradation of the natural environment is not without value, but I have tried in this chapter to give it more precision. The ecological crisis is not simply a matter of humanity dominating nature, but a matter of some humans dominating others, and many humans coming to be enthralled by and subjected to human creations. Subjection can be seen as a consequence of the attempt to dominate; as Gen 3 makes plain, the Fall is a direct consequence of the human attempt to put humanity first, to "be like God."[62] The solution can only be the restoration of right relations among humans, other parts of the creation, and God. Rather than an anthropocentric or commodity-centric world, we need a theocentric world, in which we are able to see and experience our fellow humans and our fellow creatures as icons of the living God.

---

60. Chryssavgis, *Creation as Sacrament*, 133.
61. Benedict XVI, *Caritas in Veritate*, §39, emphasis in original.
62. Gen 3:5.

Bibliography

Aquinas, Thomas. *Summa Theologiae*. Translated by Fathers of the English Dominican Province. Online ed., 2017. https://www.newadvent.org/summa/.

Benedict XVI. *Caritas in Veritate*. Encyclical Letter, June 29, 2009. https://www.vatican.va/content/benedict-xvi/en/encyclicals/documents/hf_ben-xvi_enc_20090629_caritas-in-veritate.html.

Carnes, Natalie. *Image and Presence: A Christological Reflection on Iconoclasm and Iconophilia*. Stanford, CA: Stanford University Press, 2018.

Cayley, David. *Ivan Illich: An Intellectual Journey*. University Park, PA: Pennsylvania State University Press, 2021.

Chryssavgis, John. *Creation as Sacrament: Reflections on Ecology and Spirituality*. London: T. & T. Clark, 2019.

Douglas, Mary, and Baron Isherwood. *The World of Goods: Toward an Anthropology of Consumption*. Rev. ed. London: Routledge, 1996.

Francis. *Laudato Si': On Care for Our Common Home*. Encyclical, May 24, 2015. https://www.vatican.va/content/francesco/en/encyclicals/documents/papa-francesco_20150524_enciclica-laudato-si.html.

Jhally, Sut. "Advertising as Religion: The Dialectic of Technology and Magic." *Advertising and Society Review* 1.1 (2000) n.p.

———. *The Codes of Advertising: Fetishism and the Political Economy of Meaning in the Consumer Society*. New York: Routledge, 1987.

Johnson, Junius. *The Father of Lights: A Theology of Beauty*. Grand Rapids: Baker, 2020.

Kantor, Jodi, et al. "The Amazon That Customers Don't See." *New York Times*, June 15, 2021. https://www.nytimes.com/interactive/2021/06/15/us/amazon-workers.html.

Lears, Jackson. *Fables of Abundance: A Cultural History of Advertising in America*. New York: Basic Books, 1995.

Leiss, William, et al. *Social Communication in Advertising*. 3rd ed. New York: Routledge, 2005.

Marchand, Roland. *Advertising the American Dream: Making Way for Modernity, 1920–1940*. Berkeley: University of California Press, 1985.

Marion, Jean-Luc. *God without Being: Hors-Texte*. Translated by Thomas A. Carlson. Chicago: University of Chicago Press, 1991.

———. *The Idol and Distance: Five Studies*. Translated by Thomas A. Carlson. New York: Fordham University Press, 2001.

Marx, Karl. *Capital: A Critique of Political Economy*. Vol. 1. Translated by Ben Fowkes. New York: Vintage Books, 1977.

Shachar, Ron, et al. "Brands: The Opiate of the Nonreligious Masses?" *Marketing Science* 30.1 (Jan.–Feb. 2011) 92–110.

White, Lynn. "The Historical Roots of Our Ecologic Crisis." *Science* 155.3767 (1967) 1203–7.

www.ingramcontent.com/pod-product-compliance
Lightning Source LLC
Chambersburg PA
CBHW051642230426
43669CB00013B/2406